COACHING FASTPITCH SOFTBALL SUCCESSFULLY

Second Edition

Kathy Veroni
Western Illinois University

Roanna Brazier
Ohio University

Human Kinetics

Library of Congress Cataloging-in-Publication Data

Veroni, Kathy J.
    Coaching fastpitch softball successfully / Kathy J. Veroni, Roanna Brazier.– 2nd ed.
        p. cm.
    Includes index.
    ISBN 0-7360-6010-3 (soft cover)
    1. Softball–Coaching. I. Brazier, Roanna. II. Title.
    GV881.4.C6V47 2006
    796.357'8–dc22

                                    2005020459

ISBN-10: 0-7360-6010-3
ISBN-13: 978-0-7360-6010-3

Acquisitions Editor: Jana Hunter; **Developmental Editor:** Amanda M. Eastin; **Assistant Editors:** Christine Horger and Carla Zych; **Copyeditor:** Patrick Connolly; **Proofreader:** Erin Cler; **Graphic Designer:** Nancy Rasmus; **Graphic Artist:** Sandra Meier; **Photo Manager:** Dan Wendt; **Cover Designer:** Keith Blomberg; **Photographer (cover):** Sarah Ritz; **Photographer (interior):** Photos by Sarah Ritz unless otherwise noted. Photos on pages 2, 5, 11, 14, 18, 26, 32, 48, 58, 59, 61 (figure 7.6), 63, 67, 83, 96, 99, 104 (figures 10.2-10.4), 106, 112 (figure 10.10), 115, 142, 197, 200, 206, 210, 215 courtesy of Western Illinois University/Larry Dean; photos on pages 66, 77, 78, 79, 81, 90, 92, 93 (figure 9.4), 94, 104 (figure 10.1), 108 (figure 10.7), 112 (figure 10.11), 113 (figure 10.13), 114 by Laurie Black; photos on pages viii, 38, 53, 123, 205 © Human Kinetics; **Art Manager:** Kareema McLendon-Foster; **Illustrators:** Tom Roberts and Kareema McLendon-Foster; **Printer:** Versa Press

We thank Western Illinois University in Macomb, Illinois, for assistance in providing the location for the photo shoot for this book.

Human Kinetics books are available at special discounts for bulk purchase. Special editions or book excerpts can also be created to specification. For details, contact the Special Sales Manager at Human Kinetics.

Printed in the United States of America   10 9 8 7 6 5 4

The paper in this book is certified under a sustainable forestry program.

Human Kinetics
Web site: www.HumanKinetics.com

United States: Human Kinetics
P.O. Box 5076
Champaign, IL 61825-5076
800-747-4457
e-mail: humank@hkusa.com

Canada: Human Kinetics
475 Devonshire Road, Unit 100
Windsor, ON N8Y 2L5
800-465-7301 (in Canada only)
e-mail: info@hkcanada.com

Europe: Human Kinetics
107 Bradford Road
Stanningley
Leeds LS28 6AT, United Kingdom
+44 (0)113 255 5665
e-mail: hk@hkeurope.com

Australia: Human Kinetics
57A Price Avenue
Lower Mitcham, South Australia 5062
08 8372 0999
e-mail: info@hkaustralia.com

New Zealand: Human Kinetics
Division of Sports Distributors NZ Ltd.
P.O. Box 300 226 Albany
North Shore City, Auckland
0064 9 448 1207
e-mail: info@humankinetics.co.nz

This book is dedicated to the youngest generation in hopes that they will be given great opportunities to learn to play fastpitch softball from teachers and coaches who love the game. It is also dedicated to my personal heroes and to the men and women who have motivated and inspired me.

Kathy Veroni

Every day in coaching has been an experiment. Like life itself, coaching is a process. Every decision made affects the future, and coaches are in constant reflection on the past to ensure a better tomorrow. This book is dedicated to all the players who have stuck with me through this process of trial and error and who have helped me learn many lessons on and off the field. I also dedicate this book to my father, who tirelessly worked with me to help me become the player I was and who taught me how to be my own best teacher. Here's to the voice behind the backstop!

Roanna Brazier

CONTENTS

FOREWORD

Kathy Veroni has long been a mentor and a role model to young coaches, male and female. I personally have had the opportunity to compete against her teams as both a player and a coach. Her teams not only were well coached and highly competitive, but they also always noticeably played with great conviction and an obvious passion for both the sport and their team.

Coaching Fastpitch Softball Successfully provides much more than the specifics of the X's and O's of the game. It speaks to the heart and soul of coaching. In this book, Coach Veroni presents her values of coaching young women, and she clearly demonstrates that leadership and communication are the qualities that enshrined her forever in the NFCA Hall of Fame.

Coaching Fastpitch Softball Successfully is a reflection of the ever-present inspiration and motivation in the coaching philosophy of Kathy Veroni. I enjoyed reading the book and recommend it both to aspiring young coaches as well as those who have been in the game for many years.

Carol Hutchins
University of Michigan

PREFACE

Thomas Henry Huxley wrote, "The rung of a ladder was never meant to rest upon, but only to hold a man's foot long enough to enable him to put the other somewhat higher!"

Having been involved in the game of fastpitch softball for more than 40 years, I have been blessed with the opportunity to work with great athletes who have shared my commitment to enhancing performance and enjoying the game. They are the ones who have taught me how to teach. Through the trial and error, success and failure of these athletes, I have become not only a coach but also a student of the game. The knowledge they instilled in me is now shared with you in the second edition of *Coaching Fastpitch Softball Successfully.*

In coaching, both the teacher and the learner have the same goal in mind. Teaching and learning occur simultaneously, and both the coach and the athlete strive to reach the goal or objective. The athletes must learn the game and their role in it, and we as coaches must teach better. Coaching is teaching but with more focus and passion.

As teachers, our primary mission is to impress upon our athletes that they should be perfect at practice and in drills, because the game brings challenges and anxiety. Each of us must know our part in victory and defeat as well as how to do things better.

Those of you who have read the first edition of this book will find new and better drills in the pages that follow. Also, teaching techniques have been updated, and they are presented in a more clear-cut and concise manner. Those sections are beneficial for the athlete, the teacher, and the coach. As an added bonus, this edition includes the presentation and breakdown of innovative skill development techniques.

The learning process never ends as long as there is someone willing to pass on all that she has learned. As a student of the game, I have always been interested in seeking out ideas and styles that work for other gifted coaches. Therefore, for this edition, I have asked Coach Roanna Brazier to collaborate and contribute to the book. Roanna brings her experiences as an elite pitcher and hitter as well as her knowledge of instructing athletes to be the best they can be. Roanna has a genuine love and respect for the game, as well as a sense of responsibility to share what she has learned for the benefit of others.

ACKNOWLEDGMENTS

I would like to thank Mindy Dessert for her knowledge, wisdom, and assistance in writing the first edition of *Coaching Fastpitch Softball Successfully* and for helping put our system of coaching and training into this book. I would also like to acknowledge the work and friendship of Jen Tyrrell, a gifted player and coach who helped guide this second edition along.

I am so happy that this book is now in the hands of teaching coaches. Writing this book was a labor of love, but unfortunately my best teacher will not be able to read it—my mother passed away on October 21, 1997. Josephine Lillian Veroni was my hero, my teacher, and my best friend. She was a softball player in the 1940s as well as an equestrian, bowler, and super sports fan. For 28 years she watched as I coached softball teams, from Western Illinois University to the Macomb Magic. She saw many tremendous athletes play the game she loved.

As coaches, we are all dream weavers, and we have the ability to make young girls sparkle as

The 1943 Roper Manufacturing softball team, with my mom, Josephine Cascio Veroni (front row, far left), and aunt, Dorothy Cascio Mahle (back row, second from right).

they realize their dreams. My mom bought me my first glove. She let me play sports whenever I wanted. She watched me throughout my playing and coaching career with the Rockford Comets and later with the Pekin Lettes. She came to Connecticut to see the Falcons win a world professional fastpitch title and saw every Western Illinois and Macomb Magic team play.

She made me laugh, and we rarely argued. If we got into a disagreement, she would soon change the subject. She taught me how to cross the street when I was very little and how to go to school by myself. She taught me to be grateful for all we have in our lives . . . and to remember not to take anything for granted, not a person or even one moment in time.

She loved to read, and she shared that gift with her twin granddaughters. My brother Jim recalled how he would sit and watch the love our mom showed Kayla and Kelly whenever he took the girls over to visit her—with the girls sitting on either side of her, she would read them the book she had bought them. As teachers and coaches, we are kindred spirits with our mothers. We must pass on a legacy from one generation to the next, and from one season to the next. The important lessons my mother taught me, I, in turn, try to teach my young athletes. Just as we want our mothers to be proud of us, so too, do our players want us to be proud of them. Reward them with your praise.

At one of our school's basketball games, I was asked to speak with the television announcers during halftime about the upcoming softball season. I called my mom and told her I would be on TV and that I would tug on my ear, which meant "Hi, I am thinking about you." By the time I got home after the game, she had already called and left me a message on my answering machine. She told me I had done a very nice job and that she was proud of me. She said, "I saw that little ear tug you gave me." Well, Mom, I write this book in your honor and memory, as a thank-you for all you gave me and taught me. You gave me the gift of life and the support I needed. I hope that I have passed that support on to other young women who want what you and I wanted—to have fun and to play the game to the best of their ability.

Thanks, Mom, for all of the wonderful memories. Until we meet again.

Kathy Veroni

KEY TO DIAGRAMS

First baseman	1B	Pitcher	P
Second baseman	2B	Catcher	C
Third baseman	3B	Hitter	H
Shortstop	SS	Receiver	R
Left fielder	LF	Coach	CO
Center fielder	CF	Path of fielder	————
Right fielder	RF	Path of throw	– – – – –
Fielder	F		

CHAPTER 1
DEVELOPING A SOFTBALL COACHING PHILOSOPHY

A coaching philosophy involves your beliefs about the way your program should be run. You should have a solid, consistent philosophy. As a coach, you touch people's lives, beginning with your players and extending to their families, along with administrators, the media, and others. By being consistent, you ensure that your players understand what is expected of them.

One of the most important jobs of the coach is to bring the team together. All coaches seem to use the adage "Together we can," and this idea is best implemented through the consistent guidance and support from the coach. Consistency sends the message to the athletes that you are going to be fair in all decisions because you will base each decision on the principles and values that you have created and followed. When you are consistent, the athletes as well as the media and administrators can expect certain behaviors from you. This knowledge will enhance the athletes' performances both on the practice field and during games. A cohesive team cannot be formed if you change your philosophy and standards depending on the athlete or the situation.

DEFINE YOUR PHILOSOPHY

My philosophy is the sum of my coaching beliefs. I believe a lot of things have to combine for a team to win a conference championship or a national championship. Some are obvious factors: hard work, dedication, teamwork, discipline, and skill in the fundamentals of the game. Other factors for success are more subtle: the emergence of leaders, the development of the team's "chemistry" and confidence, and the surprise of young players growing into roles with enthusiasm and ability. And some components are intangible but no less real, such as spirit, tradition, and the will to win. My philosophy is to attempt to bring these aspects together every season in a way that is consistent with my belief that the most important part of coaching is to give athletes the opportunity to participate and to be the best they can be.

I have always stressed performance rather than winning. Through our team objectives, I ask the athletes to do only the best they can. If circumstances combine for a victory, we can

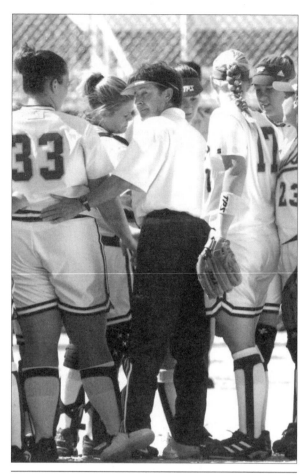

Many things must come together for a team to be successful. A team is greater than the sum of its parts.

celebrate; however, sometimes events that occur in the game are beyond the athletes' control. Performance then becomes the ingredient to team success. I believe in putting athletes first, winning the game second.

During my years of coaching, I have had my coaching philosophy tested on different occasions. I try to stress that winning is not everything and that if the athletes do the best they can, then they can be congratulated on a job well done. It is this belief that has been tested the most. After playing great softball but losing, athletes often come off the field and hang their heads. I always want them to be proud of their performance, and though I do not expect them to cheer or smile, I do expect them to respect the game. After performing at their optimal level, they should be able to applaud their efforts, congratulate their opponents, and respect the competition. They should feel the loss, but I also ask that they acknowledge the efforts in

the game—their efforts, as well as those of the coaches, umpires, fans, and opponents.

In developing my philosophy, I realize that with my position comes the power to influence those I teach—with that power I hope to elicit a positive change. My father once told me to "go for it" when I was debating whether to change softball teams. I had the option of staying home to play or moving away to play for a great traveling team. Those three little words sent me on a journey of many positive experiences. My mother taught me not to be afraid and to try new things. She taught me strength and courage and determination. My sister taught me to dream dreams and to trust in the future, and she taught me that roots are strong and that you can be anything you want. My brothers taught me kindness and sensitivity, and that nothing is impossible. My assistant coaches taught me to laugh and to give my all. All of these people have influenced me, and I try to incorporate what they taught me into my philosophy so that I can influence my players in the same way.

THE BASICS OF A COACHING PHILOSOPHY

Your coaching philosophy should not be developed overnight. You should gather different views of coaching the way you would visit a buffet—choosing and trying different methods and observing what works for others, as well as remembering certain techniques that worked (or didn't work) for you both as an athlete and a coach. Once you have gathered what you feel is right for you, then try it out. You will no doubt have to throw out some beliefs, but others will become the backbone of your coaching style and success. When putting your philosophy together, remember to look for tools that will cover what is important in a team, that is, how to lead a team to success and how to make the most of the game for everybody.

Be Yourself

Sometimes you will find yourself playing a role that fits a situation but that you cannot support in your heart. I find these situations in coaching to be rare. The coach who follows her heart and does what she believes is right will come out ahead. Athletes are smart, and they spend a lot of their time trying to figure you out. They will test you, push you, pull you, and see what they get from you in return. If you try to respond in a way that is truly not you, they will see through your facade. They want you to be genuine, just as you want them to be genuine.

Many first-time coaches want to do a great job, and thus, they put on a serious face when they hit the field. They see coaching as strictly business. Sometimes they hesitate to let down their guard and laugh with the athletes. But it's important to show your full personality when coaching. The athletes want to see that you are real so they can relate to, trust, and confide in you. As a coach, you are their teacher, their friend, their confidant, and you sometimes serve as their parent. You must be honest with your athletes and your staff if you wish honesty in return. So when in doubt, be yourself and listen to your heart. You will not always be right, but at least you can say, "I did what I believed was the right thing to do."

You must develop and follow your own coaching style. It is good to have mentors but not to imitate them. If you look at successful coaches, you will see that each one is different. Some are quiet and use their body language, while others are more vocal. They motivate in different ways as well as teach with different tools, yet all have found success. Their diversity shows that there is no one way to coach. You must find what will work for you from within yourself. By all means, learn some coaching techniques from others, but build them into *your* style.

Be Willing to Listen

As a coach, it will benefit you to become a communicator and to recognize the needs of your team and balance those needs with yours. Open communication is critical between the coach and the athlete and among the athletes. The coach should encourage everyone to express themselves honestly about team standards, feelings, and expectations. Encourage your athletes to communicate both their compliments and complaints. An open-door policy demonstrates to everyone that you are interested in seeing how the team members are doing and feeling.

Coaches expect the athlete to listen to all directives, but a coach must also possess a keen ability to listen. Listening shows that you care what your team members are saying and that their thoughts and feelings are important. The athletes should feel comfortable expressing their opinion when asked. I try to make it clear that there are appropriate times and places to address issues on which an athlete does not agree with the coach. If an athlete disagrees with something I have done, or wants to question a coaching decision I have made, I prefer that she comes to me to discuss her concern on a one-on-one basis. Because this discussion is about my thoughts and hers, it should occur away from the team.

Athletes often find it difficult to approach their coaches with questions that require a clear yes or no answer. I'm not sure why this happens, but it may be the result of an intimidation factor combined with the obvious fear of hearing the dreaded "no." It is my philosophy to say yes whenever I can. If an athlete comes to me with a legitimate question and is passionate about something that she is proposing, then I will back her by saying yes. As a coach, I know the athlete has certain wants and needs, and by working together, listening, and asking, a win–win situation is created.

Touch People's Lives

As I look back at the players I have coached, I am rewarded by their success in coaching and in life. Many of my players have gone on to coach teams of all ages and are sharing their love of the sport. I know these women are making a positive imprint on the young lives they touch because I know the kind of athletes they were when they played for me.

Coaches need to use the influence they have on their athletes to help them make good life decisions. I try to influence the athletes in a way that helps them increase all positives in their lives. I want our team to be filled with women of character; the ideal athlete for our program is one who is caring, dedicated, and a team player. I want our program to be highly professional and a class operation. I want the team to play the game the way it should be played, graceful in victory and defeat. If your athletes can walk away from your program feeling they have learned important life tools that will help them in the future, then you have done your job.

On the field, I stress leadership and responsibility. These two characteristics are critical not only in sports but also throughout life. If I demand these things from my athletes, they will take these values with them out onto the field and also into life situations. They will all leave having learned some valuable lessons and with some newly found strength to face future challenges.

Our mission as coaches is simple: We will challenge the athlete to be a winner in all that she does, because we're not just teaching her lessons for softball . . . we're teaching her lessons for life.

1. Keep in mind that it doesn't matter that much who's on the other side of the field. We have to control what we can do, and if we play up to our full potential and do our best, then the results will take care of themselves.

2. Do not overlook an opponent. Our goal is to play at our full potential all of the time.

3. Try to earn respect from your opponent and in rankings and on a national level. (I want our players to know that we will teach them how to compete at the very highest level.)

4. Know that we are going to play to win and we will back it up with performance.

5. Be mentally and physically tough, cool under fire, and make great decisions. We must have a killer instinct, an instinct of putting people away.

6. Be a leader, be committed to the game, and don't overlook any opponents. Have a very businesslike approach.

I guarantee that my players will work harder than they ever have, but I also promise that the coaches will all work hard to make the game of softball fun for them. I assure the players that they will be treated with respect and dignity at all times, and that we will place a high priority on character. As coaches, we never know how and when we will make an impact on our players' lives, but if we give them every opportunity to grow and develop life skills, we have touched their lives in a positive way.

It's Never Too Late

I once had an athlete call me and leave the message that she had finally gotten her degree. She had left school five years earlier, and the only thing keeping her from graduating was an Illinois constitution test for the out-of-state student. That athlete was Jenn Jackson. She had told me several times she was going to come up and take it, but things never seemed to work out. She had earned a job as a St. Louis police officer without the official degree and had been doing well. It was not until she came up for our fall tournament that a friend talked her into taking the test. She did and she passed! She would receive her diploma and a considerable raise in salary. She was excited and really proud. It felt good that she wanted to share the accomplishment with me even after being gone for five years. I called her back and congratulated her on a job well done! She told me that she knew I would want to know and that I had always been there for her, encouraging her along the way.

Have Fun

Martha Ewing and Vern Seefeldt of the Youth Sports Institute of Michigan State University conducted a study with the cooperation of school systems in 11 cities. Questionnaires were filled out by more than 10,000 young people, aged 10 to 18. The study underlined a number of truths about children and sports:

1. Fun is pivotal; if it is not "fun," young people won't play a sport.

2. Skill development is a crucial aspect of fun and is more important than winning, even among the best athletes.

3. The most rewarding challenges of sports are those that lead to self-knowledge.

4. Intrinsic rewards are more important in creating lifetime athletes than are extrinsic rewards. Intrinsic rewards include the self-knowledge that develops out of self-competition, and extrinsic rewards include victory or attention from others.

Remember these "truths," and plan activities with them in mind. Try to keep the fun in all

Players will work hard for their performances, and the coach must work hard to make the game fun for them. Nothing brings smiles like a little salsa dancing, for example.

practices, and encourage laughter and smiles. When the coach laughs and smiles, the team relaxes and executes with less stress. Laughter is a great reliever of pressure. Give your players a reason to smile at practice, during warm-up, and in games. If the team plays hard and smart and yet loses, the athletes may not be satisfied with the ending, but somewhere within the game they will have experienced enjoyment. If athletes play hard and smart, they will have more fun than if they do not.

ESTABLISH OBJECTIVES

Your objectives come after you establish your philosophy. You should have objectives for yourself, your staff, the athletes, and the team. These objectives will surface from what you believe is important in the game and will be in your mind at every softball hour: during practice, pregame, games, and the off-season. The athletes will have the most objectives because they play the game. Many of those objectives are set to help the athletes reach their optimal performance. Team objectives help you decide

if you have really won or lost the game, beyond the scoreboard. If the team accomplishes the majority of its objectives, you will often feel victorious even when the scoreboard reads defeat. I believe it is the coach's goal to help the athletes reach their goals.

Player Objectives

I have several objectives that I expect players to meet, although I also want them to develop objectives on their own. Here are some possible objectives for players:

- Treat other players, officials, and coaches with courtesy and respect.
- Represent your team and school with pride and respect.
- Always cheer for and support your teammates.
- Arrive everywhere early.
- Run if you arrive late.
- Always be honest.
- Work hard and give your all.

I want the players to be the best they can be as athletes, as students, and as people. They should use our program and coaching staff to add to their talents and strengths, and to minimize their weaknesses. I want them to be team players in life, to be worthy employees in the future as they are worthy athletes now, and to find happiness in all they have accomplished and in what they strive to conquer tomorrow.

A Losing Effort?

Sometimes we win and sometimes we lose. In a recent game, I felt like a spectator with a passionate interest in the events but who was not truly concerned with the outcome. When the game began, there was an overwhelming sense of calm, and it seemed that everyone was totally connected and on the same page. A very special aura was present.

I watched our hitters. They were totally focused. They looked so athletic and confident in the batter's box and seemed to swing at every good pitch. Our outs were crushed, and all of our hits went to the opposite field. I watched and marveled in a deeply connected sort of way. As the hitters looked at me from the outside of the batter's box, their faces were "poised" and awash with promise. No fear. No concern. No press. I looked back at them and wondered what they saw in me.

Every defensive play was made. Every catch and throw was precise. There was no hurry, no wonder if the out would be recorded. There was a feeling of defensive "connection." The game just flowed. And I watched. Absorbing. Soaking it all in. I watched our pitcher rock and fire. Perfect timing. Thoughtful, yet gathered. Working with her catcher and me and all those around her. In the center of her universe. Owning and trusting her intuition and her talent. Shooting the ball to all corners of the zone. Precise. Powerful. The game went too fast, like a great concert. I was drawn in to the tempo and pace, drawn in to the talent and energy. I watched as a privileged observer. It was awe inspiring. We may have lost the game, but the scoreboard did not tell the whole truth.

Team Objectives

Team objectives will develop from what the team wants from the season. The most important objective is for the players to work as a team and support each other. Members of the team are not all going to be best friends. Although friendships are important, the most critical element of a successful team is respect. Players can earn the respect of their teammates through the attitudes and actions they display both on and off the field.

Softball is like an assembly line—if everyone is doing her job at the highest level, the end product is quality. For a softball team, the desired end product of all its efforts is quality team play. A team's players will set their sights on a goal in hopes that, with each team member giving her best, the goal will be reached. Some common team objectives follow:

- Be completely focused as a team at practice and games.
- Support and respect each other.
- Represent the team first and yourself second.
- Play one pitch at a time.
- Give a winning effort.

In addition to the objectives listed here, the following three sections describe my three main messages to each team I coach.

Play Hard A coach should never have to speak these two words: "Play hard." As coaches, we need to instill in our athletes the concept of playing hard, but then it should be something every athlete does without being told. That is what sports are all about. If a player is out on the field and does not play hard or give it her all, someone else eager for the moment will give what it takes to be "out there" and will pass her by.

What does it take to be out there? What is playing hard? It is giving 100 percent of what you've got. That is what I tell my players I want from them. I ask this not only from my starting nine but from the whole team. You never know when a smart pinch runner is going to score the winning run or when a pinch hitter is going to bring in your runners. Everyone has to be prepared to give 100 percent when opportunity knocks.

Play Smart Playing smart wins ball games. I say it all the time to the athletes: "Be smart." I want them to think ahead, not only to want the ball, but also to know where to go with it when they get it. We have won crucial games because we have outsmarted our opponents. It can be as simple as your hitters not swinging at bad pitches and drawing a walk, or your fielders faking a throw with an aggressive runner on second and just holding onto the ball. It is about judgment and thinking ahead.

You and your players have to communicate with each other and make sure you see the same things. If you communicate, think ahead, and trust your instincts, then you are playing smart.

Practice As You Play Coaches know that "perfect practice makes perfect." Players have to give 100 percent in practice so that when game time arrives, the game pressure becomes routine. Fundamentals must be executed correctly in practice. Intensity must be planned for in practice, and hustle and determination must be incorporated into practice drills. If players take practice too easy, the game will become hard, so practice must be intense and fun at the same time. You should utilize pressure drills during practice and have a consequence if an error is made.

After "perfect practice," the athletes will go onto the field with confidence. Your shortstop will know she can field the short hop because she did 50 of them at practice the day before. Your outfielders will get good jumps on the ball because they spent time with you going over technique. The practice is the foundation for the game, and your players can only go as high as their foundations will hold them.

A Winning Effort

I have discussed winning with my assistants, and we do in fact talk about the wins and the losses and match them up in our hearts. Winning the game gives us something that losing could never give us. In one such discussion, my assistant and I ended up talking about our most recent win. The whole team had been elated. The athletes got on the bus, played a tape, and sang along at the top of their lungs. We were all laughing as they began dancing up and down the aisle. I even began dancing with them. This feeling that winning gave us, which caused us to want to dance and sing, we had never gotten from losing and playing well, nor do I think we ever will.

Coach's Objectives

The objectives of the coach are similar to those of the athlete and can include the following:

- Keep getting better as a coach.
- Know your strengths as a coach.
- Believe in your abilities.
- Stay committed to your plan.
- Keep a balance in your life.
- Be yourself.

You want to be able to give it your all, enhance your strengths, and minimize your weaknesses. I try to be a constant student of the game. I want to be able to give quality time to my athletes. To do this, I make sure that if I do not have the answer to what they need or want, I will find it. I believe my number one objective is to love what I do. By showing your athletes your dedication to them and to the profession, you will let them know you are in the coaching profession because you truly love it.

CHAPTER 2
COMMUNICATING YOUR APPROACH

Coaches can teach and learn only if they are effective communicators. Successful coaches must be able to exchange information with players, assistant coaches, umpires, players' parents, and the media. As a coach, you play a major role in the development of young athletes, and it is crucial that you effectively communicate with your players.

Communication is the essence of the team structure. The better you communicate, the stronger the fabric of your organization. It is your responsibility as a coach to help the athletes understand how to play the game and how to relate sport to life.

COMMUNICATION OFF THE FIELD

One of the most important aspects of coaching is to have good communication with the athletes off the field. A coach and her players can reach an understanding about each other off the field and away from the stress that sometimes surrounds games and practices. Through off-the-field communication, you can show the players your concern for them and the respect you have for them.

In addition to your athletes, there are a number of other people you'll have to communicate with on a regular basis, including assistants, parents, members of the school faculty and administration, and other students. Communicating effectively with all of these different groups will help you spread the word about your softball philosophy and program.

Communicating With Players

I teach the athletes that we need to have good communication. If the coaches and players are not communicating, the coaching staff will have a difficult time knowing where people are, how they are feeling, what is going on in their classes, and how their families are doing. One of my expectations is that the athletes greet the coaches when arriving at practice. This greeting opens up the door for further conversation, which will give a sense of how things are going for both parties that day.

The best chance for the coach and athlete to really get to know each other occurs during planned one-on-one conversations. I meet each student-athlete once a week for a 15-minute conversation. This gives me a chance to praise and encourage her performance on the field and to find out how college life is treating her and how her classes are going. It also provides a chance for her to express her thoughts.

Four times a year, I have a one-hour meeting with each player. These meetings take place partway through the fall season, at the end of the fall season, at the beginning of the spring season, and at the conclusion of the spring season. At these times, we discuss the athlete's goals and expectations as well as my evaluation of her practice and performance.

Within these conversations, the athlete will find her comfort zone with the coach and will discover that the coach values her as a person, not just as an athlete. These one-on-one conversations are when both the coach and player forget their respective roles and become people.

I have a policy that my players can always drop in to talk with me—appointments are not necessary. Communication involves both parties getting the opportunity to talk and share thoughts, concerns, and ideas. I try to define what communication is for the athletes so that they know I want their input and that they know when I am speaking I want them to listen. Your athletes want to be able to talk with you and know that you will listen, just as you want that from them.

Unfortunately, there are no definite, black-and-white answers regarding how coaches should communicate with their players. Coaches create their own styles to try to communicate what they think is important. You should keep the following four tips in mind when communicating with your players:

1. Work to gain your players' trust. Coaches have many expectations of their players. Usually, you will be able to explain your expectations in a way that the players understand; however, sometimes players may not completely comprehend the reasons for your expectations. If your players believe that what you teach is necessary and trust that they will eventually understand it, they will give you the benefit of the doubt and try to meet your expectations.

2. Teach your athletes to put the expectations on themselves (with a little guidance). Sometimes players do not put as much effort into reaching goals and expectations that they think are just the coach's idea. If it is also their goal, they might work harder toward reaching it. The art of coaching is figuring out a way to make your ideas become ideas that are shared by the players.

3. Teach your athletes to trust their training so that you can coach the game and not the skill. You should convince the players that the thousands of repetitions in practice will be transferred to the game if they can clear their mind in competition, thus allowing for this subconscious transfer to occur. Make your athletes aware that they are free to make instinctual decisions, allowing for what was practiced to come out in the game. This blend of trusting the training, clearing the mind, and allowing natural instincts to take over enables the athlete to play "in the zone" where performance flows.

4. Have an open mind. Many coaches are set in their ways and believe "doing it their way" is the best way. However, a team changes year to year and even from early on to later in the season, and you have to be willing to adapt with it.

Communicating With Assistants

I always try to incorporate my assistants in every aspect of the game. I give them their time to teach as well as try to teach them all that I have learned. I have had a great variety of assistants who have taught me different aspects of the game. Most of my assistants have been former players of mine who shared my love for the game and my philosophy of developing athletes to be the best they can be. I want my assistant coaches to have a vested interest in the program and to know that their ideas matter. I give them responsibilities and allow them to develop programs and plans for the team.

Some assistants have a specialty, such as pitching, which allows them to work in their area of expertise. If they begin in an area in which they have had success, it helps develop their confidence. I make sure that no one feels totally responsible for any one area of the program. I oversee all aspects and will request progress reports on any "assignments." I work hand in hand with my assistant coaches in planning the schedule, the budget, the workouts, and all other aspects of the program.

From the first day, I give feedback to my assistants about their strengths and weaknesses. I always have more positive than negative feedback, and the constructive criticism helps them to learn more about the game.

Sharing ideas on the field will lead to mutual respect and understanding between coach and staff.

The communication between you and your assistants is a give-and-take. You will not always agree, but this is healthy and will always be a learning experience. Keep the communication lines open and find value in your assistants' opinions, skills, and insights. Listen to everything your assistants are trying to say, and think about what they are trying to relay. Remember, it is your program, and you want good people representing you. Trust your judgment and confront all problems head-on. Loyalty is critical in this relationship; build it with honesty and communication.

Communicating With Parents

Work with parents and make them a part of the team rather than view them as critics to be avoided. Parents must be able to approach you, ask questions, and talk with you about their daughters. However, make it clear that you will not talk about playing time. The parents are not with the team on a daily basis to see where each member of the team will fit best in the lineup. In most cases, they just want to know that their daughter is doing well and that she is in good hands. Take the time to approach the parents also. It is a nice feeling when the coach initiates the conversation and lets the parents know that their daughter is a fine young athlete. Successful communication will provide great fans, volunteers, and supporters of their daughters.

In the beginning of each year, we have a picnic where all the athletes and their families come together and meet one another. Every year there are new athletes and families, and I feel it is important for these new people to get the chance to meet the other athletes and families before the first competition. This allows them to ask questions, get to know each other, and learn what the program is about. It is a mixer in the truest sense because they are the ingredients of the upcoming team. It is nice to have the opportunity to recognize how well we will blend. Also, at the beginning of a season, I prepare a parent roster with names, addresses, phone numbers, and e-mail addresses so that parents can develop relationships with each other. This also allows me an opportunity to communicate travel arrangements, itineraries, and scheduling information directly with them.

Communicating With School Faculty and Administrators

Regardless of the ages or abilities of your athletes, you want them to receive a great education. My coaching staff tries to create a working relationship with the professors who teach our athletes. We ask our athletes to introduce themselves to their professors as student-athletes. We write a letter that tells the professor the days the athletes will miss because of competitions and asks for the athlete to be excused. The athlete is to arrange with each professor how to make up the work. We realize not all professors are going to be fans of athletics, and we try to work the best we can with them so that everyone understands the role of the student-athlete.

Without the "student" there will be no "athlete." I believe coaches are teachers first and should share academic monitoring with other faculty members. In my program, we request feedback from professors and work directly with student-athletes, and we try to ensure that our athletes are attending classes, getting the help they need, and staying on schedule. Staying abreast of each athlete's classroom performance shows your interest in the student first.

When communicating with administrators, my assistant and I meet with the athletic director or other administrators on a regular basis regarding particular athletes or issues relating to my program. That way our administrators get to know our team and how well they are doing. If there is something I need for my team or an important issue has come up, they are kept "in the know."

You must be organized when meeting with an administrator. Be sure to bring the necessary paperwork with you to the meeting and realize their time is valuable. Communication is an integral part of success when dealing with administrators. The athletic director is a key staff member and needs to be informed of every major issue concerning your team.

Communicating With the Community

Coaches at the high school and college level need to communicate with the community. For one month each summer and two months each spring (usually in June, January, and February), one of our team's goals is to be the center of attention in our community. People are very active and busy these days, and numerous activities compete for their time and attention year-round. But for a short time, we work with individual community members to keep the spotlight on our team. We want to gain their support for our team and for the sport itself, because this helps build a better program for Western and for the young athletes. We work with the community in the following ways:

- Our athletes and coaches do clinics for young athletes.
- Our athletes and coaches periodically do a local radio show one day a week with ticket giveaways.
- Our athletes deliver our posters, media guides, and schedule cards to area businesses.
- We have designed a program called "Community Corporate Teammates."

A more in-depth discussion of community projects can be found in chapter 4.

Communicating With the Media

You should give the members of the news media your time and patience. This might be easier said than done, but it is critical if your athletes are to get the exposure they deserve. I want the media to talk to the players so people will better understand what it takes to be a strong Division I female athlete. I do not keep the media waiting. Immediately following our game, if there is anyone present from the media, I tell them I will be right with them. I then gather my thoughts and meet for the interview. At this time, the players are packing their equipment prior to our team meeting.

If we have a unique story, I try to notify the media members first. They enjoy getting a "scoop." I encourage the reporters to call me at home as well, and if they would like to call us on the road, I let them know where we are staying.

COMMUNICATION ON THE FIELD

The athletes learn the game on the field, during practices and games, through the communication the coach has with them. What you say and how you communicate with each athlete can determine the outcome of the game and the success of your program. If the athlete understands that you are on her side and that you want to help her be the best she can be, then the communication line is open.

Communicating With Players

My main objective with my athletes is to let them know that I respect them and the efforts they make, and that I am concerned about the forces that affect their ability to play to their potential. When the coach is on the field, she is visible to all who watch the game or watch the practice, so I try not to overreact or embarrass the athletes—they try to play their positions with poise and technique, and so do I. Many others view the image that you project on the field, and you must conduct yourself at the highest level of professionalism.

Never Humiliate

The coach has the right to be passionate, but she must choose the right moment and express herself with respect and dignity. I have made it a point in my career to never yell at a player during a game. I will not raise my voice to them when there are other people and fans around. I may do that during a practice but never when the athlete could be embarrassed in front of nonplayers. I work with my assistants to make sure they follow this philosophy. If a player is having a difficult time hitting or fielding, I will pull her aside between innings and talk quietly. Most of our game communication is praise, leaving criticisms for practice.

Always remember that the athletes are young adults who need to be treated respectfully. If you treat them otherwise, they will eventually lose trust and respect for you, thus, affecting their performance. Keep the communication lines clean and clear. Do not damage those lines with humiliation, but rather strengthen them with words that instruct.

Linking

I have noticed an interesting phenomenon that I call "linking." It occurs when a player asks a routine question directly of the coach. This may not sound special, but have you ever corrected or criticized a player and then a few minutes later she asked a basic question? I believe the player is trying to reconnect with you on a one-on-one basis. She wants to have you acknowledge her again in a positive light, and so she asks you a question, usually a simple one, so that you can respond in a nonthreatening manner. I call this "linking" because the player wants to reestablish her relationship with you.

Instruct, Don't Dictate

Go out every day of practice with a lesson in mind. Follow that lesson plan by telling the team what that day's objectives are and then, at the end of each practice day, reviewing what was accomplished. This method will help you feel prepared to teach what you want to teach that day. Coaches should give direction to their athletes to help them reach the optimal outcome of each day's lesson. Students, in general, learn from instruction when they have input and can work together with the person in authority. Usually, giving a command or ordering a desired behavior does not reinforce that behavior or teach it to the student.

Coaches must be sure they have taught a skill before they can criticize the athlete for her failure to execute a skill or to carry out a play. I try to always remember that I am a teacher first and foremost and that it is my responsibility to instruct the student in how to play the game at the highest level. Both the teacher and the learner have the same goal in mind—doing things better. Teaching and learning occur simultaneously, and both the coach and the athlete strive to reach the goal or objective.

Comprehension is accelerated with transfer learning. Transfer learning occurs when an athlete learns from the instruction given to another athlete. That is why you should stress listening and paying attention as all instruction is given. You can make the best use of teaching moments by ensuring that everyone can hear. For example, if an athlete throws to the wrong bag on a batted ball, you can benefit everyone by instructing all players on the appropriate decision. That player will inevitably not be the only one put in that situation in the future.

Communicate During the Game

In softball, there are communication lines going on all over the field. On defense, the pitcher gets signals from the catcher, who might be getting signals from the coach. The shortstop and second baseman get signals from the catcher and give them to the outfielders. When on offense, the batter and the base runner receive signals

During the game, the coach should be clear in the instructions she gives. Now is the time to coach the game rather than the skill.

from their coach on what play to execute. This communication goes on for every pitch of the game. This type of communication is verbal and nonverbal. The game relies on the use of communication so that all participants are informed and receive the right message.

As the players come off the field to get ready to bat, our team has a quick huddle to praise the defense and discuss the upcoming ways to score. This is a time to unite during the game.

At the conclusion of each game, we meet as a team in the outfield to briefly discuss the game. We sit in a circle in assigned spots; this way, I know where each player is and can look at her to address her. I use this time to acknowledge the "well hits" (well-hit balls), the good execution of plays, the RBIs, and the defensive plays that stand out. If the team made mental errors, we talk about them at this time as well. The focus of this meeting is on praise and instruction.

Communicating With Assistants

My assistant coach and I make it a point not to disagree in front of the team. We present a united front to the players, and if we have disagreements, we use a more private opportunity to discuss them. I do make game decisions based on my assistant's input. I feel two heads are better than one, so I try to confer with her often during the game. As a general rule, I coach third base and determine the particular plays. I will discuss any pinch-hit or pinch-run possibilities throughout the game. I feel that we know what it takes for our squad to be successful because we have talked about our opponent's strengths and weaknesses prior to the contest. During the game, I do not hesitate to call time-out or take my assistant aside to discuss changes in our game plan.

We plan out every practice together and do a follow-up evaluation after practice. We take notes from the evaluation and work in our suggestions for future practices. We share the same office so our discussions are free flowing, but we do plan our day in blocks of time with the first task of the day being to plan that day's practice.

Each Monday we evaluate the previous week's games and practices, and we determine the emphasis for the upcoming week. We ask the athletes to notify us in advance if they are going to be late or unable to attend a practice. In this way, we are better able to plan around those occurrences.

Communicating With Umpires

Let the catcher set the rapport with the plate umpire in determining balls and strikes. Quiet conversations between the two will establish a strike zone the battery can work with. I may ask the catcher if a particular pitch was a strike, and I want an honest opinion back. If an umpire makes a call I disagree with, I will go onto the field slowly so that I can gather my thoughts. I will try to present my remarks in a calm manner, knowing that I will not win any judgment calls, but might win a rules decision. Conversations versus confrontation will develop a better relationship with an umpire.

The coach must be able to ask the umpire a question about a play and then have a brief discussion. Often, however, the umpire is too sensitive to hear the question or the debate is too highly charged. My approach is to make my point quickly and then move on. For example, if it is a situation where the umpire says my player missed a tag, on my way out to the umpire, I will first quickly ask the player if she did indeed apply the tag. If the player says yes, I will continue my trip out to the umpire. I believe in this manner the umpire has heard it from the player and then from me. There is little to talk about after that, but the umpire knows we know a call was missed. The umpire is just trying to do the best job possible, and it does not serve a purpose to embarrass her or argue with her.

Don't Call Me Honey

In a regional Amateur Softball Association game where my summer team was vying for a chance to win the title and go on to nationals, I had to draw the line in order to keep my starting pitcher, Margie Wright, on the mound. The game was highly charged, and neither Margie nor our catcher felt the umpire was as sharp as he should have been with balls and strikes. They showed their displeasure to him with facial expressions and quiet comments. In the sixth inning, as I was walking to the coach's box, he said to me, "Listen, honey, you better do something about your pitcher." As soon as he said the word *honey*, I knew I was going to win an argument with an umpire. I stopped, spun around, and said, "You can call me Kathy, or you can call me Coach, but you can never call me honey. I am not your honey, never was, and never will be." The crowd within earshot roared, and the umpire blushed. He spent the rest of the game apologizing to me. The best part was, my pitcher stayed in the game, quite a bit more relaxed, and we went on to win the regional title.

CHAPTER 3 MOTIVATING PLAYERS

Motivation means helping players improve to a higher level of performance. I do this by calling on skills and strategies that assist each player in reaching for, meeting, and stretching beyond her expectations as an athlete. My job as the coach is to find the mechanisms that challenge my athletes to work harder to be the best. These tools, or motivational devices, must keep the job at hand fun and interesting or no growth will occur. I try to motivate the athletes so that they can reach the goals they set.

I often use our competitive schedule as motivation. An athlete is going to work harder when she knows her opponent might be a little bit better. Haven't we all often heard that the team will play up or down to the competition? I also try to do things for my players that make them feel special and unique. In this chapter, you will find some of those techniques that can help motivate your players.

WHAT MOTIVATES YOUR ATHLETES?

In many ways, softball is an individual sport. When the athlete is the batter, there is little a teammate can do to enhance her performance. She must work long and hard on her individual skills and often delay gratification throughout many months of training. This requires intrinsic motivation that must come from within the player. Some intrinsic motives are success, recognition, self-worth, and peer acceptance. A high level of motivation results in athletes who are committed and driven toward success.

There are essential elements needed to get the most out of your players. Although some athletes already possess these qualities, you should try to instill and further develop them in all your athletes as a motivational technique.

1. Players need the ability to work for delayed rather than instant gratification. The great athlete separates herself from the good athlete when she shows a willingness to practice hard now for a payoff later.

2. Players must have the ability to take feedback as help, not criticism. To achieve her maximum, the athlete needs to receive coaching and instruction—this is the coachable player. The athlete must recognize that progress, not perfection, is the goal. She must accept instruction openly rather than defensively.

3. Players must have a vision of where they want to be and could be. Success and greatness come with a vision of being so. The athlete must have a sense of purpose, a vision to guide her efforts. This vision is the fuel that drives the delayed gratification. The athlete's motivation must not be external, but internal.

4. Players must have the ability to look for solutions, not problems. These are the athletes who love a challenge, who see opportunity in difficulty, and who persist with hard work and alternatives rather than quit.

Athletes must learn from the coach that success is ensured when they perceive a loss or mistake as information that will prepare them for the next event. When they learn to *learn* from their mistakes, they will not dwell over a failure. This is what we have all experienced as constructive criticism.

Motivation can be passed from player to player through small gestures, such as a touch or a tip of the visor. Athletes with high levels of motivation will be driven toward success.

VERBAL REINFORCEMENT

Reinforcement means to strengthen with new assistance. When using verbal reinforcement to strengthen a player's focus or confidence, you are saying something in a positive light about her performance. There are several different ways to go about this. In this chapter, I will share with you what has been most successful with my athletes. One of the most common ways I reinforce my athletes is through verbalizing their strengths. When addressing the whole team, I will often choose one athlete and name her as a great leader, hitter, or defensive player. I do this so that she gets the recognition she has worked hard for and also so that her teammates see that hard work is acknowledged.

Approaching an athlete at practice and reinforcing her efforts with one-on-one communication is important for me. One-on-one communication has a place in every game as well. I find that those athletes who give the extra effort day in and day out need to be applauded by the whole team. Athletes like hitting home runs in the game, where everyone can appreciate their talent. The same principle applies here. If a player has hustled all practice, point out in front of everyone that you see and appreciate her efforts and that you feel the team should recognize them as well and should follow her example.

Verbal reinforcements are not always expressions like "good job." They can be skill related also—for example, telling a hitter, "Great hands," because she kept her hands stationary on a bad pitch. Overall, I verbalize more about the skills that are being polished during practice time. This is appropriate because I want the athlete to know why I said, "Good job." So I go straight to the skill and say, "Britt, great hands." That way I am saying, "Great job" about the skill she performed.

When you need to correct an athlete, the best way is to sandwich the criticism between two positive reinforcements. For example, you might say, "Sarah, great balance (positive reinforcement). You need to keep your bat still (constructive criticism), but your hands are coming through the zone nicely (positive reinforcement)." This helps the athlete better absorb criticism because she is also hearing things she is doing correctly.

Everyone has a strength. It could be that they are quick or strong, or have good balance, a good eye, or even keen insight into drills. Make sure to point out that not only does your starting lineup have great skill but so do those players on the bench.

Team Praise

There are crucial times when you want to make sure you verbalize the team's strengths both as a whole and individually. It might be before a big game, after a tough loss, or if the season seems to be a roller coaster of ups and downs. These times represent crucial moments when the group needs to be reminded of its talent and effort. I sometimes take the time to pull out each individual's strengths for display. When I have touched on everyone, I combine all those attributes and talk about the team as a whole. This technique helps the team members respect each other for their own individual strengths and illustrates how they all make up the team they are a part of. With this in mind, they may find a comfort zone on the field and begin performing at an optimal level. Verbal reinforcement is the quick and easy high that an athlete or a team needs. As coaches, we are the providers. You will also see other athletes picking up on it and using it daily to support their teammates.

Individual Attention

Individual attention is a special way to motivate players. The motivational power an athlete receives when she feels like the coach is paying attention to her in practice is great. I believe the coach and the athlete need to have a 10-second contact within the first 10 minutes of practice. The trick to this is requiring the athletes to say "Hello" when arriving at practice. This provokes a response from you and even possibly a small exchange of a smile, pat on the shoulder, or short conversation about their day. Saying "Hello" is the doorway to communication, comfort, and caring.

I try to make sure our staff provides some type of verbal reinforcement to everyone. The easiest way to reach everyone is when they are working in small groups. If your staff can work at different stations, they are likely to have the opportunity to teach and provide insight to the athletes on a more individual level. As the athletes move through the practice stations, they should be reached by at least one of you and receive some individual attention about the task at hand.

NONVERBAL REINFORCEMENT

Coaches are always looking for ways to send a message and make it stick. Verbal reinforcement is good, but I feel it is a quick fix. Nonverbal reinforcement can be both a quick fix and a lasting message.

Physical cues or body language can send a message and be a nonverbal reinforcer. These might include clapping, patting a back, a high five, or a nod of approval. These types of nonverbal reinforcement are very good but are something of a quick fix also. They convey your approval or congratulations, but within moments the athlete and you are doing something different and the transaction is over.

Token reinforcement—that is, the use of a token such as a sticker to reward a player for an accomplishment—has been a fun motivator for our athletes. We have stickers for singles, doubles, triples, home runs, stolen bases, RBIs, Ks, great defense, great offense, and great hustle. After every game, our staff votes on an offensive and defensive player of the game, sometimes picking more than one in both categories. These athletes receive a sticker picked out for their specific accomplishment. The other stickers are allotted to the athletes who earn them during each game. After an athlete receives the sticker, she places it on a sign with her name on it that hangs on her locker. This allows other athletes to see each player's talents and contributions.

Everyone needs daily inspiration. I like to start practice by taking a quote I feel is relevant to what we need to accomplish that day and handing out copies to the athletes to all read silently. Taking the quote-of-the-day approach with my athletes is like fishing for their attention. The quote I offer is the bait, and their thoughts are the fish. It is a true exercise of focusing. For a moment, we are pulled to one common thought and what it means to us. I sometimes read the quotes, but many of the players like to have them written down. I type them up and sometimes add a few graphics and then hand them out. Several of the athletes put them in their handbooks; this is an excellent place to keep them, since they can return to the quotes and refocus.

Trading Cards and Posters

I once saw a great poster of Dot Richardson with the caption DESIRE at the bottom of it. I thought that my athletes should have a poster of themselves with an inspirational message as well. I let them choose their saying, and then I located the action picture of them that best depicted their abilities and designed a poster for them. I took the 8 1/2-by-11-inch sheets to a color copier and made 11-by-14-inch posters. I then laminated the posters and gave them to the athletes. The athletes used some as Christmas presents, and many hung them on their walls.

I also designed trading cards for them. Again, the color copier did a super job! On the front, I put each athlete's name and position along with our school's name and an action photo. Information about their career and statistics appeared on the back. When they saw their cards, they beamed!

PRACTICE AS A MOTIVATOR

When your athletes are practicing in the gym at 6:00 a.m. on a cold January morning, you sometimes need to remind them that they are fortunate to be there. You can talk about the ones who are not fortunate enough to play on a softball team—those athletes who got cut or just were not seen. Competitors work harder when facing a challenge. Athletes need to hear about their opponents who are practicing every day to beat them. I sometimes wear the sweatshirts of the teams we cannot wait to play in the upcoming season. It is a subtle reminder that those opponents are out there practicing and preparing for us, just as we must do today for them. As competitors, we motivate ourselves by staying focused on the competition.

Many times I bring in a video of the country's high-profile athletes in competition. We watch these games as a team and critique them. This helps my team see that there is always room for improvement. It also helps them relate to those athletes, since they find themselves facing some of the same stumbling blocks in the game.

In practices, you want to hit all the important details, but you also want the athletes to come to practice with their own personal agendas. I believe each athlete has an idea of what she wants to work on, who she wants to outhit, who she wants to strike out, or how many ground balls she wants to make a play on without making an error. Let these things be part of practice. Create competitions. Congratulate your freshman pitcher in front of the team when she gets your best hitter to fly out. Hit your shortstop ground ball after ground ball, and let the team applaud her as she makes the plays. There should be clapping and cheering during practice. It is at those instances that the athletes recognize why they love the game and its intensity.

Fix the Problem With Sweat

I had a pitcher who could not get her drop ball to drop. In practice, it was unmatched by the other pitchers, but in the game she seemed to lose faith in it. We felt it was psychological, that she did not believe in her pitches, or herself. She was more inclined to argue that it was something else. After listening to every excuse and tolerating bad performances, I decided she needed to throw the drop ball so many times that throwing it in the game would be easy. I sent her over to a brick wall with a strike zone painted on it and gave her a bucket of balls. Her practice that day consisted of throwing drop balls to a designated area on the wall. After she threw a ball, it would bounce off the wall, and she would have to pick it up and then throw another. In the end, she had thrown hundreds of drop balls. She was sweaty, tired, and disciplined. We both got what we wanted out of the experience. She got a drop ball, and I got an athlete who realized the game is easy. In a game, the pitcher gets to throw to a catcher and batters; she doesn't have to pick up every ball. This pitcher valued the experience and did not fear throwing her drop ball in the game again.

GOAL SETTING

Every practice, every day, every week, the athlete needs something to inspire her. I believe a goal is a pep talk an athlete gives herself.

To get somewhere, you must first know where you want to go. Some of the teams I have coached have gone to a national tournament, and some have not. But it was not always based on talent or lack of talent. I believe those who go believe they can and never consider the possibility that they won't. The team sets the goal to win it all, and though they might come up short, they do go a lot further than they would have if they had never strived to be champions.

Performance Goals

Athletes should stay away from outcome goals and focus on performance goals, which they can control. Some things in the sport of softball are out of the athletes' hands. For example, a pitcher might want to throw a shutout. This is an outcome goal and one over which she has little control. She might be pitching great, getting batters out, having good ball movement and location, but the team may make some errors and allow a run to score. The pitcher had no control over the players on her team and how well they were fielding that day. If her goal was based on the outcome—the shutout—she will not have achieved her goal, even though her performance was outstanding.

On the other hand, performance goals are specifically within the athlete's control. When setting performance goals, the athlete should ask herself (1) what her individual softball goals are, (2) what goals she will meet in order to be a successful student-athlete during the semester, and (3) what action she is going to take to accomplish these goals. Examples of performance goals might be to hit the ball hard, to stop swinging at bad pitches, or to stop 10 grounders in practice without an error. These are all goals that the athlete can meet without depending on the performance of others.

Goals should be set up like a pyramid. The *now* goals make up the base of the pyramid. These goals are abundant and create a strong base for the others to rest on. Athletes need

to constantly strive for something during each moment of practice or competition. A now goal is one that an athlete wants to accomplish at this present moment. In softball, a player might say she wants to follow every ball into her glove for the entire practice. These are goals that the athlete makes in the present and attempts to accomplish in the present.

Short-term goals occupy the center of the pyramid. They are the most important portions of the pyramid, the building blocks. They work off the base of now goals and require a real commitment from the athlete. They are goals the athlete expects to meet in practice or within a two-week period. If they are accomplished, the heart of the pyramid is strong.

Much of the athlete's goal setting needs to involve short-term goals since these are the building blocks of the success pyramid. Short-term goals must be realistic and attainable, and they can be verbal or written. Every 2 weeks I have my athletes fill out a "goal card," which they carry with them at all times. On this card they list four short-term goals for the 14-day period: a personal goal, a family goal, a school goal, and a softball goal. I put a motivational quote on the bottom of the card every 2 weeks.

Long-term goals make up the peak of the pyramid. This is the highest point of goal setting. If the athlete reaches the peak successfully and she has followed the steps correctly, then she is probably playing up to her "peak" performance. Once the athlete has met her long-term goal, she can see and feel all the great reasons why goal setting is important. Having been to the top once, she will create another pyramid to conquer.

Team Goals

Team goals are developed and discussed by the team. They could be spoken or written words, such as "Let's have the best defense in the conference." During this discussion, our athletes create a list of all the team goals for the season. This list is made into a large poster with the opponents for the season across the top and the goals down the side. This chart is then posted after every game with a star next to the goals the team met.

Changing Goals

If a goal set in the beginning of the year becomes unattainable at some point in the season, a new attainable goal needs to be set. If, for example, one of your athlete's goals was to have a fielding percentage of .970, and there is now no possible way to raise it that high, she needs to change her goal. You can first help her evaluate why she did not meet her original goal. After she has reflected on the first goal, let her put it away and create a goal that can be met in the remainder of the season. This allows her to still have something to shoot for and also to learn from her failure to fulfill the first goal. She might realize that she did not reach her first goal because it was unrealistic for the position she plays or possibly that she did not follow the steps needed for the end result desired. When goals are made in the beginning or in the middle of a season, they first need to be attainable to be effective.

Misdirected Goals

Misdirected goals are those that are either unattainable or too obvious. It would be ineffective to set a goal such as going undefeated in a season. Although everyone hopes for it to happen, it's not a goal that can be controlled. Though being undefeated in a season is attainable, it is a misdirected goal because it is controlled by too many other forces. An example of an unattainable goal is for your weakest hitter to say she wants to hit .380 for the season. You know she struggles to keep a .250 average. This goal is too lofty and will most likely collapse this athlete's goal pyramid. It would be better for you and the athlete to find an attainable goal.

An example of an obvious goal is to say, "I want to do the best I can." Of course most athletes usually want to do the best they can. To make this a goal is an easy way out. They need to strive for something to increase their level of play. "I did the best I could" is often an excuse for not rising to the occasion.

DISCIPLINE

Discipline has a dual meaning. Coaches both teach and perform types of discipline during their careers. They teach time management, healthy eating, and behavior control, for example, which affect the athletes' everyday lives whether in practice, at school, or on personal time. Coaches perform discipline in cases where an athlete has broken a rule. The two mingle with each other and help strengthen each other.

When prompting an athlete to perform at the level I feel she can, I have to use several motivating tools to get the end result. Every sport has its rules, and every team has its own laws or code. Discipline in one's behavior is the first discipline I address. The athletes are informed of a formal code of ethics put out by the university, and then they are introduced to a code that has been put together by me and many former athletes. (See chapter 4 for an in-depth discussion of my rule-setting process.) They are codes that teach the player to be self-disciplined and help her become an elite athlete.

10-Mile Run

I have always tried to impress on my players the importance of class attendance. One April we had an off day the last Friday of the month. Early that April, I announced to the team that we would not practice on the last Friday in April, but that they must go to class. Our game schedule was such that we did not play that Saturday or Sunday. Halfway through April, I again reminded the team that we would be off the last weekend but that they must go to class on that Friday. The night before the last Friday, we were returning home from a trip to Iowa, and I again reminded them about class attendance. At that time I said, "If you don't go to class, be ready to run 10 miles." We gave our closing cheer, and the next morning I sent my assistant to see who was and who was not in class. Seven players decided not to attend class! That Sunday night, I called each of those athletes and told them to be at the field the next morning at 5:30 a.m. Monday morning I loaded those seven into my van and drove 10 miles out of town. I dropped them off and said, "See you at practice this afternoon." It has been a few seasons since anyone has missed a class.

It also takes discipline to perform the movements of an athlete. The athlete learns certain motions, styles, and techniques of how to perform no matter what sport she is participating in. For example, in softball the athlete learns a batting position. This position requires the hitter to be disciplined at keeping her eye on the ball, remaining balanced, and many other techniques that lead to successful hitting. This skill discipline is something that is taught using forms of discipline to reinforce the correct action.

In practice, I will use a physical task as a form of discipline to motivate athletes to develop their skills. For example, we play a hitting game and ask that each hitter perform a certain skill. It might be taking the ball to right field or putting it on the ground. When the hitter is unsuccessful, she must do an assigned amount of sit-ups. When she is done, she gets another try at performing a hitting skill. This puts pressure on the athlete to perform, so when game time arrives, she has already successfully executed the skill under pressure. If the hitter cannot put the ball on the ground in the game when we need it, there will be a negative outcome much greater than sit-ups.

CHAPTER 4 BUILDING A SOFTBALL PROGRAM

Many considerations go into building a successful program. These include deciding on a system of play, utilizing and nurturing outside support, setting up rules, and recruiting athletes. I've learned about these ingredients throughout my playing and coaching career. I played under Chuck McCord with the Pekin Lettes for seven years. I then had the opportunity to compete professionally with the Connecticut Falcons. That roster read like a "Who's Who" of coaches in Division I athletics. This opportunity happened while I was coaching at Western Illinois University. In 1979, I decided to build my own women's major premier fastpitch team, the Macomb Magic. I began by setting a goal that it would be a professionally run team that would compete against the very best in the country, that would be exciting to watch with tremendous athletes, and that it would represent our community at the elite level. Many hours went into this dream, and the outcome was a club that played in two United States Olympic Festivals, twice finished fourth in national tournament play, qualified for five national tournament participations, and won state championships and regional titles as well. All of this occurred during the seven-year existence of the program.

When I decided to put this team on the field, my first obligation was to find the players who would be its heart and soul. This was accomplished by selecting two WIU players,

Robin Lindley-McConnell and Jackie Crescio, who were finishing up their senior years. The next player I chose was my assistant coach, Kathy Welter. With these three players, I had the nucleus of talent and desire. The four of us then brainstormed ideas for the vision, the team makeup, and the team image. I rounded out the team with players whom I had coached in the past as well as other players from the Western Illinois team. It was a small squad but one with the ingredients I thought were necessary for success. The team members liked each other and respected each other's talent. They knew my style of coaching and brought to the program solid pitching, strong defensive tools, and offensive power.

With the players on board, I asked Kathy Orban to serve as the business manager. The two of us worked with a local marketing person, Steve Yeast, who helped us target the professional image we were after. He designed our media guide and helped us with marketing strategies. He also taught us how to link with community members and earn community support. With his ideas and our own, we began our fund-raising efforts. From the very beginning, we competed with a strong schedule and traveled from coast to coast.

Our main financial support came from gate receipts and sponsorships. The Macomb Magic played evening games and weekend games at home whenever possible, and we drew people from area cities and towns. Attendance at home games was outstanding.

Along with every coaching philosophy comes a coaching style, and from this a certain system or method for playing the game. My coaching philosophy has always been to handle my team in the fairest possible way. I try to treat each player differently because each player's personality is different. At every practice, a lesson of "how to" is delivered. These lessons reflect the coaching style, and from there a system is born. I hold five points as the standards within my system: to be myself; to be honest; to give respect; to let the players know they are people to me, not just softball players; and to stay positive.

My system and style of play have always mirrored the Macomb Magic teams. I want to find and recruit great ballplayers, athletes who are talented enough to play more than one position. I have always believed that if a player can hit, there will be a defensive spot for her. I believe that a player should either bring a great bat to the team or a great glove. I want the player who has both, of course, but more often the athlete has more of one than the other. When I recruit,

I look for the athlete with strong hitting and throwing mechanics. I know I can teach and refine those skills, but I want that strong base to start with.

In this chapter, I discuss developing a system, gaining support for your program, implementing the system, and instilling pride in your program.

GAIN SUPPORT FOR YOUR PROGRAM

There are many avenues to pursue to gain support for your softball program, from your school's administration, faculty, and students to other members of your community. Without the friends and families of our players, as well as administrators, faculty members, trainers, and members of the community, our program could not be successful. Their support is what we count on at Western, and in the following sections, I'll talk about some of the ways I've gained that support. Keep in mind that your number one goal should be to gain people's respect for you, your program, and your athletes.

Team fan clubs help create community awareness of, and support for, the team. They also give players the opportunity to pass their talents and enthusiasm to the future stars of the game.

Administrative and Faculty Support

The softball program is a representative of the university. When making decisions about the team, uniforms, opponents, fund-raisers, and other issues, you should keep the administration informed and ask for their input. Communication is essential. If you have good communication lines, it will be easier for athletic directors, counselors, principals, and superintendents to support you. Working together will bring about a better relationship. I want my administration to get to know the softball players on a personal level. To that end, I include the administration in many of the events we put together in a social or professional setting.

Because we have always stressed the importance of academics to our players, I decided that I would show the professors how much I cared about our players' classes. I gathered up our players' class schedules one spring and made a list of included professors and their campus office address. I also drafted a letter noting the athlete that the professor had and the days the athlete would be missing class. Most important, I brought a schedule and a softball brochure in hopes that the teacher would find time to attend a game or two. I visited each professor, introduced myself, and engaged in a brief conversation regarding the softball team and the specific player the professor had in class. This was my chance to meet each professor face to face and form a positive connection between academics and athletics. We also dedicate a home game to the professors where they are the special guests for the evening. It allows them to see the many talented facets of their students. This effort to inform teachers of absences and provide information about the program shouldn't be limited to the college level. In high school, the teachers and students spend more time together, and this closeness should lend itself to athletes supporting teachers and teachers supporting athletes.

Student Support

There is nothing like hitting the ball hard and hearing the roar of a big crowd. It's a great feeling to have the stands full of your peers supporting you and your talent. Our staff tries to always inform the student body of our game times and team successes. We also have people working on promotions to entice the students of Western to come out and watch some pretty amazing women playing softball. We involve the crowd with games that go on in the stands and drawings that give them a chance to try to hit a ball over the fence in between games. There are prizes and giveaways and chances to mingle with the athletes after the game, not to mention action-packed softball with diving catches, balls going over the fence, pitches at 65 miles per hour, and headfirst slides into home plate. All these things combined help us gain the support of the students.

Community Support

There are many ways to involve your community in your program. To increase community awareness and support for our team, we have a fastpitch softball club for fans. We put together a package that would allow fans the opportunity to get to know the players and the coaching staff on a personal level, and to let them experience the various "stories" behind the scenes. I have included an example of our Fastpitch Club's description and benefits in figure 4.1. We also have a Diamond Club for the young fans that gives them softball experience along with the chance to get to know the players and coaches (see figure 4.2).

We have also been fortunate enough to obtain business sponsorships for our home games to boost our community support. We structured a plan called Community Corporate Teammates (CCT), which works like this: For each of our home games, we involve a local community group to assist in both the promotion of the game and in giving away prizes they have donated. For each of the CCTs, we do radio announcements and newspaper coverage. In exchange for a cash contribution or free products, the CCT receives a certificate, a picture of the team and the CCT's employees taken in the CCT's establishment, a public address announcement, and a program listing.

There are many activities you can organize with corporate sponsors: free squeeze bottles, gift certificates, and magnets from area restaurants; sponsorship of youth clinics by area businesses; prizes from area merchants for returning

---

You are invited to join the Western Illinois Fastpitch Club

Who:

A Board of Directors and Officers govern the WIU Fastpitch Club. The membership consists of alumni, friends, and supporters of Westerwinds softball.

Why:

The WIU Fastpitch Club is being formed as a friends group for the Western Illinois softball program. As financial constraints continue to rise in college athletics, support from friends groups such as the Fastpitch Club becomes critical. In addition to the financial support, members have an opportunity to support and promote the team. Loyal backing from alumni, family, and friends has a tremendous meaning for the student-athletes.

Membership options:

Individual $30 yearly
Student $20 yearly (high school or college)
Lifetime $200

Membership benefits:

- The opportunity to promote and support the WIU softball program
- The opportunity to meet and interact with the coaches and players at club functions
- Newsletters mailed throughout the year, which include updates on the team, feature stories, notes from the WIU coaches, and upcoming club activities
- T-shirt, decal, schedule card, poster, media guide, and trading cards
- Acknowledgment in the game program
- Social opportunities such as tent gating, invitation to the "Big Game Breakfast," Fan Van, and postgame socials

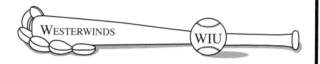

Figure 4.1   Western Illinois University Fastpitch Club information.

foul balls; and so on. We've involved nearly 30 community corporate teammates in one season with little expense for them and a win–win situation for all of us.

IMPLEMENT THE SYSTEM

Once you have developed your own softball system and have the school and community behind you, you are ready for the final step in building a softball program: implementation. In this step, you concern yourself with hiring assistants, establishing team rules, and passing the pride you have in your program on to your players.

Hiring Assistants

When searching for an assistant, you must look for someone who will complement you and the program. Just as you recruit a certain style of

athlete for a certain position, you should search for a certain type of person to come in and assist you in the coaching duties. Your assistant will bring knowledge, experience, and support to the team. Take your time when looking for an assistant, and make sure that she has all the attributes you are looking for. For example, I look for outgoing and personable characteristics in assistant candidates I evaluate. You should look at her dominant characteristics and decide if they will mesh with yours. Even if your assistant is a volunteer, you should still make sure you are comfortable with her.

Check into the background of a potential assistant to make sure she is qualified. Talk with former employers and ask about the characteristics you are most interested in. It would be in your best interest to call people who are not on the reference list. The two most important qualities to me are loyalty and trustworthiness, and with time and a solid working relationship, these feelings begin to grow. Once you feel you can trust your assistant, you can begin to relinquish more responsibility to her, and then she

You are invited to join the WIU Diamond Club

Who:
The WIU Diamond Club is open to girls in grades 2 through 8.

Why:
The WIU Diamond Club provides four clinics to help you be the best fastpitch player you can be. You will learn from the Westerwinds softball players and coaches. You will be playing with other players in your age group and skill level. Each clinic will cover all aspects of the game of fastpitch. You will be working with fun equipment and learning from the best athletes around—the Westerwinds!

Membership cost = $70

Note: If you do not wish to join the Diamond Club but would still like to attend the clinics, they are three hours long and cost $20 each.

The cost of joining the club and not attending the clinics is $20.

Membership benefits:

- Free admission to all home games
- The opportunity to meet and visit with the coaches and players at club functions and games
- Four clinics
  December 29   1:00-4:00 p.m.
  January 19   1:00-4:00 p.m.
  February 15   6:00-8:00 p.m.
  April 19   6:00-8:00 p.m.
- Decal, schedule card, poster, and media guide
- Trading cards
- Social opportunities such as tent gating and postgame socials
- T-shirt

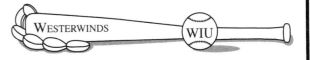

Figure 4.2 Western Illinois University Diamond Club information.

is able to give ideas and put more time into the program. Offer her tons of teaching opportunities and room to grow. Remember, no relationship is perfect, but with open communication and trust, you should be able to pull through the disagreements.

Establishing Rules

Every organization has a goal or a purpose. To reach our goal, I feel we must have guiding principles or rules to help direct us. These rules are ways of governing our team, and they give us an opportunity to discuss how we can best represent our university and play softball at the highest Division I level.

I believe rules are necessary and give unity and an identity to a program. The rules and standards you set for yourself say something about you, your program, and your team. That is why it is important that the team as a whole develops rules and commits to them. Judi Garman, the

former coach at Cal State Fullerton, once told me she has a simple rule, and that is, "If a team member makes another member unhappy, she is asked to leave the team." I have come to realize the importance of this rule, and I also use it.

The Rule-Setting Process

When developing rules and setting standards, I provide the athletes with a team handbook. This handbook outlines the student-athletes' rights, expectations, softball rules, plays, academic information, and so on. I let the team members give their input on the rules dealing with alcohol consumption and drug use. When talking about alcohol use and drug use, we ask each player to stand up and express her feelings and beliefs. This often leads to testimonials from upperclassmen that have a very strong message for the younger athletes. The players discuss what they feel are appropriate standards, I write them up, and then they sign their names to ensure we are all committed.

I also give each athlete a code of ethics. The purpose of intercollegiate athletics is to provide the opportunity for the athlete to develop her potential as a skilled performer in an educational setting. Following is a list of the ethical considerations:

1. Develop and maintain personal habits that enhance healthful living.
2. Objectively acknowledge your own strengths and weaknesses, and recognize that each person has both.
3. Value your personal integrity.
4. Respect differing points of view.
5. Willfully abide by the spirit, as well as the letter, of the rules throughout all practices and competitions.
6. Uphold all standards and regulations expected of participants.
7. Treat all players, officials, and coaches with respect and courtesy.
8. Accept victory or defeat without undue emotion.
9. Graciously accept constructive criticism.
10. Respect and accept the decisions of the coaches.
11. Be willing to train in order to achieve your full potential.
12. Respect the achievements of your teammates and opponents.
13. Be honest, work hard, and give your all.

Rules are sometimes broken. I get together with the team, and we decide as a group on a discipline for when the rules are broken. I let the players discuss and brainstorm their ideas. I want the team to feel involved in deciding anything that deals with their health and well-being. I want the athletes to know the ramifications of their actions and what is expected of them. I ask them to read the rules carefully, and if they have any questions or concerns regarding these rules, to speak to the team captains or the coaching staff. They are then asked to sign a contract stating that they have read, understand, and are willing to abide by these rules.

Being a member of the WIU softball team affords the athlete many benefits but also involves many responsibilities. One of these

Where's the Rake?

I had a player who had some personal problems during her sophomore year. She could not obey team rules and was dismissed from the team. The following summer she begged to be given another chance. After a few meetings with her, I agreed to let her try out. She then said, "If I make the team, will I get to play?" She was so persistent in her demands that I finally stood up and said, "You should be begging me for a chance to rake the infield." On that note, she asked, "Where's the rake?"

I told her where it was, and she left the office. Later that night, I drove by the field and noticed my player raking away. The temperature was over 100 degrees that day. That night I called her up and told her she had done a great job on the field and to show up at practice.

The player who raked the field did earn a uniform that fall. She drew up a contract for herself to make some positive changes in her life, along with helping set up and take down practice each day. She went on to earn a starting spot in the lineup and was the consummate practice player: came early, stayed late, and worked hard.

We traveled to our first game that fall, played great, and came away victorious. This player went three for three, had three RBIs, and had a fine defensive game. As we walked over to shake hands with our opponents, the game ball was sitting on the ground. I bent over, picked it up, and found myself looking right into that player's eyes. I handed her the ball and said, "Great game." She took the ball and immediately brought it in to her body, toward her heart, and tears filled her eyes.

It was in that instant of the softball going to her heart that we both realized the importance of the game to her. Later, she told me that she woke up to her clock radio playing "One Moment in Time." That game was truly one wonderful moment in time, and it demonstrated the heart of a champion. The player was Venus Taylor, who was selected by her teammates twice as their most valuable player and who went on to become a professional fastpitch player and a Division I head coach.

responsibilities is adhering to high standards of physical training. Being an athlete is a 24-hour-a-day commitment, and as a full-functioning team member, the athlete must be willing to make that commitment. She is asked to obey basic training rules such as getting eight hours of sleep each night and extra rest before a game, eating a balanced diet, and drinking plenty of water.

The Unwritten Rules

We were on the bus after a very hard loss, and I heard laughter from a few rows away. At first I ignored it, but then it continued. I asked my assistant coach to please let that player know that it was not appropriate to laugh after a loss. The athlete apologized and said she didn't realize that was a rule. My assistant, Mindy Dessert, told her it was an unwritten rule. The next day the athlete again apologized and quietly asked if she could have a list of the "unwritten rules." I realized there are things we expect as coaches but may not let the athletes know in a timely manner. I now have "The Unwritten Rules" in their handbooks. They are the following:

1. Be five minutes early.
2. Say "Hello."
3. Hustle everywhere.
4. Lend a hand in practice setup.
5. Turn in your uniform immediately after the game.
6. Keep a ball in your glove.
7. Always have your uniform shirt tucked in.
8. If you are not playing, cheer for those who are.
9. If you are going to be late or are going to miss a practice, give 24-hour notice.
10. Always tell the coaches the truth.
11. If you disagree with something, set up an appointment to meet with the coaches.
12. If you make other people on the team unhappy, you will be asked to leave.
13. Treat equipment with respect.
14. Always run when arriving late.
15. No headphones while in uniform.
16. No laughing after a loss.

The unwritten rules are all about respect—respect for the game, for coaches, and for teammates. Members of the team are not all going to be best friends. Although friendships are important, the most critical element of a successful team is respect. Players can earn their teammates' respect through the attitudes and actions they display both on and off the field.

The Coach's Input

The coach should set boundaries for several different areas of the program. I try to give my input when I feel that decisions being made by team members or by the team are not beneficial to the team as a whole. This does not happen very often. It is a good feeling for the players and me when they make correct decisions because I then feel we are on the same page. When they stumble off that page is when I use my authority to pull them back on.

I give my input only when asked for it. When an athlete comes to me and says, "Coach, what do you think about . . . ?" I tell her what I think. This is my favorite way to give input because it is absorbed better when it is asked for.

Captains

I prefer that the team elect the captains. These captains are players to whom the team can turn as a liaison between themselves and the coaching staff. We have captains' lunches every week where the coaches and captains can discuss the status of the team and any issues the captains wish to bring up. This allows a very informal, open sharing of ideas that helps to keep the team healthy. I believe healthy teams talk, and this is one forum that we count on each week to work together.

The captain must know what is required of her in this position. By providing the captain with a detailed job description, you can ensure that there will be no discrepancy regarding what the coach expects from her. Responsibilities of the captain include the following:

1. To be loyal to the coaches and teammates
2. To lead drills, warm-ups, and so forth
3. To set the mental and emotional tone for the team

4. To keep the coaches informed
5. To provide input on team decisions
6. To talk with struggling teammates
7. To handle team conflicts
8. To organize team activities

Inherent risks and challenges must be discussed with your captains, such as the following:

1. They are always being watched.
2. Their teammates' trust and respect are fragile.
3. They must deal with conflict, and they will not always be liked or be popular.
4. Their teammates might be jealous.
5. They must be willing to take the heat when things go bad.

Having captains is vital for the team because it gives the athletes someone to go to with a problem before approaching the coaching staff. If the problem can be worked out without the coaches' interference, then everybody gains. The athletes develop a trust in the captains, the captains feel a sense of internal reward for being able to help out a teammate, and the coaches can carry on with coaching. There are certain situations when a problem might be too big for the captains to try to fix themselves. It is the responsibility of the captains to make the judgment about when it is the right time for them to bring the issue to the coaches.

On the field, the captains are leaders and teachers. In practice, they offer their insight and enthusiasm. During the game, they give direction with their actions and create team unity with cheers, talks, and actions. The job of a captain is a crucial one. The team members must know all that they are asking from the athletes chosen as captains, and those chosen must look inside and see if they can perform all that will be asked of them.

INSTILL PRIDE

I have a wall of honor behind my desk and on it are pictures of former players who have graduated from the softball program; each year it is bittersweet to put up the recent set of graduates. When prospective student-athletes come into the office for a visit, they can look at me or look behind me to see the former Westerwinds. Even after they have signed on, every time they return to the office, it is gratifying for me to watch their eyes as they look at all of the pictures. Our office is covered with pictures: images of the present and memories of the past. We do not keep trophies in our office—we keep people instead.

The more the players of today know about their team's tradition and heritage, the more special their role becomes. They are continuing a great tradition of excellence when they wear the purple and gold and represent our university.

Talent can fail and so can mental toughness at times, but if your players have pride in

Talent and mental toughness may fail at times, but if players have pride in themselves and the program they are sure to pull through the tough moments.

themselves, their team, and the program, they are sure to be able to pull through the tough moments. These moments could be during games or when a team crisis arises. Your team needs to feel its worth. The players need to know their efforts are appreciated and that they are part of something important. It is the coach's job to build this feeling by showing them that she is willing to stand up for the athlete, the team, and the program.

Former Players

Western has many former players who return to the program as great fans, volunteers, and coaches. They always set a precedent with their support and words of encouragement. It is nice for the new team to get the chance not only to meet past women athletes, but also to be supported by and learn from them.

Fans in Florida

One spring break we took the team on a softball-blazing trail and headed down to Tampa, Florida. We were going on a 17-day road trip, and we were anxious about the upcoming action. When we arrived at our first game in Tampa, I was very excited to see four past players sitting in the stands waiting to cheer us on. I knew two of them lived in Tampa, but the other two had flown in from St. Louis. It was a great feeling for me as well as for the team to see former athletes being such great supporters. After the games, I invited them to eat dinner with us. I introduced the former players to the team, and we all talked for hours about softball. For some people, it may seem shocking that these women took their vacation days from work to come watch the team. But for the team and me, it is not shocking because we all know how great it is to be part of the Westerwinds tradition and to play fastpitch softball.

These types of interactions let our new athletes see the great pride the athletes of the past have in the Westerwinds tradition. As each year passes, each player builds more onto this tradition with her contributions as a student-athlete. Although many players see what their efforts do for themselves or their team, not many of them think about the impact their hard work and actions will have on the players of the future. When former athletes come back and visit, the current players get the chance to see what impact they had and continue to have on the program. I have always felt fortunate to see so many of our past athletes at games. It is nice to bring them down after the game and introduce them to the team. Many of the past athletes come around often enough that they establish friendships with the new athletes. But even former athletes who do not frequent the games as much leave a lasting impression with their presence. If you are particular about whom you recruit as athletes, making sure they are also good people, you will be rewarded not only in the years that they are part of your ball team but for many years to come.

A Classy Operation

When we put on our uniforms, I expect total representation of the university. I want our players to know that they represent something bigger than themselves: the athletic department, the players before them, future players, and the school itself. Players' names may slip from memory as time passes, but the school, community, and program will continue into the future. In the athletes' team handbook, this is the statement that serves to introduce them to our expectation: "Wearing the team colors is a privilege not a right. As a member of this softball team, you are representing not just yourself, but our university, your coaching staff, and your teammates. Acting accordingly is the most important thing you can do every day. We will strive to win with integrity and class. We will earn each other's respect through listening, communicating, and caring about each other as people, not just coaches and players."

I remember the year when the Macomb Magic won 60 games and at one time had recorded 44 wins in a row. We were playing in a tournament in Chattanooga, and we all walked into the complex together—I was somewhere in the middle of the group. I realized at that moment that I was exactly where I wanted to be, and I felt so proud to be associated with such tremendous athletes. During that streak, I know some people came to see us play, wondering if we were going to lose. When we did lose game 45, we had our usual team meeting highlighting the game, the players changed their shoes, and we all agreed, "Well, it wasn't going to last forever." The players showed me "class."

Every day that you spend with your team, you need to remind them that it is a privilege to play intercollegiate athletics. They need to hear that they are great athletes playing a difficult sport at one of the highest levels of competition. I believe they need to know these things because it is easy to have class when you have pride in what you do, who you are, and what you represent.

CHAPTER 5 PLANNING FOR THE SEASON

In this chapter, we will discuss the importance of creating a master plan for the season. Some of the topics we will cover are planning with your staff, scheduling fair competition, and designing a master conditioning plan. Some people may view the coaching professional as one who conducts practices and games during one season of the year. However, coaching softball is a full-year commitment to planning and preparation. If you have done these two things completely, the season should run smoothly.

STAFF RESPONSIBILITIES

My staff and I plan the responsibilities of each of the staff members. I will delegate certain responsibilities, but I am the one who is ultimately responsible. I try to be sure my assistants and managers are working in the areas they enjoy and in the areas of their expertise. We discuss our plans and programs throughout the year and continually review and evaluate all aspects of the program.

Assistants

You cannot run a successful program alone—you need the assistance of a strong staff. Do not be afraid to delegate certain responsibilities and then adjust your assistants' duties depending on their ability to fulfill them. The general responsibilities of my assistant coaches are as follows:

- Monitoring academic progress
- Generating scouting reports on opponents
- Arranging team travel
- Creating goal charts and locker room charts
- Administering summer camps
- Directing student managers
- Maintaining current media files
- Purchasing uniforms, equipment, and supplies
- Cooperating with the booster club
- Completing team testing and charting
- Organizing the recruiting process (evaluating prospects, organizing contacts and visits, maintaining correspondence)

Student Managers

For any program to be a success, it needs "hired hands" and hearts to work for it. These people are the coaches and others behind the scenes—people who love athletics. One such person who helps the program run smoothly is a student manager who assists the coaches with specific duties.

I have always found that the managers do not have to know everything about your sport to succeed; they just have to be eager to learn about it. They must want to contribute and to be a part of a successful program.

When putting together a list of the student manager's duties, I try to look at what could be done without coaches present and what activities would offer us more coaching time if another person were to perform them. The general responsibilities of my student managers are as follows:

- Assisting in practice and setups
- Assisting in closing up practice and making sure everything is put away
- Videotaping games and practices as needed
- Performing game duties as assigned
- Coordinating while traveling (locating restaurants, locker rooms, and training facilities)
- Laundering

The student manager is a valuable resource for the coaches. When managers perform their

A "Jeff" of All Trades

I once had a volunteer student manager who could do stats, catch the pitchers in the bull pen, videotape, and hit fly balls—in practice he even filled in at positions when athletes were injured. The list was endless. All these things were a blessing, but what made Jeff Mison stand out the most was his love for the game. He wanted to learn as much as he could from our program. He traveled with us whenever he could, and besides being our manager, he was our biggest fan. His great effort and heart allowed us to get many things accomplished. The second year that Jeff helped out, he went with us to the conference tournament, and we won the championship. It was a great feeling for all of us. To celebrate the victory, we ordered conference championship rings. As I handed them out to the team, it was very special to hand one to Jeff. I hope when Jeff looks at the ring he realizes how his helping hand played a part in all of us being champions.

duties well, they earn the respect of the team and become a part of the experience. I expect the same thing from a student manager that I do from the athlete—a winning effort.

COMPETITION SCHEDULE

It is your responsibility to build a schedule based on fair competition for your squad. Playing all levels of competition helps prepare your team for your conference schedule. Fair competition consists of playing teams you can definitely beat, those you might beat, and those you may not. By layering in this manner, your team can reap the benefit of winning games—mental growth, confidence, and rhythm—but also improve by playing the best teams possible. We play in three or four tournaments each spring. We look to play in tournaments that give our athletes exposure, as well as to play opponents from different regions. Ideally, our schedule would have a balance between away and home games. I want to play as many home games as possible so that our fans have the opportunity to cheer us on. In this way, we can build a strong fan base that supports our athletes on and off the field.

EQUIPMENT AND FACILITY NEEDS

It is essential to have plenty of the necessary equipment, such as balls and bats. Having an adequate supply of equipment ensures that practice time is efficient and productive. The following is a suggested checklist of the equipment a team should have.

- Regulation, game, Wiffle, tennis, and machine balls
- Catcher's gear
- Bats
- Protective screens
- Bases, pitcher's mound, plate
- Batting tees
- Pitching machine
- Field rakes

- Specialty equipment if affordable, such as swing analysis equipment, harness, soft hand gloves, and hoppy balls

Work first at obtaining the necessities, such as bats, balls, catching equipment, and protective screens. In your equipment closet, you should also have some batting tees and a pitching machine. The machine not only offers relief to your pitching staff but also allows the batter to focus on a moving ball when practicing her swing. Screens are necessary for protection for the coaches and players from batted balls or errant throws. Big buckets of regulation softballs will always be needed, but a bucket of tennis balls can also provide you with several different drill opportunities. If affordable, specialty equipment adds variety to practices while reinforcing skills.

And a Dream Comes True

The idea of writing this book was overwhelming. I had not yet decided when to begin when I was called to the bedside of Mary Ellen "Mickey" McKee, a dear friend and tremendous fan of softball. Mickey asked me to pick up a notebook, and as I sat down with it, I realized it was a book she was writing about her brother. She instructed me to get a piece of paper and pencil, and then she proceeded to dictate the conclusion of the book. We worked together for a couple of hours, sharing stories and thoughts. Before I left, I picked some lilacs for her. The next morning, I told Lu Harris, my assistant coach, about my afternoon with Mickey, and it was right then that Lu and I decided to begin outlining the first edition of this book. We had just begun our labors when we were told that Mickey had just passed away. We sat for a while in disbelief, then we cried and went to Mickey's home—her spirit and the lilacs were still there. On that day, we planted a lilac bush next to our softball field, and on that day the book and the bush took root. Mary Ellen McKee's memory lives on as she gave the profit from the sale of her home to enable us to build our softball field. It is named in her honor.

It is also essential to have a safe facility. First and foremost, practice and playing fields should be safe and regulation in design. What I look for in a safe field is regulation fences, dugouts, a level outfield with no holes, and a level infield with smooth dirt. A rest room facility should be close by for players and fans. Planning ahead for inclement weather is a must. Rakes and a field drying substance should be on hand to help reduce moisture on the field. If affordable, a weather alert radio can be helpful to track storms.

BUDGET ITEMS

The coach must anticipate the financial needs of the program by itemizing expenses that will be incurred during the season. This would include hotel costs, meals, gas, rental cars, entry fees, uniforms, bats, balls, catching gear, helmets, training equipment, umpiring fees, and correspondence expenses, among other things. To offset the expenses, revenue can be generated through gate receipts, entry fees, sponsorships, and donations from alumni and the community. Many teams will look toward fund-raising activities to offset the expenditures. Ideas that my teams have depended on in the past include camps, clinics, car washes, magazine sales, bingo night, raffles, alumni contributions, and 100 innings games.

CONDITIONING PROGRAM

A complete conditioning program is vital to softball performance. An inclusive plan will incorporate anaerobic and aerobic conditioning, flexibility, strength and power building, and speed and agility training. All of these will be used to attain a quicker, stronger, and faster athlete.

Determine Player Fitness Levels

Before we begin our season, the players go through a battery of 10 tests. These baseline scores illustrate the players' beginning level of

A conditioning program that incorporates endurance, agility, footwork, and speed will produce a quicker, stronger, and faster athlete.

fitness and strength and provide a good way for each player to see her improvement through the training period. Using these scores, we divide our team into miniteams for other activities. These tests can be done inside or outside. Prior to the tests, the athletes do a complete warm-up and stretching routine. The tests are as follows:

1. **Home to home**—The athlete starts at the plate with a rockaway foot pattern and sprints from home to home. Two stopwatches are used, and the average time is recorded. After all athletes have had one try, they repeat, and the best time is recorded for each player.

2. **Agility run**—From a starting line, the athlete runs through cones that are set up in a zigzag pattern. The course is approximately 60 feet (18.3 meters) long. The foot pattern calls for changes of direction, and the finish line is next to the starting line. Two stopwatches are used, and the average time is recorded. After all athletes have had one try, they repeat, and the best time is recorded for each player.

3. **Jump and reach**—The athlete measures her standing reach. Then, from a balanced position, she takes one step and jumps up. That measurement is taken, and the first measurement is subtracted from the second to determine the vertical jump distance.

4. **Chin-ups**—The athlete uses a reverse grip and stands on a chair at the chin-up bar. She does as many as she can and steps down on the chair when she is finished.

5. **Chest pass**—The athlete sits in a chair with both feet on the floor and a belt holding her hips to the chair. A tape measure is laid out on the floor in front of the athlete, and she chest-passes a medicine ball (about 10 pounds [4.5 kilograms]) out along the tape measure. Each athlete gets two tries, and her best distance is recorded.

6. **Triceps dip**—The athlete places her feet (toes up) on a chair or other support that elevates her lower body parallel to the floor. She is positioned straight-armed between two benches or chairs, supporting herself with her hands on the seats. She slowly lowers her body, keeping her elbows together, and exhales as she pushes up. The on-deck player can hold the benches to keep them stable. This drill is performed for one minute, and the number of dips is recorded.

7. **Decline push-ups**—The athlete places her feet on a bench or chair and her hands on the floor in the push-up position. While inhaling, she lowers her body slowly until her chest touches a cone (about 10 inches [25.4 centimeters] high). Exhaling, she slowly pushes herself back to the original position. This exercise is performed for one minute, and the number of push-ups is recorded.

8. **Flexibility**—The athlete sits on the floor at the front of a flexibility box (a wooden box

with a ruler extending from the top of the box toward the athlete) and places her feet against the box. She then reaches forward as far as possible over the ruler. The distance reached is recorded.

9. **Sit-ups**—The athlete sits on the floor with knees bent at a 90-degree angle and feet flat. A partner holds her feet. The player crosses her arms over her chest, places her hands on her collar, and curls her trunk so that her shoulder blades are off the floor. She does as many sit-ups as possible in one minute. The partner counts, and the score is recorded.

10. **Running**—Each athlete runs one lap around the track, and her time is recorded.

The results of these tests will tell us where our athletes are physically and where they need to be. It takes a certain level of fitness to succeed, and we need to know where to start when conditioning our athletes.

Plan Conditioning Program

The demands on the athlete's skill and stamina must be considered when developing a conditioning program. This regimen builds discipline, mental toughness, cardiovascular endurance, strength and power, agility, footwork, and speed. The softball year is typically divided into three segments: off-season, preseason, and in-season. In the off-season, the focus is on high-intensity strength building, speed, agility, and endurance. In the preseason, the focus is on transferring strength to sport-specific actions—power, speed, agility, and endurance. In the in-season, the focus is on speed, agility, and strength maintenance. Strength training will be minimized during the season, but we will continue working on power. We will work around our game schedule, conducting shorter workouts while we incorporate speed and agility drills in practice.

The role of weight training in our conditioning program is to prepare the athlete for competition, to prevent injury, to rehabilitate, and to produce a quicker, stronger, and faster athlete. Olympic-style lifting works specifically on the core body strength, which is what softball players use to perform every skill.

Multijoint lifting will allow for improvement in all areas. Our goal is to provide our players with skill and technique development, and to couple that with a combination of strength and conditioning exercises in order to enable each of them to reach their highest athletic potential.

Our players do additional core body strengthening every day in the form of an abdominal workout. The core is the trunk. Having a stable trunk will allow unimpeded movement. The body recovers from these conditioning exercises very easily, so the exercises can be worked on daily either in or out of the weight room without fear of fatigue.

Figure 5.1 presents sample conditioning plans for each of the three segments of the year. These plans include conditioning exercises, core work, and weight training programs. Specific conditioning drills can be found in the next section in this chapter.

Conditioning Exercises

These exercises should be incorporated into a training program as a means for increasing strength, speed, and quickness. The following can be built into a practice or can serve as the basis for an entire conditioning workout.

Medicine Ball Exercises

• **Twist and toss**—The athlete starts with the ball cradled next to her body at waist level and her feet spaced slightly wider than her shoulders. She twists her torso in the opposite direction of the intended toss, then quickly and powerfully changes direction of the twist and releases the ball with her arms outstretched. Make sure the athletes use their hips, shoulders, and arms for this exercise.

• **Sit-up throw**—Two athletes start by sitting on the floor facing each other with their feet interlocked. Keeping their arms extended, they use their abdominal muscles to both throw the ball with an arc and absorb the shock of the catch by rocking back.

• **Ball scoop and toss**—The athlete starts in a semi-squat stance holding the ball low and between her legs, with her arms fully extended,

Figure 5.1 Sample Conditioning and Weight Training Plans for the Off-season, Preseason, and In-season

	Sample off-season conditioning and weight training	
	September to early October: Emphasis on fundamentals with practice.	
Day	**Conditioning**	**Weight training**
Monday	30 min. run	Shoulder stabilization routine Hang clean: 4 × 3 @ 67-76% Back squat: 4 × 5 @ 64-73% Glute-ham: 2 × 10 Alternate dumbbell shoulder press: 3 × 6 Pull-ups: 20 Bar hang: 40 sec. Abdominal workout
Tuesday	Run and dives: 15 min.	
Wednesday	Run foul pole to foul pole: 5 ×	Shoulder stabilization routine Medicine ball Russian twist: 20 Hanging leg raise: 25 Medicine ball overhead throw sit-ups Clean pull: 3 × 5 @ 79-91% Lateral squat: 8 each Front squat: 4 × 4 @ 76-91% Incline bench press: 4 × 8 @ 50-76% Alternate dumbbell row: 12, 10, 8 Close grip push-ups: 2 × 20 sec. Grippers: 30 sec.
Thursday	First-step quickness drills Cone and bat drills Plyometrics	
Friday	30 min. baserunning drills	Shoulder stabilization routine Abdominal workout Power clean: 4 × 3 @ 67-76% Box step-ups: 3 × 5 Eccentric hamstring: 2 × 10 Dumbbell bench press: 3 × 8 Chin-ups: 20 Push-ups: 20 sec. Wrestler's twist: 20
Mid-October to mid-December: Emphasis on high-intensity strength building, speed, agility, and endurance.		
	Conditioning	**Weight training**
Monday	Speed drills Plyometrics Cone drills Medicine ball drills	Shoulder stabilization routine Hang clean: 4 × 3 @ 67-82% Back squat: 5 @ 64%, 3 @ 70%, 7 @ 76%, 7 @ 70% Glute-ham: 2 × 10 Dumbbell shoulder press: 3 × 5 Pull-ups: 25 reps Bar hang: 40 sec.

	Conditioning	Weight training
Tuesday	3-mile run First-step quickness drills Bat drills	
Wednesday	Speed drills Plyometrics Cone drills	Shoulder stabilization routine Medicine ball Russian twists: 20 Hanging leg raises: 25 Medicine ball overhead throw sit-ups: 12 Clean pull: 3 × 3 @ 55-100% Lateral squat: 8 each Front squat: 4 × 3 @ 76-91% of clean Incline bench press: 5 @ 50%, 4 @ 67%, 4 @ 76%, max. @ 82% Dumbbell row: 3 × 8 Close grip push-ups: 2 @ 30 sec., 20 sec. Grippers: 45 sec. Abdominal workout
Thursday	Interval training	
Friday	Speed drills Plyometrics Cone drills Medicine ball drills	Shoulder stabilization routine Power clean: 4 × 3 @ 67-82% Box step-ups: 3 × 5 Eccentric hamstring: 2 × 10 Dumbbell bench press: 3 × 6 Chin-ups: 25 2 sets of push-ups: 30 sec., 20 sec. Wrestler's twist: 20 Abdominal workout

Sample preseason conditioning and weight training
Emphasis on transferring strength to sport-specific actions—power, speed, agility, and endurance.

	Conditioning	Weight training
Monday	First-step quickness drills Plyometrics Cone drills	Shoulder stabilization Jump shrugs: 4 × 3 @ 67-76% Back squat: 4 × 5 @ 67-82% Romanian deadlift: 2 × 8 @ 76-91% Pull-ups: 4 × 5 Bar hang: 40 sec. Abdominal workout
Tuesday	3-mile run	
Wednesday	First-step quickness drills Bat drills Plyometrics	Shoulder stabilization Push jerk: 3 × 5 @ 58-70% Front squat: 4 × 4 @ 76-91% Incline bench press: 5 × 3 @ 64%-max. Inverted row: 2 × 10 Explosive push-ups: 2 × 15 sec. Walking grippers Abdominal workout

(continued)

Figure 5.1 (continued)

	Conditioning	Weight training
Thursday	Interval training	
Friday	3-mile run	Shoulder stabilization Hang clean: 5 @ 64%, 3 @ 73%, 3 @ 79%, 2 @ 85%, 1 @ 85% Lateral squat: 2 × 8 Dumbbell bench press: 3 × 8 Dumbbell walking lunges Chin-ups: 4 × 5 Reverse wrist curl: 2 × 10 Wrestler's twist: 20 Abdominal workout

Sample in-season conditioning and weight training		
Emphasis is on speed, agility, and strength maintenance. Strength training will be minimized, but we will continue working on power. We will work around our game schedule, conducting shorter workouts while we incorporate speed and agility drills in practice.		

	Conditioning	Weight training
Monday	Speed drills Cone drills Medicine ball drills	
Tuesday	Run foul pole to foul pole: 5 × Baserunning drills	Shoulder stabilization routine Power clean: 4 × 3 @ 61-70% High box step-ups: 8 each Lateral lunge: 6 each Incline bench press: 3 × 5 @ 64-73% Romanian deadlift/eccentric hamstring supersets: 2 × 6 + 6 Dumbbell row w/pull-ups: 2 × 6 Dips: 20
Wednesday	First-step quickness drills Bat drills Plyometrics	
Thursday	20-min. run	Shoulder stabilization routine Squat: 20 reps, 6 min., 64-70% Dumbbell bench press: 3 × 5 Plate pull-over/upright row supersets: 2 × 10 Lateral raise/hammer curl: 2 × 10 pull-ups Pull-ups: 15 × 5 eccentric Abdominal workout
Friday	Speed drills First-step quickness drills Cone and bat drills	

her back straight, and her head up. She scoops up the ball and tosses it up using her shoulders, arms, back, hips, and legs, then moves back into a semi-squat position to catch the ball.

- **Chest pass**—Two athletes start by facing each other while standing, sitting, or kneeling. One partner holds the ball at chest height with her arms flexed and the back of her hands touching her chest; she pushes the ball outward toward the other partner, fully extending her arms. The other partner anticipates the catch with her arms extended horizontally at chest height, and she absorbs the shock of the catch by bending her elbows but not allowing the back of her hands to touch her chest. The catching partner immediately returns a throw in similar fashion.

- **Throw**—The athlete starts by kneeling on the floor and holding the ball behind her head with her elbows bent. She slowly leans back and then quickly flexes forward using her torso muscles and follows through by throwing the ball as far as possible. Make sure the athletes concentrate on thrusting their arms forward from the shoulders and chest.

Plyometric Exercises

Plyometrics is a method of developing explosive power. Speed and strength combined is power.

- **Double-leg bounding**—The athlete begins in a half-squat stance, with her shoulders forward and out over her knees, her back straight, and her head up. The athlete jumps outward and upward, thrusts with her arms, and reaches maximum height and distance by fully straightening the body. Upon landing, she goes into the next jump.

- **Alternate-leg bounding**—The athlete starts with her knees bent and one leg slightly in front of the other. She drives that leg up and out in front of her, jumping as far as possible. Upon landing, she repeats with her other leg.

- **Lateral bounding**—The athlete starts in a ready position, one long step from an incline. She pushes off with her outside foot and lands on the incline, then immediately pushes back off of it, trying to gain as much lateral distance as possible.

- **Side hops**—The athlete sets two 18-inch (46-centimeter) high cones 2 feet (61 centimeters) apart. She starts on the outside of one cone with her feet together, and she jumps sideways over both cones, one at a time. The athlete changes direction and jumps back over the cones, keeping her arms at a 90-degree angle throughout the drill.

- **Side jump and sprint**—The athlete sets one cone 15 yards (13.7 meters) from the finish line and starts in the same position as the side hop. She jumps back and forth over the cone 10 times then sprints to the finish line.

Speed Drills

Speed and first-step quickness are beneficial for all defensive positions as well as for baserunning. They can mean the difference between out and safe at first base and taking away a potential base hit.

- **Forward, backward, and linear run**—Use tennis balls and a training partner. A1 starts from a two- or three-point start position. A2 stands about 15 feet (4.5 meters) from A1 (this distance can be adjusted according to each athlete's abilities) with a ball held out at shoulder height. A2 drops the ball. A1 then explodes forward and catches the ball before it bounces twice.

- **Backward run and turn and run**—A1 now stands with her back to A2. A2 holds a ball out, drops the ball, and gives a verbal command. A1 then takes a step backward, turns, and explodes forward to get the ball before it bounces twice. There is no crossover step used in this movement. Make sure A1 practices taking a step back with both the left and the right foot.

- **Crossover to run**—A1 stands facing sideways from A2. The distance between A1 and A2 can vary according to ability. A2 drops the ball. A1 immediately uses a crossover step. If she needs to go left, she will take her right foot and cross it over her left and go to get the ball before it bounces twice.

- **Infielder start**—A1 gets into an athletic position 10 to 12 feet (3.0 to 3.6 meters) from A2. A2 rolls balls to each side of A1 as A1 shuffles to get the balls and roll them back. Every three or four balls, A2 holds up a ball and says, "ball." A1 breaks forward, touches the ball, and returns to the start position as A2 continues to roll balls.

- **Figure eight sprint**—Place two cones 5 yards (4.6 meters) apart. The athlete sprints in a figure eight pattern around the cones, making sure to take tight turns and make crossover steps when changing directions. (See figure 5.2.)

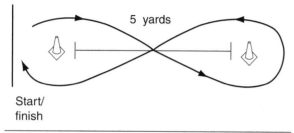

Figure 5.2 Figure eight sprint drill.

First-Step Quickness Drills

Like speed, first-step quickness is beneficial for all defensive positions as well as for baserunning.

- **Falling starts**—The athlete starts with both feet together and leans forward until she must take a step. She then sprints 30 feet (9.1 meters).

- **Jump and sprint**—The athlete jumps up off of both feet, lands, and sprints 30 feet.

- **Front roll and sprint**—The athlete does a somersault and sprints 30 feet.

- **Sprint off belly**—The athlete starts lying on her belly, gets up, and sprints 30 feet.

- **Standing long jump and sprint**—The athlete bounds forward and lands on both feet, then sprints 30 feet.

Agility and Footwork Drills

The following drills are designed to assist the athlete in improving both quickness and the ability to change direction while increasing foot speed.

Cone Drills Do these drills in single-file formation five times.

- **Three cone drill**—Number three cones 1, 2, and 3 and then put an athlete across from the number 2 position. A coach calls out a cone number, and the athlete responds to the command by running and touching the cone. (See figure 5.3.) The commands are given off as quickly as the athletes can respond. Make it a competition by having two athletes facing each other and racing to touch the cones before the other athlete.

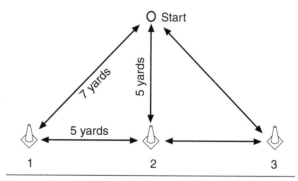

Figure 5.3 Three cone drill.

- **Three corner drill**—The athlete starts in a ready position on the first line. She sprints to the first cone, plants and drives off the left foot, shuffling right to the second cone. At the second cone, she backpedals to the third cone. Once at the third cone, she plants her left foot and breaks at a 45-degree angle to the right as if she were breaking for the ball. (See figure 5.4.) Make sure the athletes use good acceleration while sprinting to the first cone, don't cross their legs on the shuffle step, and stay low on the backpedal.

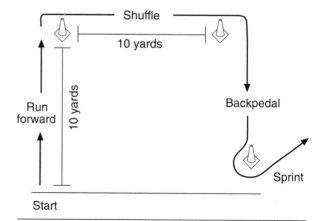

Figure 5.4 Three corner drill.

• **Zigzag**—The athlete starts on the right side of the square and runs forward. At the first cone, she makes a reverse pivot by throwing the right shoulder clockwise. She grapevines to the second cone. She then reverses pivot and backpedals to the third cone, and then reverses pivot and grapevines to the finish. (See figure 5.5.) Make sure the athletes are facing the proper direction when doing the grapevine, and that they back pivot and have good acceleration and deceleration while sprinting to the cones.

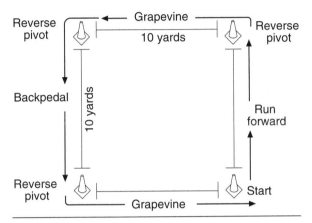

Figure 5.5 Zigzag drill.

• **Backward zigzag**—The athlete starts on the right side of the square and backpedals to the first cone. At the first cone, she grapevines to the second cone and then backpedals to the third cone. At the third cone, she grapevines to the finish. (See figure 5.6.) Make sure the athletes stay low on the backpedal.

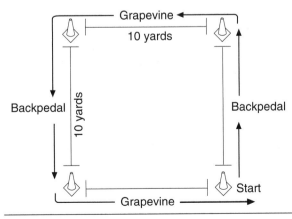

Figure 5.6 Backward zigzag drill.

• **Combination zigzag**—The athlete starts on the right side of the square and backpedals to the first cone. At the first cone, she sprints diagonally to the second cone and then backpedals to the third cone. At the third cone, she sprints diagonally to the fourth cone. (See figure 5.7.) Make sure the athletes stay low while backpedaling.

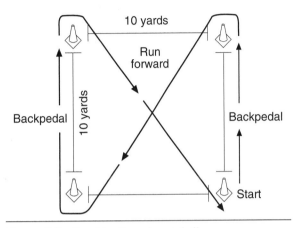

Figure 5.7 Combination zigzag drill.

Bat Drills Do these drills in single-file formation five times.

• **Change of direction**—The athlete starts at either the right or left side at one end of the bat and runs forward to the other side of the bat. The athlete plants her outside foot at the end of the bat, exploding forward toward the other end of the next bat, and continues through all bats. (See figure 5.8.) Make sure the athletes push off with the outside foot.

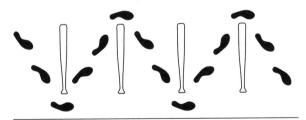

Figure 5.8 Change of direction drill.

• **Forward-backward**—The athlete is in a ready position with her knees slightly bent, upright torso, her head up, and her hands and arms away from her body. On command, the athlete runs forward to the end of the bat. She then backpedals through the bats to the opposite end, and then forward. She repeats through all bats, ending with a five-yard (4.6-meter) sprint. (See figure 5.9.) Make sure the athletes stay low throughout the drill and that their weight is forward on the backpedal. Encourage them to eliminate false steps when changing directions.

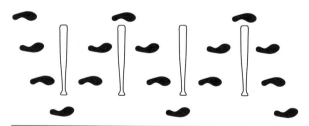

Figure 5.9   Forward–backward drill.

• **Zigzag**—The athlete starts at either the right or left side at one end of the bats, facing the row of bats. She shuffles diagonally beyond the first bat and then changes direction and shuffles to the end of the second bat. She continues shuffling through all bats. (See figure 5.10.) Make sure the athletes stay low throughout the drill and do not cross their feet, but that they do push off with the outside foot when changing direction.

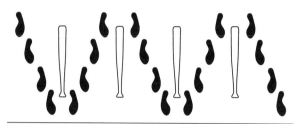

Figure 5.10   Zigzag bat drill.

• **Bunny hop**—The athlete laterally hops over the first bat, keeping her legs and feet close together. After contact, she quickly hops again over the second bat and continues hop-

ping over each bat. (See figure 5.11.) Make sure the athletes pull their knees up high and move their feet quickly.

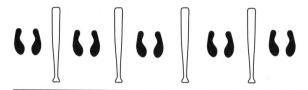

Figure 5.11   Bunny hop drill.

• **Combination lateral**—The athlete is in a two-point stance with her knees slightly bent, upright torso, her head up, and her hands and arms away from her body. She runs laterally over the first two bats and then sprints five yards (4.6 meters) to the third bat and laterally steps over it. She backpedals five yards and laterally steps over bats four and five. She should continue through the bats doing this pattern. (See figure 5.12.) Make sure the athletes have good acceleration and stay low during the backpedal.

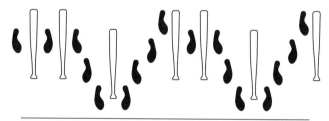

Figure 5.12   Combination lateral drill.

• **High knees**—The athlete starts at either the right or left side at one end of the bats, facing the row of bats. She sprints to the first bat, pulling her knees up to her waist and pumping her arms. She continues through all bats. (See figure 5.13.) Make sure the athletes keep their knees high, backs straight, and pump their arms.

Figure 5.13   High knees drill.

CHAPTER 6
PREPARING FOR PRACTICES

I have always believed that the game is for the player, and practice is for the coach. For practice to be productive, the team needs clear objectives. I want practice to be quick paced and challenging, and I prefer to work in small groups. The players and coaches must know what is to be accomplished. For example, if we are hitting off a tee, I want to teach the drill so that each player knows what her focus should be (such as hands inside the ball, short stride, and so on). You should save every practice's notes and make additional notes on them after practice so that a great practice can be repeated.

COACH PREPARATION

Taking into consideration the amount of preparation time the team has before competition, the coach should develop a progressive plan that she will implement from the first practice until the first game of the season. To develop this plan, the coach must consider the amount of time and space allotted for team practice, as well as the size of the squad. The coach should assess the strengths and weaknesses of individuals and the team as a whole in order to decide the amount of practice time that should be spent working on each aspect of the game.

Coaches must be mentally and physically ready for practices. Make sure each staff member knows his or her role in the overall operations of the team as well as the day-to-day practices. Plan each practice together as a staff, taking into account facility issues, player attendance, and any equipment or personnel constraints. Ensure that each coach has a copy of the practice plan.

PLAYER PREPARATION

I expect the athletes to come prepared for practice and to bring a high level of energy, intensity, and focus. They must come with all gear and clothing necessary for full participation and a mind-set to give 100 percent effort.

To aid the athlete in attaining that mind-set, I post the day's practice plan. I always tell my players that when they walk on the practice field they should shed their problems as they shed their jackets. Two hours in a 24-hour period is a reasonable amount of time to stay focused on the tasks at hand, not on their car problems, tests, or an argument they had. Athletes should come to the understanding that they can have a good practice on a bad day and even turn the bad day into a good one as a result of a productive practice session. I have worked with my assistants to make these two hours a valuable experience for the athletes, so I expect them to respect our efforts and to put 100 percent of themselves into the practice. Players with injuries should talk to the coach ahead of time about what type of participation they will be allowed.

The athletes prepare for practice in a three-step process. First, they arrive in the visitors' dugout where they change their shoes and organize their equipment. Second, they take their bat and glove and move into the home team dugout where they reflect on their hitting and defensive goals as well as visualize the successes they will experience in practice. The third step is to begin the prepractice drills.

MAKE PRACTICE COMPETITIVE AND GAMELIKE

By their nature, athletes are competitive and love a challenge. It is your job to make each practice day just that—a challenge. By challenging I do not mean having players merely survive practices, but instead, having them face competition built into practice.

I build competition into each practice by creating segments where players go head to head. I make the competition gamelike by giving the winners an external reward (such as stickers for their lockers) to go along with the natural, internal reward of winning. Conversely, if the athletes fail in the competition, there can be a consequence such as a run or jumping jacks.

I also use drills to simulate gamelike conditions during practice. One way to bring the game to practice is by focusing on doing a drill correctly the first time. For example, during an at-bat in a game, I want my athlete to be ready to hit the first good pitch she sees. I apply this concept when the athlete is in the batting cage at practice. If she is not ready and takes a strike, or if she lacks focus and swings at a bad pitch, she will get kicked out of the cage and must wait until her turn comes up again.

Sometimes in a drill we offer the athletes the chance to "answer back." For example, if the drill calls for successfully fielding three ground balls in a row and the athlete bobbles the last one, we give her the chance to field five more. The athlete does not end on a miscue, but rather "answers back" with success. This draws a valid comparison between practice and the game. If an

Practices that are challenging and gamelike will prepare the athlete for stressful, high-pressure game situations.

error is made in the game, the athlete must regain her composure and successfully handle the next fielding opportunity that comes her way.

By making daily practice more competitive, you help the athletes to be better prepared for all of the stressful situations that will arise in the game. By creating competitive drills in practice, you give the athletes an opportunity to gain experience with stress, which will in turn make them feel more comfortable when they are standing in the batter's box or on the pitching rubber with the game on the line. If athletes experience success within a competitive practice environment, the game will not seem so far removed from what they have been doing day in and day out in practice.

COVER ALL THE BASES

To make sure she hits all the key points, a coach should make a list of essential skills to cover (see figure 6.1). The coach should keep track

Figure 6.1 Practice Checklists

DEFENSE

Infield

- Sacrifice bunt defense
  - runner on first
  - runner on first and second
  - runner on second
  - runner on third
- Running slap bunt defense
  - runner on first
  - runner on first and second
  - runner on third
  - no runners on base
- Slap bunt defense from the right side
  - runner on first
  - runner on first and second
  - runner on third
- Holding runners
  - runner on second
  - runner on third
  - hold and get the out
  - check and hold the runner
- Fake throws
  - runner on third, ball hit to the third baseman
  - runner on second, ball hit to the shortstop
- Backhands, forehands, balls in front
- First and third situations
- Rundowns
- Squeeze bunt defense
- Pickoffs at first, second, and third
- Fundamentals of fielding ground balls
- Fundamentals of catching fly balls
- Double plays
- Defensive situations with ground balls to infielders
  - runner on first, force play at second
  - runners on first and second, force play at third
  - runners on first and second, force play at second
  - bases loaded, force play at home
  - runner on second, hold and go to first
  - runner on third, hold and go to first

- Runner interference on ground balls
- Sun drills
- Wild pitches and passed balls
- Pitchouts
- Fence or dugout drills
- Communication
  - between first and second baseman
  - between shortstop and third baseman

Outfield

- Positioning and depth
- Defensive situations with balls hit to the outfield
  - runner on first, fly balls to right, center, and left
  - runner on second, fly balls to right, center, and left
  - runner on third, fly balls to right, center, and left
  - runner on third, fly balls, when to let ball drop
  - runner on first, single to right, center, and left
  - runner on second, single to right, center, and left
  - runner on third, single to right, center, and left
- Fundamentals
  - grounders: balls in front, to the side, in the gap, down the line, foul balls
  - drop step
  - angles
  - diving: headfirst, seat slide
  - playing the fences
  - lanes
  - sun balls
  - balls over their heads
  - backing up
  - communication with infielders and other outfielders

Team defense

- Balls hit between
  - outfielders
  - infielders
  - infielders and outfielders

(continued)

49

Figure 6.1 *(continued)*

Team defense *(continued)*
- Communication priorities
  - on all bunts
  - on all fly balls
  - between infielders
- Cutoffs
- Relays
- Piggybacks
- Rundowns
- Throwing wet balls

OFFENSE
- Hitting fundamentals
- Hitting, ball location: out, in, up, down, change
- Hitters' responsibility on steals and first and thirds
- Bunts: sacrifice, base hit, push, slap, squeeze, bunt and run, run and bunt
- Hit-and-runs

- Sacrifice flys
- First and thirds
- Hitting behind runners
- Baserunning
  - leadoffs
  - dive backs
  - sliding: headfirst, force, figure four, slide by, hook
- Steals, straight and delay
- Tagging up at bases and drawing throws
- Rundowns
- Running to bases
- Rounding
- Breaking up double plays at second and home
- Coach as a communicator
  - players receiving signs
  - directing runners
- Situational running

of what is being accomplished at each practice session so that she will be sure to cover every aspect of defensive and offensive play before the first scheduled game. The number of sessions devoted to each fundamental and the time spent on each should be determined by the coaching staff. This will depend entirely on the experience level of the team as well as that of the individual position players.

Weather is a factor in our sport, and unfortunately, it can necessitate changing our plans. On bad weather days, we move into our indoor area and scale down the practice to fit the space allowed. As coaches, we have to be flexible and creative at these moments. We still accomplish our objectives for that day's workout.

Figure 6.2 includes a detailed practice checklist for each defensive player and the defensive skills required for that position. You can put down whatever defensive skills you wish to cover with each position. Next to the skill, record the date and time spent on each

particular item. When game time is getting closer, pull out your checklist and make sure you have covered all the important aspects of each position.

Everyone knows the feeling of being "unprepared." You never want to go to practice without something written down to follow. You might make adjustments once practice starts, but you still should have an outline of what you want to cover and how much time should be allotted. I schedule activities in the same order when planning my practices. For example, we always stretch, run, and throw in the first half hour so that we are physically warmed up and prepared to do other drills. Following is a list of the basics we cover at practice with suggested time frames.

1. Pitchers and catchers report early for a half-hour workout prior to the team stretch.
2. Team stretch (10 minutes)

Figure 6.2 Individual Defensive Skills Checklist

Catcher

- Blocking
- Handling pop-ups and bunts
- Tag and force plays at the plate
- Giving signs to the pitcher and the infielders
- Communicating with the umpire
- Pitchouts and intentional walks
- Framing the pitch
- Bunt defenses
- Pickoff plays, called and automatic
- Suicide squeeze
- Throwing to second and third
- Using the cutoff player
- Rundowns
- Throwing balls from the backstop
- Throwing mask
- Finding the fence

Pitcher

- Glove work and footwork
- Fielding bunts
- Double play situations
- Backing up bases and the plate
- Covering home plate
- Fielding ground balls
- Fly ball and ground ball communication
- Rundown responsibilities
- Intentional walks and pitchouts
- Pop-ups
- Pitching in the rain

First baseman

- Glove work and footwork
- Positioning
  - normal
  - bunt situation
  - power hitter
  - slapper
- Cutoff responsibilities
- Bunt defenses
- Double steal plays

- Pickoff plays
- Double plays
- Playing the fence on pop-ups
- Ground ball and fly ball communication
- Rundowns
- Piggyback responsibilities

Second baseman

- Footwork at first and second
- Charging balls, angles and pop-ups
- Positioning
  - normal
  - bunt situation
  - weak hitter
  - slapper
- Backing up throws from the plate
- Covering second on steals and throws from the outfield
- Cutoff responsibilities
- First and third coverage
- Bunt defenses
- Pickoff plays at first and second
- Making tag plays
- Piggyback responsibilities
- Rundowns
- Double play footwork
- Fly ball and ground ball communication

Shortstop

- Footwork at second and third
- Charging balls, angles and pop-ups
- Positioning
  - normal
  - pull hitter
  - slapper
- Backing up throws from the plate
- Bag coverage, steals, throws, double plays
- Cutoff responsibilities
- Double steal plays
- Bunt defenses
- Pickoff plays

(continued)

Figure 6.2 *(continued)*

Shortstop *(continued)*
- Double play situations
- Making tag plays
- Fake throws
- Rundowns
- Piggyback responsibilities
- Fly ball and ground ball communication

Third baseman
- Positioning for pull hitter, bunter, slapper, late in the game
- Bag coverage for force outs, tags, steals
- Cutoff responsibilities
- Bunt fielding
- Pickoff plays, called or impromptu
- Double play situations
- Making tag plays
- Playing the fence on pop-ups
- Fake throws
- Rundowns
- Fly ball and ground ball communication

Outfielders
- Positioning depth
- Fundamentals
  - blocking
  - scoop and shoot
  - angles
  - coming into the catch
  - reading bat angles
  - sun drill
  - power hops
- Fielding to the side, gappers, down the line and foul
- Using cutoff and relay players
- Throwing to bases
- Playing the fence
- Fly ball responsibilities and communication with infielders and other outfielders
- Backing up bases
- Rundowns

3. Conditioning run (10 minutes)
   - Jog laps.
   - Line jogging—All players jog single file around the field; the last player in the line sprints to the front. When she is almost to the front of the line, she yells, "Go" to repeat the sequence.
   - Progressives—Each player sprints to first base, then sprints from home to second, then sprints from home to third, and then sprints from home to home.
   - Interval runs—The players sprint a predetermined distance and then rest. Repeat.
   - Fitness 15 (see page 55)
4. Plyometric drills (10 minutes)
5. Baserunning drills (15 minutes)
6. Warm-up throwing (15 minutes)
   - Loosen up—Partner catch

   - One-hop drill—Partners throw one-hop ground balls back and forth.
   - Short fly drill—Partners throw lateral fly balls back and forth.
7. Infielders, pitchers, and catchers (15 minutes)
   - The coach works with infielders on ground balls and specific situations.
   - Pitchers and catchers throw back and forth in the bull pen, or pitchers take ground balls from the coach, and catchers take balls from infielders.
8. Outfielders—Fundamentals (15 minutes)
9. Team defensive drills (15 minutes)
10. Hitting drills—Circuit training (45 minutes)
    - Toss stations
    - Tee stations
    - Machine station
    - Live pitching station

By incorporating conditioning runs into the beginning of each practice, the coach ensures that the athletes are warmed up and prepared for drills.

11. Alternate hitting and fielding to maximize either skill.

12. Scrimmage days.

For some coaches, getting started is the most difficult part of organizing practice. To make it simple, we prepared two sample practice itineraries shown in figure 6.3. They are examples of a preseason and an in-season practice. For each practice session, one softball field with some adjacent space is utilized during a two-hour time frame.

INCORPORATE CONDITIONING IN PRACTICE

I am always looking for a new and challenging way to condition during practice. I like to have our drills serve a dual purpose: (1) to develop skill and (2) to condition the athlete. One of the plans I like the best is called "Fitness 15" and involves a 15-minute workout that is packed with activities and events. We may do the Fitness 15 often in practice throughout the preseason. It serves a different purpose than the preseason workouts, because it ties in softball athletic movements as well as isolates specific skills. A pre-test and a post-test are conducted with our players, and I have been very impressed with the improvement in strength, speed, and agility. This circuit of drills accomplishes many things: a cardiovascular workout, development of foot speed along with leg power, development of agility, and training in softball skill technique.

You can tailor this circuit to meet your needs by inserting different activities for variety and specific problem areas. It utilizes space the size of a basketball court and can be done indoors or outdoors. The Fitness 15 is composed of 15 stations at 1 minute each, with a changing period of 15 seconds, allowing the athletes to go from one drill to the next. This is the only time they can walk or get a drink. I have them take their water bottle or cup with them so that they can get a drink during the changing time.

Figure 6.3 Preseason and In-Season Sample Practice Plans

Preseason Sample Practice Plan

3:00 Jog and teach stretching

3:15 Teach Fitness 15

3:35 Hitting circle—teach hitting fundamentals (players form a circle around the coach to copy her hitting motions)

3:50 Hitting circuit (demonstrate) with players in nine groups (see chapter 8 for drill descriptions)

- Long Tee
- Two Tees
- Push-Throughs
- Balance Beam
- Front Toss
- Self Toss
- Two-Ball Toss
- Snap Backs
- Lightweight Bat

4:15 Demonstrate receiving techniques

4:20 Practice receiving techniques using the wall

4:25 Demonstrate throwing techniques

4:30 Practice throwing techniques with a partner

4:35 Demonstrate fielding techniques

4:40 Practice ground balls—fielding mini-drills (see chapter 11 for drill descriptions)

- Soft Hands
- Up and Back
- Short Hop

4:50 Baserunning—home to first

In-Season Sample Practice Plan

3:00 Run, stretch, throw

3:15 Hitting circuit (demonstrate) with players in nine groups (see chapter 8 for drill descriptions)

- Inside-Outside
- One Hand, Small Bat
- Drop Toss
- Bounce in Front
- Front Toss
- Reverse Tracking
- Basketball Toss

4:00 Baserunning—steals

4:15 Defensive circuit (see chapter 11 for drill descriptions)

- Soft Hands
- Find the Fence
- Triangular Ground Balls
- Reaction Fielding
- Up and Back
- Throwing drills (Right Leg Drive and Hops; see chapter 10)

4:30 Infielders Work—Outfielders Run

4:45 Outfielders Work—Infielders Run

Hint: Give your drills a name so you can refer to them by that name and do not have to review them every time.

In this circuit, the name of the station is written on a three-by-five-inch index card and placed on the floor at that station. I also use small cones to help lay out the activities. There are five exercises for leg workouts, five for softball skills, and five for agility. Figure 6.4 shows the Fitness 15 layout.

You may want to substitute other activities for variety, such as push-ups, sit-ups, medicine ball throws, or wrist roll-ups. Keeping the format of five stations each for three skills allows you to maintain balance and an organized tracking system. We also play upbeat music during the Fitness 15, and when the music stops after one minute, the athlete moves to the next station. You may not be familiar with my terminology for the stations so a brief description is presented here.

- **Cone jumps**—Place a 12-inch-high (30 centimeter) pylon 40 feet (12 meters) away from a base. The athlete stands next to the cone and jumps sideways over the cone for 10 jumps. After the last jump, she sprints to the base, then jogs back and repeats.

- **Soft hands**—Use a soft hand paddle and a wall. The athlete stands about 15 feet (4.5 meters) from the wall and makes low throws to the wall. As the ball rebounds from the wall, the athlete makes the catch and throws the ball back.

- **Forward-backward**—Place seven markers about five feet (1.5 meters) apart in a staggered diagonal (see figure 6.5). The player starts at the end marker, sprints forward and touches the next, sprints backward and touches the

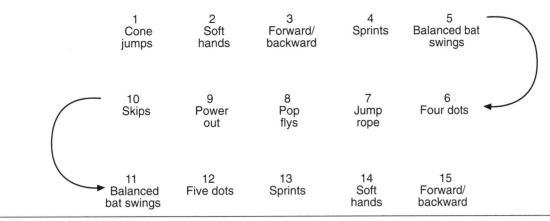

Figure 6.4 Fitness 15 setup.

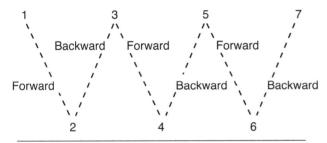

Figure 6.5 Forward-backward Fitness 15.

next, and keeps going forward and backward until all seven are touched, then jogs back and repeats.

• **Straight sprints**—Place a starting base and a finishing base about 60 feet (18.3 meters) apart. The athlete begins at the starting base in the rockaway leadoff position and sprints through the finishing base, then jogs back and repeats.

• **Balanced bat swings**—The player uses a line or a board on the floor and swings using her perfect technique while staying balanced.

• **Four dots**—Four dots or low cones are placed on the floor about five feet (1.5 meters) apart to form a square. With her feet together, the athlete jumps from dot to dot, making an imaginary box. This drill is done rapidly for the full minute.

• **Jump rope**—The athlete does a prescribed rope-jumping pattern such as jumping on the left leg only for 30 seconds; jumping on the right leg only for 30 seconds; jumping while moving the feet sideways; jumping in quick time; and so on.

• **Pop flys**—Remember how much fun these were as youngsters? Outside or inside, players throw pop flys to themselves either with or without a glove.

• **Power out**—The athlete is in her defensive ready position, as if to field a ground ball in front of her. A target cone or marker is 10 feet (3 meters) in front of her. From her ready position, she sprints quickly forward as if to field the imaginary ground ball, then jogs back and repeats.

• **Skips**—Skips are great for ankle, calf, and quad workouts. They also develop the arm to drive up, working to get the elbow high. The athlete drives her right knee up to help lift the left foot off the ground and reaches for the sky with her left arm, slightly bending the elbow. Then she repeats with the opposite leg and arm. She performs these actions in a constant motion, skipping down 40 to 50 feet (12 to 15 meters) and back.

• **Five dots**—Four dots or low cones are placed on the floor about five feet (1.5 meters) apart. Place a fifth dot or cone in the center. The athlete starts with her feet apart at the back two dots. She jumps feet together at the center dot, jumps feet apart at the front two dots, lands and then jumps and turns in the air to face back to her starting direction, jumps to the center dot, to the end dots, and then jumps and turns in the air to face back to the dots. She repeats the pattern for the full minute.

CHAPTER 7 HITTING FUNDAMENTALS

The most important objective on offense is for the team to have the ability to score runs through the use of all offensive weapons. Situation hitting (moving a runner when necessary by going with the outside pitch or hitting the long fly ball with a runner on third), bunting, and smart baserunning are keys to run production. After proper preparation, the ability to execute and perform these offensive skills under pressure is the final key to offensive success.

In this chapter, I touch on the key concepts in hitting: the mechanics of the swing, how to correct hitting errors, teaching all types of bunts, and understanding hitting situations. Baserunning principles and strategies are discussed in chapter 9.

KEY CONCEPTS IN HITTING

The key to being an effective teacher and coach is to develop a simplified, comprehensible approach to instruction. When working on batting skills, my goal is to develop hitters who understand the key concepts in hitting. What follows is a summary of those concepts, starting with the mechanics of the swing: stance, stride, swing, position at contact, and follow-through. I teach what I call linear hitting

versus rotational hitting to create more power through the ball. The following describes a linear hitting motion, with a "short to, long through" approach.

Stance

The stance may vary from player to player, but there are some characteristics of the stance that have general applications. The feet should be about six inches (15 centimeters) wider than shoulder-width apart (see figure 7.1). A stance that is too wide will inhibit weight transfer and hip rotation. One that is too narrow may produce a long stride, causing too much head movement and poor ball tracking. The knees should be slightly flexed, with the upper torso bent slightly forward (toward the plate) at the waist. The head is turned toward the pitcher with both eyes level, and the chin is near the front shoulder at the start of the swing.

There are three types of stances: open, closed, and square. In the open stance, the hitter is turned 30 to 60 degrees on the balls of her feet toward the pitcher so that her front foot is about two or three inches (five to seven centimeters) farther from home plate than the back foot. The weight is distributed evenly on both feet. In this stance, the hips are more open to allow for a shorter swing. The disadvantage of

Figure 7.1 The batting stance.

the open stance is that it limits plate coverage on the outside third of the plate.

In the closed stance, the player's front foot is moved about two or three inches closer to home than the back pivot foot. The hips are closed, restricting hip rotation. In this stance, the right-hander can drive the ball to right field. The disadvantage of the closed stance is that it prevents the batter from reaching pitches on the inside of the plate.

The square stance is the most workable because it gives the hitter the best plate coverage without any disadvantages. No matter what the stance, successful hitters stride to a square position to get maximum coverage.

Complete plate coverage is an important aspect to consider when choosing where to stand in the batter's box. The depth in the batter's box depends on the nature of the hitter and the type of pitcher throwing. The farther back the hitter is in the batter's box, the more time she will have to read the pitch. In most

situations, I'll have my players stand in the back of the box. Against average pitchers, they have the option of moving up in the box. This will decrease the reaction time for those hitters having trouble waiting on the ball.

A player's grip on a bat is equally important. The hands should be set near the back shoulder and should be no more than three to six inches (7 to 15 centimeters) from the body. The lead shoulder is pointing at the pitcher or is slightly closed in the stance. To find a proper grip that ensures maximum power at contact, the player should let her hands hang freely in front of her with palms facing each other. She should grip the bat and pull the bat up to starting position without allowing her fingers to move again. The bat should be held in the fingers of the hands with the grip placed at an angle in the top hand from the base of the pinky to the middle of the index finger. The second knuckles of each hand are aligned when gripping the bat.

When the hitter is in her stance, her focus is soft with her eyes relaxed and looking at the pitcher. As the pitcher's hands come apart, the batter should change the focus to the pitcher's release point (a hard focus). We all know what it feels like to stare with a hard glare at something. That is a hard focus.

Stride or Trigger

As the pitcher is moving toward the release, the hitter is beginning to initiate some preparatory movement—either a stride or a trigger. The stride or trigger establishes timing and helps achieve a strong and powerful position to start the swing. During the stride, the batter takes a small step toward the pitcher. If she does not use the step, she should use a movement that helps get the swing going. The stride should be soft, closed (45 to 90 degrees in relationship to the plate), soon enough in relation to the pitch, and only a few inches. During the stride, it is comfortable for some to initiate a small movement of the hands in a C pattern. As the pitch approaches, a coiling action begins. The front side (shoulder, hip, and knee) slightly turns in, and the back knee also turns inward. During this coiling action, the front shoulder should be lower than the back shoulder (see figure 7.2). The hands should always remain inside the back shoulder.

Figure 7.2 The stride should be short and balanced.

Figure 7.3 A balanced, compact swing.

Swing

The swing begins from the bottom up. The back knee will begin to move in as the hitter shifts her weight toward the ball with the legs and hips; the hands and shoulders stay back. As the ball approaches the plate, the hitter pushes off the back foot to start the linear movement. During the movement of the legs and hips, it is vital that the head and eyes remain level and still. The hands begin to move toward the pitcher, not toward the plate, to stay inside of the ball. The hitter needs to keep the bat above forearm level (a line passing from the elbow through the hand), and the front arm maintains a 90-degree angle (see figure 7.3). The shoulder-elbow-wrist motion unlocks similar to a Frisbee throw. As the bat head moves closer to contact, the top hand begins to rotate so that at contact the palm is nearly facing up. The back leg continues to drive into a now firm (not locked) front leg, and the back foot

begins to turn toward the pitcher. This method of approaching the ball helps ensure that the hands stay inside the ball to allow for a more powerful contact position.

Stress to the hitter to drive the front shoulder to the ball. If the front shoulder pulls away from the ball, one or more of the following problems will happen:

- The head will come out of the proper position, and eye contact with the ball will be reduced.
- The back shoulder will drop down, which creates an unlevel position for the shoulders in their approach to the ball.
- The hands will drop, creating a loop in the swing.
- The back leg will collapse and eliminate any positive hip action in the swing.
- The coverage of the outside part of the plate will be reduced.

The front arm starts the hands toward the ball while the back arm finishes. The batter should allow the front shoulder to track the ball from the pitcher's hand to the contact zone. As the bat is approaching the ball, the arms remain bent. If the arms are extended too early in the swing, the swing arc will be too long, and the hitter will sacrifice bat speed and power.

Position at Contact

The hitter's body position at contact may vary slightly for pitches in different parts of the strike zone. What follows here is information on the position with regard to pitches in the middle of the strike zone. At contact, the hips and shoulders should be facing the ball, not the pitcher. That camera should always be pointing at the ball, not the pitcher. The front leg is firm and slightly bent. The back leg should be slightly flexed at the knee and driving into the firm front side.

The back foot pivots with the toes facing the pitcher, and the front foot is not open to more than a 45-degree angle to the front edge of the batter's box. For an inside pitch, the hips must open early to allow the bat head the freedom to come around quickly and make contact with the ball when it is in front of the plate. At this point, the front shoulder is still driving to the ball. The outside pitch requires the hips to stay closed until the swing is made and the back hip comes through on contact.

Both the front and back arm are flexed at contact. For maximum contact thrust, the ball is struck while the arms and bat are in the process of extension. The batter should allow the wrist to roll naturally *after* the swing. The action of the wrist during the swing should be a snap, like hammering a nail. The palm of the bottom hand faces the ground while the top hand is nearly palm up in a position facing the pitcher. The ball is hit slightly in front of the plate and across from the front foot (see figure 7.4).

Follow-Through

At contact, the swing through the ball is not over. Too many hitters start their follow-through before they have finished hitting through the

Figure 7.4   Position at contact.

ball. There must be an extra 18 to 20 inches (45 to 50 centimeters) of "pop" through the ball. The extension of the arms, snap of the wrist, and rotation of the lower half now come into play. The bat head should be continuing toward center field until full extension is accomplished. This increases the hitter's impact zone. The bat continues to move in the direction the ball is hit. A full weight transfer occurs with the majority of the hitter's weight over the firm front leg. This weight transfer and the additional drive through the ball help ensure a long, full follow-through over the shoulder and a quicker time to first base. The hitter's body should be stacked with the back shoulder over the hip and the hip over the back knee (see figure 7.5). Balance, tempo, and rhythm take on a new level of importance and greatly improve when players focus on swinging to a good finish position.

Figure 7.5 Proper alignment at follow-through.

What's the Problem?

After you've watched your hitters' swings, you may detect some problems. Chapter 8 contains not only detailed descriptions of a variety of individual and team offensive drills to improve your players' skills, but also a drill finder that will help you quickly locate specific drills for your hitters' technique problems. As a coach, you may also need to correct hitting problems quickly in game situations. Notice in figures 7.6a and 7.6b how the athlete has made important adjustments in her swing during the same game based on her coach's feedback. You can also refer to figure 7.7 for a checklist of the most important mechanics at each stage of the swing.

Figure 7.6 Hitting problems can be corrected in game situations. Note (*a*) how the hitter's back leg is collapsing along with her front leg, and (*b*) how she is able to correct this later in the game by hitting off a firm front leg with a strong back leg drive.

Figure 7.7 Mechanics of the Swing Checklist

Stance

1. Eyes and head are level.
2. Eyes are focused on the pitcher's delivery point.
3. Position is comfortable and balanced.
4. Chin nearly touches the front shoulder.
5. Hitter grips the bat with the pads of the fingers.
6. Hitter looks over the front shoulder.
7. Muscles are relaxed.
8. Front shoulder is pointed at the pitcher and slightly closed.
9. Middle knuckles are lined up.

Stride

1. Stride is soft, short, and soon enough.
2. Front side is closed.
3. Stride is short so the center of gravity doesn't move.
4. Body remains balanced. Hitter picks up the front foot and steps out toward the pitcher (less than eight inches [20 centimeters]).
5. Head remains steady with little or no movement.
6. Hands stay back.

Swing

1. Back knee begins to move in.
2. Hands move toward the pitcher, not toward the plate, to stay inside of the ball.
3. Back foot pushes to transfer weight, then rotates.
4. Hips rotate toward the ball and remain level.
5. Arms remain flexed.
6. Chin goes from shoulder to shoulder.

Contact

1. Arms flex.
2. Palms take a position almost palm up and palm down.
3. Wrists do not roll on contact; they will roll naturally during follow-through.
4. Hitter hits up against a firm yet bent front leg.
5. Hitter finishes rotation of lower half of body.
6. Hitter extends through the ball 18 to 20 inches.

Follow-through

1. Begins after full extension through the ball.
2. Majority of weight is over the front leg.
3. Hitter is balanced, with the body stacked shoulder over hip over knee.
4. Bat creates a long arc from full extension to a position over and above the shoulder.

BUNTING

The bunt can alter the outcome of many games each season. The entire team should know the importance of bunting and that a game could be won or lost with proper or improper execution of a bunt. Stressing the idea that a hitter will not be called upon to bunt unless it is important can help in the team's understanding of this strategy. Just as in hitting, the degree of success in bunting will depend on mechanics and good pitch selection. The bunt is a good offensive weapon because it can move runners into scoring position. It can also put pressure on the defense by catching them off guard or by forcing them to make an error as a result of a hurried play.

Bunting must be practiced in gamelike situations. Bunting stations with lines drawn or targets established to emphasize good bunts can be a tremendous help. Mix bunts into batting practice by having the hitter swing away a few times, then bunt, then swing away, and then bunt again. In this section, I discuss five types of bunts: the sacrifice bunt, the base hit bunt, the push bunt, the slap, and the squeeze bunt.

Sacrifice Bunt

The sacrifice bunt gives up an out by the batter not reaching first base, but advances other runners. The batter should not attempt to make a base hit out of a sacrifice bunt unless the defense allows her to do so. Although players should not try to be too perfect in the placement of the sacrifice bunt, we generally want them to put it down between the pitcher and first baseman in order to advance the runner. With a runner at first and second, or second only, the ball should be placed on the third-base side of the infield. One other detail—the batter should only bunt strikes.

To execute the sacrifice bunt, the hitter does the following:

1. The batter positions herself in the front of the batter's box to increase the chances of the ball going forward and fair.

2. The batter moves into the bunt position at the correct time; the correct time is when the pitcher separates her hands and the ball is in the downswing position of her pitch.

3. The batter should pivot and open her hips toward the pitcher. Her feet are in a forward-backward position, and her toes are pointing at the pitcher (see figure 7.8a).

4. At the time of the pivot, the batter moves her top hand up the barrel and grips the bat at the taper while the bottom hand moves up to the top of the tape.

5. The batter should make sure the barrel remains higher than the hands at all times, and to reach a low pitch, the batter should lower her hands while bending at the knees. The end of the bat should meet the top half of the ball (see figure 7.8b).

Figure 7.8 Two key steps in the sacrifice bunt: (*a*) The bunter separates her hands and pivots her feet, and (*b*) she keeps the barrel higher than her hands when making contact with the ball.

Base Hit Bunt—Left-Hander

The base hit bunt is designed to get the batter to first base without giving up an out and to advance any runners who are on base. The ability to bunt for a base hit can add 25 to 50 points to a hitter's average. I allow players to bunt for a base hit on their own if the player believes the infield is not expecting a bunt or if the corners are positioned near their bases. The hitter must wait for a good pitch and then get the ball on the ground near the foul line six feet (1.8 meters) in front of the plate. The best pitch to bunt is a low strike.

To execute the base hit bunt, a left-hander should follow these steps:

1. The batter begins with her head, eyes, and shoulders level, and she has a hard focus on the ball. The right leg triggers off the pitch by taking a slight step and angling the toe toward the left foot. The left leg crosses over, and the left foot points toward third base. This helps prevent pulling out. After the feet begin to move, the left hand should slide to the taper while the

bat is being dropped into the zone. The right hand position remains the same, but softens. (See figure 7.9.)

2. Although the hips have turned to face first base, the batter makes sure her head and the barrel remain over the plate. The hands control the bat and direct the ball down. The bunter uses soft elbows to cushion the rebounding effect of the bat. The barrel needs to be above the ball, and contact should be at the top half of the ball.

Base Hit Bunt—Right-Hander

For a right-hander to base hit bunt effectively, she must maintain her batting stance until the last possible second. No movement occurs until the ball is five to eight feet (1.5 to 2.4 meters) from the plate.

To execute the base hit bunt, a right-hander should follow these steps:

1. A simultaneous movement of the feet, hips, and hands starts the bunt. The

Figure 7.9 The left-handed base hit bunt.

batter steps the left foot away from the plate about six inches (15 centimeters); she steps the right foot in a forward movement toward first base. This foot placement aligns the hips, knees, and toes with first base.

2. The batter slides the right (top) hand up to the taper. (This position is identical to the sacrifice bunt position.)

3. The batter keeps the barrel above the knob.

4. At contact, the head of the bat should be behind the barrel, and the batter's left hand should be near the left hip. The right hand controls the bat head over the plate.

5. The batter strikes the top of the ball with the end of the bat. The ideal ball position is three to six feet (91 to 182 centimeters) in front of the plate down the first-base line.

Push Bunt

The push bunt functions as an attempt to get a base hit while using sacrifice bunt techniques. The push bunt is used when the batter can push the ball between the pitcher and the charging first or third baseman. It must be hard enough to get by the pitcher, yet soft enough that the second baseman or shortstop must charge in to field the ball.

The batter must get the barrel out, firmly extending the bat toward the ball, and then push the ball off the bat. The location of the pitch will dictate the location of the push. For instance, a right-handed batter should push an outside pitch to the right side of the infield. The hand position on the bat and the body position in the push bunt are the same as in the sacrifice bunt.

Slap

The right-hander and left-hander will execute the slap differently. The slap is an alternative for the left-handed batter to produce a hit in an RBI situation or to get on base when a bunt may not be appropriate. This tool catches the infielders in a shifting position, having to commit to the coverage of either a bunt or a hard ground ball. This technique was designed to add confusion about the responsibilities of the infielders. With no one on base, they must decide who covers first on this would-be bunt or ground ball. It is the responsibility of the second baseman to cover first on bunts, yet it is the responsibility of the first baseman to cover first on routine ground balls.

The challenge continues for the infielders when there are runners on base. The shortstop may now be called on to field the slap or to cover second base if there is a runner on first base. Probably the most difficult situation for the shortstop is when she needs to cover second on a possible steal and the batter slaps the ball to the glove side of the third baseman. This is also an opportunity to hit the ball past charging corners.

What the slap must do is pull the defensive players away from their assigned positions and force them to try to field and throw the ball under the pressure of a very quick batter running to first base. A left-handed slapper is a triple threat: She can drop a bunt, she can slap the ball between infielders, and she can hit the ball in the gaps for base hits.

What follows is a pictorial summary of the key techniques of the left-handed slap bunt. In step one (figure 7.10a), you'll notice the following:

1. The slapper has opened and stepped with the right foot.

2. The left leg continues the run to open the hips.

3. The eyes remain perfectly level.

4. The barrel of the bat remains back.

In step two (figure 7.10b), you'll notice the following:

1. The left leg is planted.

2. The eyes remain perfectly level.

3. The right hip and hands are ready to drive the ball.

4. This slapper uses a choke position with both hands together.

5. The barrel of the bat is ready to be driven forward.

In step three (figure 7.10c), you'll notice the following:

Figure 7.10 The left-handed slap bunt: (*a*) The slapper opens up and steps with her right foot, (*b*) plants her left leg and begins the swing, and (*c*) drives the ball, keeping her left arm extended.

1. Contact is made.
2. The left arm is extended and the barrel is an extension of the arm.
3. The left foot is planted.
4. The left hip is open and driving the ball.
5. The head and eyes are perfectly level.

As the pitcher starts her delivery, the right-handed batter must look as if she is going to hit. When the pitcher's hands come apart, the hitter quickly squares around to show a believable bunt position. As the pitcher's arm is at the top of the backswing, the batter must quickly get her hands back to the hitting position. No motion change with the feet occurs except for a slight pivot as in a sacrifice bunt. The hitter is attempting to move the infielders on the show of the bunt and to create some holes, which the hitter might be able to take advantage of with a ground ball. It is now the hitter's job to drive the ball hard and down.

Squeeze Bunt

There are two types of squeeze bunts, the safety and the suicide. Both are used with a runner on third base. In the suicide squeeze, the base runner is going on the pitch, whereas in the safety, the base runner goes to the plate when she is sure the ball has been bunted down.

In the safety squeeze bunt, the batter can be selective on the pitch and bunt a good strike. This skill is similar to the sacrifice except the batter should wait to square until the ball is on its way to the plate. The longer the batter can wait, the more the element of surprise for the infielders. The base runner must get a good jump off third in anticipation of a strike and the bunt.

In the suicide squeeze, the base runner leaves third base on the pitch. In essence, she is stealing home. For the batter, everything is exactly like the safety squeeze except that she must put any pitched ball on the ground (fair if at all possible). Three problems that need to be avoided are committing to the bunt too soon, not putting the ball on the ground, and missing the ball.

SITUATION HITTING

The hitter must take into consideration the game situation when going to the plate. A team with good pitch selection and discipline jumps on mistake pitches. Teach your players to use the time in the dugout when waiting to bat to study the pitcher for types of pitches thrown, what she throws when she is ahead in the count, what she throws when she is behind, what her best pitch is, and so on. Time spent teaching hitters to prepare mentally for what they must do at the plate will add runs to the final score.

Hitters can watch the pitcher for patterns. Does she follow certain pitches with other pitches, such as throwing a change-up after a rise ball or a change-up after the batter pulls a long foul ball? Hitters can also learn to detect the type of pitch thrown by the grip the pitcher uses.

The Count

To establish discipline, the hitter must learn to consider the ball–strike count. Each count presents a different hitting challenge. Sometimes the advantage is with the pitcher, and sometimes it is with the hitter. By knowing what to expect, the hitter gains the edge. When the pitcher has to throw a pitch over the plate, usually that pitch is her best control pitch. The prepared hitter will know what type of pitch the pitcher generally throws when behind and when ahead in the count. Pitchers will establish some type of pitch pattern during the game, and the smart hitter looks for certain pitches in the various ball–strike counts. Here are some key things to look at regarding the ball–strike count.

Hitter Is Well Ahead in the Count When the count is 3-0, 3-1, 2-0, or 3-2, the hitter is ahead

Each hitting situation presents a different challenge. A disciplined hitter considers every ball and strike count while at bat.

in the count. Therefore, the pitcher must get the ball over the plate for a strike. Even the 3-2 count is to the hitter's advantage since the pitcher must throw a strike to avoid walking the batter. In this situation, the hitter should look for a pitch that the pitcher has good control over. If the pitcher has a good off-speed pitch, this is an excellent count to throw the change-up.

Hitter Is Behind in the Count On the 0-1, 1-1, and 1-2 counts, the pitcher has a distinct advantage over the hitter. On these counts, the pitcher will try to get the hitter to chase a bad pitch. With the 1-2 count, the pitcher will try to strike out the batter. The hitter should look for a ball that moves down and out hard or up and in hard. Teach hitters to stay disciplined and not to expect to get a good pitch to hit with these counts.

With the 0-2 count, the hitter must stay disciplined and not swing at a bad pitch in her effort to protect the plate. She should look for a pitch in the strike zone that she can make good contact with. The pitcher will try to pitch out of the strike zone and will attempt to throw waste pitches.

Hitter Is Even or Just Ahead in the Count On the 0-0, 1-0, 2-1, or 2-2 counts, the pitcher is trying to even the count or to keep from throwing a ball that will put her behind the hitter on the count. The 0-0 count is placed in this category because a strike thrown on the first pitch will quickly put the batter at a disadvantage. Pitchers will often utilize the in-out or up-down location for a strike in this situation. An off-speed pitch is also an effective pitch thrown in these counts.

Discipline A hitter who swings at the pitcher's best pitch when she (the batter) is ahead in the count is committing a serious hitting error. If she takes one of the pitcher's poor pitches when ahead in the count, she is committing the same type of error. The better the pitcher, the more the hitter must practice good pitch discipline. For example, if a pitcher possesses an excellent drop, a hitter must lay off that pitch with less than two strikes unless the pitcher happens to throw the drop into her hitting zone. Since the good pitcher will throw fewer mistake pitches than the average pitcher, the hitter cannot afford to take any mistake pitches. If a pitcher does not possess a "strikeout" pitch, the hitter can afford to have two strikes on her.

The plate umpire is a factor in pitch selection and discipline. The nature of her strike zone will dictate what the batter can and cannot do with a particular pitcher on the mound. For example, if the umpire is a high-pitch umpire, the hitter must take this into consideration when evaluating the pitch on its way to the plate. With two strikes, she needs to protect the high part of the strike zone.

An umpire with a "small" strike zone affords the hitter the opportunity to practice much better discipline than if the umpire has a "big" strike zone. Ideally, the umpire will establish his strike zone early in the game and will maintain that zone throughout the game. If the strike zone constantly changes, then the hitter needs to protect the plate a little more when she has two strikes.

"Happy Zone"

Every hitter has a certain area of the strike zone that she likes to hit the ball in—the "happy zone." But there are also areas of the strike zone where the hitter has a tough time making solid contact with the ball. Players need to realize that even great hitters have a difficult time making good contact in certain parts of the strike zone. They also need to realize that some hitters can make good contact on pitches outside the strike zone, while other hitters need to have the ball in the strike zone. Every hitter is different, and every hitter must understand her limitations and capabilities. To become a successful hitter, the batter must make adjustments and understand her hitting zones. Hitters can improve their averages by being selective while still maintaining their aggressiveness.

Pitch Selection and Discipline

Each at-bat during the course of a game has its own unique set of circumstances. In the following sections, I will take you through some of these game situations and the hitting strategies that should be considered. For a summary of additional game situations, please refer to the chart in figure 7.11.

Leadoff Hitter in the Inning The leadoff hitter in the inning must try to find a way to get on

Figure 7.11 Game Situations and Pitch Selection Chart

Situation	Outs	Objectives	Pitch to look for
Runner at 2nd	0	Move the runner	LH: a pitch to pull (inside or off-speed) RH: an outside pitch to drive to the right side
Runner at 3rd	Less than 2	Score the runner	LH: an off-speed pitch to produce a fly ball; an inside pitch to drive to the 2nd baseman RH: an off-speed pitch to produce a fly ball; a good pitch to hit hard through the infield
Double play possibility	Less than 2	Avoid the double play and move the runner	LH: an inside or off-speed pitch to hit between the 1st and 2nd baseman RH: an outside or off-speed pitch to hit between the 1st and 2nd baseman
Sacrifice bunt	Less than 2	Avoid a pop-up	LH or RH: a low pitch in the strike zone
Squeeze bunt	0, 1, or 2	Score the run	LH or RH: the batter must get the bunt down or foul regardless of the pitch
Tying or winning run at 2nd late in the game	0, 1, or 2	Discipline and going after good pitches	LH or RH: the pitcher may attempt to pitch around the batter to get to the batter on deck; drive a good pitch into left center or right center
Tying or winning run at 1st late in the game	Less than 2	Discipline, drawing a walk, or moving the runner to 3rd	LH or RH: strikes and an up pitch to drive for an extra-base hit
Hit-and-run	0	Use when the batter has good bat control and the runner has average to above average speed	LH or RH: count is 1-0, 2-0, or 2-1; can be run on any ball/strike with less than 2 strikes and less than 2 outs; hit to the right side
A great hitter at the plate with the opportunity to win the game	0, 1, or 2	Disciplined strike zone; the opposing pitcher may be throwing around the strike zone	LH or RH: something in the hitter's hitting zone
The team is behind late in the game	0, 1, or 2	Get on base!	LH or RH: draw walks; the pitcher will be throwing strikes to avoid walking batters

base. The easiest way is to draw a walk or to hit one of the pitcher's mistake pitches. A leadoff hitter should also be ready to hit that first pitch knowing a pitcher likes to get ahead of the hitter. The leadoff hitter for a team should be a hitter with good discipline along with a high on-base percentage.

Runner at First Base With No Outs If the leadoff hitter has gotten on, then a right-handed number two hitter should have the ability to drive the ball to the right side of the infield. A left-handed number two hitter should have the ability to pull the ball to the right side of the field. If the defense is playing the left-handed batter to bunt or pull the ball, the hitter must be able to drive the ball to the left side of the infield. However, it is more difficult for the defense to complete a double play on the right side of the infield than on the left side. The hitter must be disciplined to look for a pitch in her hitting zone, one that she can drive to whichever area will provide a better chance of staying out of a double play. This is a perfect time for a bunt of some sort.

Runner at Second Base With No Outs This situation forces the hitter to practice great discipline so that she can react to a pitch that can be hit hard to the right side of the field. The right-handed hitter should look for a pitch from the middle of the plate to the outside corner of the plate. She must stay disciplined and not swing at an inside pitch unless she has two strikes on her, because hitting this pitch may result in a ground ball to the left side of the infield, preventing the runner from advancing. The left-handed hitter must look for a pitch that she can pull while knowing that the smart pitcher will keep the ball away from the lefty. A coach may sacrifice bunt in this situation if the batter does not have the ability to move the runner to third.

Runner at Third With Less Than Two Outs In this situation, the hitter must look for a pitch she can hit hard somewhere. With less than two strikes, she should look for a "mistake" pitch. However, if the pitcher gets two strikes on the batter, the batter needs to concentrate on making contact. In this situation, a hard ground ball will have an excellent chance of getting through the infield. The hitter must make every effort to get a good pitch to hit when she has less than two strikes.

Runners at First and Third With One Out With runners at first and third and only one out, the hitter should make every attempt to avoid an inning-ending double play. If the runner on first has started on the pitch, the hitter must exercise good discipline to take advantage of the infielder's movement to cover the steal. An ideal spot to hit the ball would be to the right side enabling the run to score and the runner to advance.

When it is time to begin teaching hitting skills, keep in mind the following: The opposing pitcher is throwing up to 300 pitches each day. For the hitter to be successful, she must have the opportunity to train at an equal level. Because hitting is a reactionary skill, numerous repetitions are vital. In this chapter, I present a number of hitting drills, broken down into the following categories: no-ball drills, still-ball drills, tossed-ball drills, machine-ball drills, and pitched-ball drills. There are also drills designed for challenge and competition—games where players compete individually or as a team—as well as some bunting drills. The no-ball, still-ball, tossed-ball, and machine-ball drills can all be performed for three to five minutes at a time, while the pitched-ball and challenge drills can take as long as necessary to execute. This chapter begins with a drill finder that lists several common hitting errors and the drills in this chapter that will help correct them. The use of drills can greatly enhance technique evaluation for the coach and player. You may also want to videotape the drills and review the tapes with the team at the end of practice. A player has an easier time correcting a problem if she can see it for herself.

Problem	Drill	Page
Dropping the barrel Result: missing the ball or popping up	Barrier Behind	74
	Wall Swings	76
	Down on One Knee	76
	Regular Tee	76
	Swing Over the Top Tee and Hit the Second Tee	77
	Two Tees	77
	Partner High Toss	80
	Soft Toss—Off Back Knee	81
	Pepper Game	85

(continued)

Problem	Drill	Page
Pulling the ball Result: hitting the ball foul	Frisbee Throw	75
	Inside-Outside	76
	Target on the Fence	77
	Reverse Tracking	81
	No Pull	82
	Hit 'Til You Drop	84
	Over the Line	84
Wrist rolls too soon Result: ground ball	Contact and Pop	75
	Lead Arm Extension	79
	One Hand, Small Bat	80
	One-Hand Soft Toss	80
	Reverse Tracking	81
	Partner Fair Ball	82
Weak lead arm Result: no power and slow swing	Barrier Behind	74
	Draw a Line	75
	Frisbee Throw	75
	Push-Throughs	75
	Strength Band	75
	Wall Swings	76
	Drop Toss	79
	One Hand, Small Bat	80
	One-Hand Soft Toss	80
	Snap Backs	80
	Very Fast Pitching Machine	82
	Toss Game	85
Pulling the head Result: missing the ball	Mirror	75
	Regular Tee	76
	Front Toss	79
	Numbered Balls	80
	Self Toss	80
	Tracking and Recognition	83
	Move the Runner	84

Problem	Drill	Page
Slow hands Result: lack of power and hitting to the opposite field	Draw a Line	75
	Lightweight Bat	76
	Drop Toss	79
	One Hand, Small Bat	80
	Snap Backs	80
	Soft Toss—Off Back Knee	81
	Very Fast Pitching Machine	82
Big stride Result: swinging under the ball	Mirror	75
	Stride Box	75
	Deflated Volleyball	76
	Stride, Stop, Swing	77
	Balance Beam and Ball	78
	Front Toss	79
Lack of balance Result: weak ground ball and loss of power	Balance Beam	74
	Isometric	75
	Mirror	75
	Deflated Volleyball	76
	Shutting Eyes	77
	Stride, Stop, Swing	77
	Partner Low Toss	80
	Situation Hitting Practice	83
No trigger Result: late swing	Bounce in Front	78
	Drop Toss	79
	Two-Ball Toss	80
	Tracking and Recognition	83
	Walk-Throughs	82
Lack of hand–eye coordination Result: mis-hits and not hitting the center of the ball	Drop Toss	79
	Figure Eight	79
	Reverse Tracking	81
	Two-Ball Toss	80
	Colored Ball	82
	Gamelike Batting Practice	82
	Numbered Balls	80
	Very Fast Pitching Machine	82

(continued)

Problem	Drill	Page
Poor pitch selection Result: weak hits and swings and misses	Front Toss	79
	Colored Ball	82
	Drop Ball	82
	Rise-Ball Pitch	83
	Tracking and Recognition	83
	Target Hitting	83
	12 Strike	84
	Grand Slam	84
Pulling off the ball Result: weak hits and trouble hitting outside pitches	Two Tees	77
	Contact and Pop	75
	Basketball Toss	78
	Push-Throughs	75
	Long Tee	76
	Self Toss	80

NO-BALL DRILLS

In these drills, no ball is used. The hitter might use a piece of apparatus or use a bat to break down the swing and develop individual parts of that swing.

Balance Beam

Purpose: To get the proper feel of balance during a swing.

Procedure: The batter stands on a low balance beam made from a two-by-eight-inch (5-by-20-centimeter) piece of lumber. The beam is placed on the ground in the batter's box, and the batter takes her normal swing while trying to stay on the beam. Her goal is to not lose balance and step off the beam.

Barrier Behind

Purpose: To emphasize taking the hands directly to the ball and keeping the barrel up.

Procedure: The batter's rear foot is parallel to the side of a batting cage and in contact with the net. The batter swings by taking her hands to the ball and keeping the bat barrel up. The bat should not touch the barrier on the swing. (See figure 8.1.)

Figure 8.1 Barrier Behind drill.

Contact and Pop

Purpose: To find the perfect contact point for pitches at different locations and to emphasize extension through contact.

Procedure: The batter assumes a hitting position while down on one knee, with her back knee on the ground. She starts the bat at the position where she is going to contact the ball for either the inside pitch, outside pitch, or a pitch down the middle of the plate. From the contact point, the hitter "pops" to the point of full extension without a follow-through.

Draw a Line

Purpose: To practice moving the hands to the ball and to develop speed and a strong lead arm.

Procedure: The batter assumes her stance without a bat and with her lead hand in its normal position with the thumb up. The hitter draws a line across her chest and then extends in a "karate chop" motion toward the ball.

Frisbee Throw

Purpose: To emphasize the movement sequence of the shoulder, elbow, and wrist.

Procedure: The batter assumes a hitting stance and grips the Frisbee in her lead hand, holding the Frisbee parallel to the ground. The shoulder, then elbow, then wrist extend forward to throw.

Isometric

Purpose: To practice a complete swing and follow-through.

Procedure: The batter assumes her stance while her partner stands behind and holds the top of the bat with both hands. The partner offers resistance as the batter strides and swings all the way through.

Mirror

Purpose: To develop a picture-perfect technique.

Procedure: The batter assumes a batting stance in front of a mirror with or without a bat. She swings, focusing on length of stride, hip rotation, contact point, or any specific swing mechanic the coach suggests.

Push-Throughs

Purpose: To isolate contact point and simulate the bat staying on the ball.

Procedure: The batter assumes the hitting position, and a partner stands out in front with her hand out (fingers down). The hand simulates the ball, with the batter bringing the barrel of the bat to the hand to simulate contact point. The hand should resist, and the bat should continue to push on the hand until full extension.

Stride Box

Purpose: To concentrate on keeping the front side closed during the stride.

Procedure: Construct a stride box by forming an L from two 12-inch (30-centimeter) lengths of 2-by-4-inch (5-by-10-centimeter) lumber. Lay the stride box on the ground where it will serve as a gauge for how far the batter's foot should move during the stride and where it will make sure that the front foot stays closed. The batter assumes her normal stance and takes her normal swing, trying not to step on the stride box.

Strength Band

Purpose: To develop muscle strength for the lead arm that starts the swing.

Procedure: Attach the strength band at shoulder height to a fence behind the athlete's back arm. The athlete assumes the hitting position and grabs hold of the strength band in her lead hand. She then takes the strength band across the front of her body in the hitting path.

Wall Swings

Purpose: To avoid casting the barrel in a long, sweeping swing.

Procedure: The batter stands facing the wall, about a bat's length away. She assumes her batting stance and swings. The bat should not touch the wall if the hands are going to the ball. If the batter has a long, sweeping swing, the bat will hit the wall.

STILL-BALL DRILLS

You can use any type of balls for these drills. These drills allow the batter to work on her swing without worrying about making contact with a moving ball.

Advanced Tee

Purpose: To learn muscle memory by performing the swing the same every time.

Procedure: The batter is in her normal position at a tee. Her partner places the ball on the tee. The batter hits one, then closes her eyes and hits again.

Deflated Volleyball

Purpose: To emphasize keeping the knees together with a short, balanced stride.

Procedure: The batter assumes her normal position at the tee with a deflated volleyball placed between her knees. The batter then swings through the ball while remaining balanced and gripping the volleyball with her knees.

Down on One Knee

Purpose: To concentrate on keeping the barrel above the hands to hit the high pitch. The only way to hit the high pitch is to tomahawk the ball.

Procedure: The hitter is down on the back leg with the front leg extended straight. The ball is on a tee above shoulder level when the batter is on one knee. The batter keeps her hands down and the barrel up, tomahawking the ball.

Inside-Outside

Purpose: To emphasize taking the same stride, regardless of the pitch location.

Procedure: One tee is placed on the inside corner of the plate (in front of the plate), and the second tee is placed on the outside corner of the plate (even with the plate). While using correct mechanics, the batter alternates between hitting the inside ball and the outside ball.

Lightweight Bat

Purpose: To create an underloading effect in order to increase bat speed.

Procedure: Using a lightweight bat, the batter stands in the hitting position and takes full cuts. These swings can be taken off a tee or off a toss from in front delivered by a partner. The batter should focus on firing the bat quickly through the hitting zone.

Long Tee

Purpose: To work on achieving a smooth swing with proper extension and to minimize over-rotation of the shoulders and hips.

Procedure: Set up a tee 20 to 30 feet (6 to 9 meters) away from a screen. The tee is set up at the place of optimal contact for hitting a pitch down the middle of the plate. The athlete attempts to hit the ball into the screen.

Regular Tee

Purpose: To isolate and focus on specific swing mechanics.

Procedure: Place the tee with the ball at different locations around the plate and locate the tee where contact should be made. The batter executes the correct technique while swinging to the various contact points (see figure 8.2).

Figure 8.2 Regular Tee drill.

Shutting Eyes

Purpose: To place focus on using proper hitting mechanics rather than hitting the ball.

Procedure: If a hitter is hitting off a tee or off a toss, but is not getting the results she is looking for, have her close her eyes and feel the proper mechanics involved in the swing. When the eyes are closed, she will be able to make contact using better mechanics.

Stride, Stop, Swing

Purpose: To practice keeping the hands back in the hitting position and remaining balanced throughout the swing.

Procedure: The batter is at a tee and takes her normal stride. She holds her stride position for a split second and then swings.

Swing Over the Top Tee and Hit the Second Tee

Purpose: To emphasize keeping the barrel above the hands.

Procedure: Position two tees, one in front of the other with the rear tee three inches (7 centimeters) higher than the front tee. A ball is placed on the front tee. The batter assumes her normal stance and swings over the higher tee to hit the ball on the front tee.

Target on the Fence

Purpose: To practice a smooth rhythm and follow-through and to improve bat control.

Procedure: Place a target on the fence and a tee about 15 to 20 feet (4.5 to 6.0 meters) in front of the target. The batter tries to hit the target.

Two Tees

Purpose: To concentrate on hitting to and through the ball on the sweet spot of the bat with a line drive contact.

Procedure: Two tees are placed at the same height, one 12 inches (30 centimeters) in front of the other with a ball on each. The batter tries to drive the bat through the ball on the first tee and into and through the ball on the second tee (see figure 8.3).

Figure 8.3 Two Tees drill.

TOSSED-BALL DRILLS

You can use tennis balls or baseballs for these drills. After practicing with these smaller balls, softballs appear much larger and easier to hit. The tosser's role is vital! The toss should be made to the proper bat contact location. In all of these drills, the batter can hit into a net, the fence, or the open field. The tosser usually stands at a 45-degree angle to the batter. Sometimes the tosser will be positioned like a pitcher in relation to the batter.

Balance Beam and Ball

Purpose: To develop balance as well as a firm front leg and a powerful back leg.

Procedure: The batter stands on a two-by-four-inch (5-by-10-centimeter) board and hits a ball off a toss. She takes her normal swing and tries to remain on the board during the swing. The partner stands facing the batter about six feet (1.8 meters) away and tosses the ball into the contact position.

Basketball Toss

Purpose: To prevent pulling off the ball and to concentrate on hitting through the ball.

Procedure: The batter is in her stance, and a tosser stations herself at a 45-degree angle, six to eight feet (1.8 to 2.4 meters) away from the batter. The tosser throws a basketball underhand to the hitter. The hitter focuses on keeping her shoulder in and hitting through the ball.

Bounce in Front

Purpose: To practice the hitting rhythm and the trigger and to learn to hit the ball at the top of the bounce.

Procedure: The partner stands six feet (1.8 meters) to the side and three feet (91 centimeters) in front of the batter and tosses a tennis ball that bounces up into the strike zone in front of the plate. As the ball bounces, the batter "triggers" and gets her hands started into the swing. She waits until the ball is at the height of the bounce before swinging and driving it into a net.

Drop Toss

Purpose: To develop hand speed to the ball.

Procedure: The batter assumes her stance, with a partner facing her with the ball held at shoulder height. The batter tells the partner when to drop the ball. The partner releases the ball and pulls her arm up away from the strike zone. The batter takes a full swing.

Variations: The partner can stand on a chair or on the bleachers, which will add a challenging tracking test.

Figure Eight

Purpose: To develop a quick adjustment to the ball.

Procedure: The batter is in her stance, and a tosser is down on one knee with a ball in each hand. The tosser is six feet (1.8 meters) away at a 45-degree angle. The tosser tumbles both balls around each other and then tosses one or the other to the batter. The batter then takes a full swing and hits the ball into the net.

Front Toss

Purpose: To emphasize swing techniques utilizing proper mechanics.

Procedure: Place a screen 10 to12 feet (3.0 to 3.6 meters) in front of the plate with the tosser standing behind it. The tosser throws underhand and can control pitch location while the batter takes a normal swing (see figure 8.4).

Lead Arm Extension

Purpose: To emphasize the shoulder unlock, the elbow unlock, and the wrist unlock.

Procedure: The hitter kneels on her back leg 10 feet (3 meters) from a screen or fence, and the tosser positions herself 4 feet (121 centimeters) in front and to the side of the hitter. The hitter hits the ball hard using only the lead arm (left arm for right-handed batters and right arm for left-handed batters). The batter starts with both hands on the bat, holding it in proper position. A full swing is taken.

Figure 8.4 Front Toss drill.

Numbered Balls

Purpose: To work on keeping the eyes on the ball and seeing the ball to contact.

Procedure: Place a screen 10 to 12 feet (3.0 to 3.6 meters) in front of the plate with the tosser standing behind it. The objective is for the batter to call out the number written on each ball that is tossed to her before contact is made.

One Hand, Small Bat

Purpose: To emphasize the top hand movement by having the hand cock the wrist for full extension; the top hand grips the bat "like a hammer" and swings through the ball.

Procedure: The batter assumes her stance using a small bat that she can control with the top hand. A helper tosses balls that the batter hits with the small bat.

One-Hand Soft Toss

Purpose: To emphasize loading the lead arm in sequence: shoulder, elbow, and then wrist.

Procedure: The batter is down on the back knee with the front leg up, and she grips the bat with only the bottom hand. The tosser stands six feet (1.8 meters) away at a 45-degree angle and tosses the ball out in front of the batter's lead arm. The batter swings only at strikes and drives the ball into the net.

Partner High Toss

Purpose: To practice keeping the barrel above the hands with the weight transfer through the ball.

Procedure: The tosser stands about six feet (1.8 meters) away at a 45-degree angle. She tosses a firm chest-high toss into the hitting area in front of the plate. The batter hits into a screen.

Partner Low Toss

Purpose: To concentrate on a soft, short, and balanced stride.

Procedure: The hitter stands 10 feet (3 meters) from a screen, and the tosser positions herself 4 feet (121 centimeters) in front and to the side of the hitter. When working on the inside pitch, the hitter closes her stance, and the ball is tossed to her front hip. When working on the outside pitch, the hitter slightly opens her stance, and the ball is tossed to the front hip across the center of the plate. The toss should be low and firm, and the batter hits the ball hard and into the screen.

Self Toss

Purpose: To practice taking the hands inside the ball and going to full extension with bat control.

Procedure: The hitter takes her normal stance. She holds the bat in her top hand and tosses the ball with her bottom hand (a "fungo" hit). As the ball approaches the contact position, the hitter drives the ball to a center field target.

Snap Backs

Purpose: To develop quick hands, a small stride, and forearm and wrist strength.

Procedure: The partner stands six feet (1.8 meters) from the batter and tosses balls in rapid succession to the contact point of the strike zone. The hitter is standing up and drives one ball after another into a net by taking her swing and snapping the bat back to the starting position in preparation for the next toss.

Two-Ball Toss

Purpose: To practice keeping the hands back until the last possible second.

Procedure: The partner stands about six feet (1.8 meters) to the side of the hitter and holds two balls in the same hand. The tosser tosses both balls at the same time and commands the batter to "hit the top ball" or "hit the bottom ball." The batter hits into a screen.

Reverse Tracking

Purpose: To practice tracking the ball and keeping the hands inside the barrel.

Procedure: The ball is flipped from behind the hitter on an inside-out plane. The hitter can slightly turn her head to track the toss. As the ball comes forward, the hitter must hold her power angle until contact. The hitter must wait on the ball and then drive it with authority into the center of the net. The hitter needs to fully extend before rolling her wrists (see figure 8.5).

Soft Toss—Off Back Knee

Purpose: To concentrate on hitting down on the ball.

Procedure: The hitter kneels on her back knee, and the tosser stands about six feet (1.8 meters) to the side and faces the hitter. The tosser tosses at the hitter's contact position. The object is for the hitter to drive the ball into the center of the net while working on hand speed. This drill eliminates the lower body and emphasizes hand quickness (see figure 8.6).

Figure 8.5   Reverse Tracking drill.

Figure 8.6   Soft Toss—Off Back Knee drill.

Walk-Throughs

Purpose: To properly control weight transfer that occurs during the swing and minimize over-rotation.

Procedure: Place a screen 15 to 20 feet (4.5 to 6.0 meters) from the plate with a tosser standing behind it. The batter assumes the hitting position at the plate, but then puts her swing into motion—stepping with the front foot and then crossing over with the back foot. As the batter is crossing over with her back foot, the tosser delivers the pitch, and the batter swings at the pitch, without over-rotating.

MACHINE-BALL DRILLS

Unless stated otherwise, the machine is at a normal pitching distance from the batter and on normal speed. The machine is used in place of a live pitcher. The machine enables the hitter to perform many repetitions in a short amount of time.

Colored Ball

Purpose: To practice visual tracking as well as taking the pitch.

Procedure: Red and black colored quarter-size dots are painted on four sides of the balls. The hitter is instructed to hit the black balls and to take the red balls. This drill can be done in a batting cage or on a field with fielders.

Partner Fair Ball

Purpose: To practice hitting off the machine on a field with fielders.

Procedure: The pitching machine is on the mound and set on the hitting speed and location for that day. All players have a partner, and they take turns hitting off the machine. One hitter hits until she hits a fair ball and then it is the partner's turn. A prescribed amount of time is allotted for each pair combination. Fielders and base runners can be used.

Drop Ball

Purpose: To practice hitting a drop ball.

Procedure: Position the pitching machine on a short stand, about six inches (15 centimeters) off the ground. The pitched ball will then come from an elevated position to a low strike position. This drill can be done on the field with fielders or in a batting cage.

Gamelike Batting Practice

Purpose: To concentrate on proper techniques and execution.

Procedure: The feeder at the machine gives an offensive signal to the batter, who must execute the play as if it were a game situation. The feeder uses all plays, such as the hit-and-run, bunts, and squeezes. This can be done in a batting cage or on a field with or without fielders. Base runners are used when fielders are present.

No Pull

Purpose: To emphasize keeping the front side closed throughout the swing.

Procedure: Set the machine at normal speed to throw to the outside corner of the strike zone. The first baseman, second baseman, and right fielder are at their positions for the right-handed batter (for the left-handed batter, the third baseman, shortstop, and left fielder are at their positions). If the ball is hit to the right (or left for a left-handed batter) side of second base, the defense returns the ball, but if any ball is hit elsewhere, the batter must run and get it. Base runners are practicing going from first to third and second to home.

Very Fast Pitching Machine

Purpose: To emphasize a short, soft stride and quick hands.

Procedure: Move the hitter very close to the machine or set the machine on high speed. The batter just tries to make contact with a regular swing. This can be done on a field with fielders and base runners or in a batting cage.

Rise-Ball Pitch

Purpose: To practice hitting a rise ball.

Procedure: Take the legs off the pitching machine and position the machine on the ground. The pitched ball will then come from a low position to a high position. The batter must swing at only strikes. This drill can be done on the field with fielders and base runners or in a batting cage.

PITCHED-BALL DRILLS

Pitched-ball drills are the final step in the progression of hitting drills. In the previous drills, the swing has been built, and now it is time for the batter to test it out! A live pitcher is needed in these drills, which now place the batter in gamelike situations.

Situation Hitting Practice

Purpose: To practice offensive plays.

Procedure: The coach gives an offensive signal, and the batter must execute the play. The coach can utilize the hit-and-run, the bunt, or the squeeze or slap bunts. This drill is done off of a machine or with a live pitcher. Defensive players are at their positions and base runners are used. All swings taken must be purposeful, because swinging at bad pitches in batting practice sessions will carry over to the game.

Coaching points: Situation hitting in batting practice sessions provides the hitter and coach the opportunity to evaluate the hitter's discipline and pitch selection.

Variations: Play an intrasquad game using different counts or place the hitter in a certain count each time she steps to the plate.

Target Hitting

Purpose: To develop the right-handed batter's skill of hitting an outside pitch to right field and an inside pitch to left field, and vice versa for the left-handed batter.

Procedure: In batting practice, the batter must hit into an assigned area of the field. For example, the first pitch a right-handed batter hits must be to right field. She will need to be sure to wait for an outside pitch. On her next swing, she must try to pull the ball, thus looking for an inside pitch. This drill can be done with or without fielders and base runners.

Tracking and Recognition, or Take the Pitch

Purpose: To develop tracking skills and to recognize strikes.

Procedure: A pitcher is on the mound with a catcher behind the plate. The pitcher throws pitches, and the hitter stands in the batter's box. The batter takes her normal stride and tracks the ball as well as recognizes spin on the ball, such as drop, rise, or change-up spin. The batter does not swing at the pitch but calls out the type of pitch that was thrown.

The batter will be better prepared for game situations if the coach integrates live pitching into practices.

12 Strike

Purpose: To enable the batter to see live pitching and to practice swinging at strikes.

Procedure: A pitcher is on the mound with a full-geared catcher behind the plate, and the hitter is in the batter's box. The batter gets 12 strikes. A strike is called when a pitch considered to be a ball is swung at, when a pitch is swung at and missed, and when a pitch delivered in the strike zone is not hit. The next batter comes on deck after 10 strikes. This drill can be done with fielders and base runners.

COMPETITION AND CHALLENGE GAMES

This section of drills is the most fun! The skills the players gain from the competition and challenge that occur in these drills will carry over into the actual game. The swing that has been built in the previous drills now must be executed in pressure situations.

Coach's Challenge

Purpose: To make batting practice gamelike by introducing pressure.

Procedure: This game is played with a pitching machine in the cage and three or four players per team. Each team has an "at-bat," and the opponents determine if the result would be a hit or an out. Keep track of base runners and runs scored each inning and alternate as you would in a normal game.

Grand Slam

Purpose: To practice proper swing technique and hitting the ball to score points.

Procedure: Players can be grouped individually or in teams. Each player is awarded 10 swings with the object being to score as many points as possible in those 10 swings. Areas of the batting cage are assigned points: four points for hitting the back of the cage; three points for hitting it in power alleys; two points for hitting certain areas of the cage; one point for hitting a ground ball in front of a certain line. Zero points are given for swings and misses and for not getting the ball across the line.

Hit 'Til You Drop

Purpose: To enable the batter to see many pitched balls in a short amount of time.

Procedure: The game can be played with a live pitcher or a pitching machine. A full defense is in place, and players are partnered up. Base runners can be used. The partners get five minutes together to bat one at a time. The batter keeps her turn until she hits a foul ball or swings and misses a pitch. The players continue to alternate until the time elapses, and the score is kept by the number of balls hit into play.

Move the Runner

Purpose: To emphasize offensive play execution to move the runner.

Procedure: The game is played with a live pitcher or a pitching machine. A full defense is in place. The players are partnered weaker with stronger. One partner starts on first base, and the other is at the plate. The object of the game is to score your partner in less than three outs. The hitter can employ any strategy or play to move her partner. The hitter does not run out the play.

Over the Line

Purpose: To concentrate on pitch selection and hit placement.

Procedure: Set up the field as diagrammed in figure 8.7. The game can be played with three or four players per team. When three outs are recorded, the teams change from offense to defense and vice versa. The inning begins with a tosser tossing for a hitter who attempts to hit a line drive over the line. If the ball lands over the line, a single is recorded, and if the ball lands over the deepest line, a home run

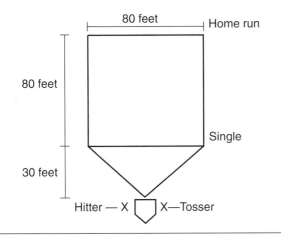

80 feet | Home run

80 feet

30 feet

Single

Hitter — X   X—Tosser

Figure 8.7 Over the Line drill.

is recorded. Outs are recorded in the following manner: (a) A fielder catches the ball in the air, (b) the ball bounces before the line, or (c) the ball lands outside the field of play. After three outs, teams change sides. Any number of innings can be played.

Pepper Game

Purpose: To emphasize putting the ball on the ground.

Procedure: Set up a hitter and a line of four or five fielders 20 to 30 feet (6 to 9 meters) away. The fielders toss underhand to the hitter, and if the fielder catches a line drive, she gets to advance one position. If a fielder misses a ground ball on her glove side, she goes to the end of the line. The batter is out (and gets only one out) if she pops up or a line drive is caught, or if she hits the ball over the fielders, swings and misses, or hits a ball foul. The fielders toss in order. When the batter is out, she goes to the end of the fielding line, and all other fielders move up one spot.

Toss Game

Purpose: To concentrate on solid contact and good swing mechanics.

Procedure: A game is played with infielders, outfielders, and the catcher. The coach stands 10 feet (3 meters) down the first-base line for the right-handed hitter and down the left-field

line for the left-handed hitter. The coach tosses to the hitters, and they run out their batted ball. Each player hits once in each inning while the defense clears the bases every three outs until all batters on the opposing team have hit.

Variations: The coach can tell the hitter where to hit or what offensive situation to play.

BUNTING DRILLS

Bunting is an important tool in the offensive arsenal. These drills will enable the athlete to practice and develop proper bunting techniques. Be sure to build ample time within your practice to perfect the short game.

Drop Everything

Purpose: To practice the squeeze bunt.

Procedure: A screen is set up in the middle of the pitching area. This drill has two pitchers and two catchers. Pitcher 1 is in front of the screen and throws to home plate. Pitcher 2 is behind the screen and throws to second base. Hitter 1 is at the plate and bunts the first pitch and runs to first base, while at the same time, hitter 2, who is at a plate where second base was, bunts the first pitch and runs to third base. Then both hitters jog to the ends of the opposite lines. If the ball is not contacted by one of the hitters, she runs to the center-field fence, touches it, and sprints to the end of the next line.

Get It Down

Purpose: To practice sacrifice bunts and bunt placement.

Procedure: A rope is placed 15 feet (4.5 meters) from home plate and in a semicircle stretching from one sideline to the other. The pitcher and catcher are at their defensive positions with base runners on the base paths. All the hitters are at home plate. Each hitter bunts the ball and tries to keep it inside the rope. The hitter gets two chances to contact the bunt. If the first or second ball is bunted, the hitter runs to first base. If the hitter misses both balls, she runs all the bases before returning to the end of the line.

Slap Them In

Purpose: To improve on the slap bunt technique.

Procedure: All infield defensive positions are filled, and there is a runner on third base. The hitters are at home. Each hitter slaps the ball and tries to put it on the ground toward the second baseman or the shortstop. The runner at third is going either on the pitch or the throw to first; the batter decides this and gives a signal to the runner. After the slap execution, the hitter goes to third and the runner goes to the end of the line at home.

Slot Shots

Purpose: To practice the push bunt.

Procedure: The pitcher, catcher, third baseman, and first baseman are in their defensive positions with base runners. All hitters are at home plate. Each hitter push-bunts the ball and tries to push it in the slots between the pitcher and the third baseman or the pitcher and the first baseman. The hitter gets two chances to push the bunt in the slot. If the first or second ball is bunted, the hitter runs to first base. If the hitter misses both balls, she runs all the bases before returning to the end of the line.

PLANNING HITTING PRACTICE

Now what? You have all these drills to help develop your hitters. How do you make the pieces of the puzzle fit into a practice plan? I like to spend two days with no-ball drills, then two days with still-ball drills. We then progress to two days of tossed-ball drills before we go into three days of machine-ball drills. When I feel our hitters have established the basics and our pitchers are ready, we will progress into pitched-ball drills. When batters have specific problems, you should start them with the no-ball drill solutions in the drill finder and then work them up to more complex drills.

After several weeks of practice when the players have had a chance to work through all of the drills in the progression and to become familiar with them, you may want to try taking a five-station approach to practice with an equal number of players at each station. I like to put athletes in the same group who have similar technique problems. I use this station plan in the preseason as well as in the regular season, but on a less frequent basis.

You can utilize a facility that is a little larger than a basketball court, along with all kinds of balls: Wiffle balls, tennis balls, "real soft" balls, and real balls. Set up five areas and use one or two drills in each area. By organizing the drills in the station approach and keeping track of "decks of drills," you can add interest to your hitting practices. Imagine numbering each drill in this chapter (by type of drill) and putting each one on a three-by-five-inch index card. Now put all the drill cards in five different decks as follows:

- Deck 1: no-ball drills
- Deck 2: still-ball drills
- Deck 3: tossed-ball drills
- Deck 4: machine-ball drills
- Deck 5: pitched-ball drills

You have five decks of such drills and five stations. Take a drill from each deck and put it at each station. For example, on one day of practice, you might do the following:

- Station 1 (no-ball)—deck 1, drill 1
- Station 2 (still-ball)—deck 2, drill 1
- Station 3 (tossed-ball)—deck 3, drill 1
- Station 4 (machine-ball)—deck 4, drill 1
- Station 5 (pitched-ball)—deck 5, drill 1

You may be using a special apparatus, and this can constitute one of the stations. Let the specialty items be station 5 instead of pitched-ball drills. If you have any special coaching or teaching items, I suggest they be utilized at station 5 or a new station. Bunting drills could also be utilized at another new station. That format would look like this:

- Station 1 (machine-ball)—deck 4, drill 3
- Station 2 (still-ball)—deck 2, drill 3

- Station 3 (tossed-ball)—deck 3, drill 4
- Station 4 (variety)—deck 1, drill 1
- Station 5 (specialty)—deck 5, drill 1

What should the timetable look like? Here's an example:

Number of players: 20

Number of stations: 5

Players per station: 4

Minutes per station: 8

Minutes to pack up balls and move to next station: 2

Total amount of time: 50 minutes

With this plan, in 50 minutes each batter will be at five different stations and experience five different drills. If each athlete gets 10 to 20 swings at each station, this plan would allow for 50 to 100 total swings in 50 minutes.

CHAPTER 9

OFFENSIVE STRATEGIES

My ideal offense is one that executes proper fundamentals consistently and under pressure. I like an aggressive offense that attacks the ball at the plate and takes the extra bag on the base paths. This type of offense puts constant pressure on the defense. The offensive strategies presented in this chapter are written with this in mind.

BASERUNNING PRINCIPLES

Smart, aggressive, instinctive baserunning is a strategic and effective weapon that can always keep the defense guessing. The first step in teaching effective baserunning is to train your athletes to make their own decisions. Many young athletes have been taught to rely on their coach to tell them everything—when to run, when not to run, and when to take an extra base. As a result, they never develop that game sense. I try to put as much responsibility on the player as possible. The athletes need to learn how to see the game while they are running, so we design gamelike drills for them to do so. We encourage them in practice to be overly aggressive and find out what their limits are so that during the game, they will know what they can and cannot do.

By continually putting your players in competition during practice, you can simultaneously teach them technical skills and decision making, training them to develop the instinctive responses they will need during the season. Coaches should not be afraid to stop a drill to point out when a player is making an error. The goal is to quickly correct the mistake by making that player, as well as her teammates, aware of the correct course of action in a given situation. Whenever we hit, we also run the bases. We always work on reading the ball off the bat, going for two bases at a time instead of one, and ensuring that our players always know that their job is to score on every ball that is hit. We regularly stop practice to call attention to something that can be applied in a game.

Baserunning circuits, which emphasize reading and reacting, can be placed into offensive and defensive drills. In the circuits, the bases are loaded and the runners focus on a different skill at each base. At first base, they may be working on base starts for a steal. At second, they might be taking a large lead or anticipating a bunt. At third, they might practice what to do when a contact play is on or practice tagging up. In each drill, the runner is forced to read the ball, no matter where it goes. We give the athletes a situation and teach them to read it, both offensively and defensively.

Leads

A base runner's leadoff stance will vary from base to base. I like the rocker step, or the sprinter start, at first and second (see figure 9.1). In this position, one foot is on the base, and one foot is behind. The base runner rocks back as the pitcher is in the downswing of the pitch. The runner should time her start so that she is leaving the base when the pitcher's heel has left the rubber. This allows the runner to be gone by the time the ball leaves the pitcher's hand. This cue lets her think about the runner's foot and the pitcher's foot. On third base, we use a traditional baseball start with one foot on the base and the other in front of the base because I believe it opens up the entire field to the runner's view.

The length of a base runner's lead is a regular sized step and a dive away from the base. If the infield area is firm and in good shape, the runner will be able to get back to first with greater ease. If the dirt is loose or wet, the runner's lead will have to be shortened.

Turns

In the ideal turn, the runner takes a right angle toward second base. But we teach three different methods according to the athleticism of our players. We start off by teaching an abbreviated turn so the runner doesn't lose speed on her approach to the base. The runner begins angling out for her turn when she is about 20 feet (6 meters) from the base. The length of the angle away from the base should be no farther than 5 or 6 feet (1.5 to 1.8 meters). Once the runner has reached her ideal angle away from the base, she must begin angling toward the base gradually so she can maintain as much speed and balance as possible. The next method is a tight circle around all bases. A small semicircle is used from bag to bag. The third and quickest method, but most advanced, is the right angle to second. All methods require a significant dipping of the left shoulder and a strong lean in toward the infield. Either foot can land on the front inside corner of the base, but the next step needs to be with the foot pointed at second base (see figure 9.2).

Figure 9.1 The rocker-step leadoff.

Figure 9.2 Turning at the base.

Tagging Up

In tagging up, the runner puts one foot on the bag and turns to face the catch. This is a simple concept of the runner putting herself in the best possible position for seeing the ball and the defensive players. It is best if she times her start so she leaves the base when she sees the ball hit the leather or sees that it will hit the ground. The base runner should see the catch herself to avoid communication problems between the player and coach.

When the base runner feels she can safely make it to the next bag after the catch is made, this will warrant a tag. When the ball is hit foul and when the right fielder is running toward the line, the runner should always tag. All other situations require a knowledge of the game situation, speed of the runner, strength of the fielder's arm, where the other runners are, and the placement of the hit. We have our players automatically think run unless a coach holds them up. This avoids a miscommunication between the coach and player.

When the situation does not call for a tag, the runner needs to get a safe lead. The runner should get far enough away from the bag that she can make it to the next safely if the ball drops, yet close enough that she can get back safely. Going "halfway" is not a phrase we use, because very few hits require the runner to actually be halfway down the line. The base runner should get set and watch the catch and not assume whether it will be caught or dropped.

Staying in the Path

The runner should stay in the path of a thrown ball on the bases. Any time a runner can legally interfere with the throw from one fielder to another, she should do so. However, she does not want to reduce her time to the next base by changing her course on the base path. For example, with the runner at first base and a ball hit to the second baseman's left, the runner needs to stay on the outside of the base path. With a runner on second and a ground ball hit to the shortstop's right, the runner should run directly toward the third baseman's glove, forcing a difficult throw from the shortstop to the third baseman.

Another example occurs when the runner is at third and the third baseman fields the ball going close to the line. The runner should stay in the inside of the base path as she runs toward home plate, making a difficult throw for the third baseman to the catcher. If the third baseman catches the ball in foul territory, then the runner would stay on the outside of the base path. The runner can never obstruct the view of the player fielding the ball by throwing up her arms or hands or by going out of the baseline.

When the runner is advancing to second base on a ground ball to the right side of the infield, she must avoid being tagged by the second baseman. The runner should make every attempt to get by the second baseman, but if she cannot, she must make the infielder come toward her to make the tag in order to avoid a double play at first.

Sliding

The desire and the ability to slide are two important facets of aggressive baserunning. Sliding must be taught so that it will be utilized in the game and so that poor techniques will not result in injuries. There are three reasons to slide:

1. To reach a base going full speed without going by it.
2. To avoid a tag at a base.
3. To break up a double play attempt.

Once the runner decides to slide, she must slide without hesitation. I will describe five slides: the "figure four" slide, the pop-up slide off the figure four, the hook slide, the go by slide, and the headfirst slide.

Figure Four Slide

The "figure four" slide allows the runner to go directly into the base. Either leg can be bent with the lower part of the bent leg crossing under the knee of the straight leg. The bent leg remains parallel to the ground in the slide. The cleats of the shoe that is underneath should be facing out away from the ground. The straight leg is extended forward with the knee slightly bent, and the foot is 5 to 10 inches (12.7 to 25.4 centimeters) off the ground. The buttocks remain fully on the ground with the upper body extended back to where the shoulder blades almost touch the ground. The neck is arched forward with the chin toward the chest. The arms are bent and the hands are up in the air (see figure 9.3).

Pop-Up Slide

The pop-up slide is very similar to the "figure four" except that the runner finishes the slide by standing on the base and being ready to advance to the next base. The runner starts the slide about eight feet (2.4 meters) from the base with the upper body remaining in a sit-up position. The body weight is on the bent lower leg and extended back to the buttocks (see figure 9.4a). The extended leg is slightly bent and raised three to five inches (7.6 to 12.7 centimeters) off the ground, and the instep of the extended leg contacts the bag. As bag contact is made, the extended leg straightens and the upper body moves forward. This movement should be enough to carry the runner back to the upward position (see figure 9.4b).

Hook Slide

The hook slide is used to avoid a tag. In this slide, the ball has beaten the runner to the base but may be off target. When sliding to the right

side, the left leg bends with the foot out away from the body and the right leg straight out in front. The player's weight should be on the right part of the buttocks with the upper body in a flat position and the head up. The bag is "hooked" with the top of the left foot's toes or shoelaces.

Go By Slide

The go by slide is another slide we use to avoid a tag. When sliding to the right side of the bag, the runner puts herself in the "figure four" position, but slides by the bag and grabs it with her hand (see figure 9.5).

Headfirst Slide

The headfirst slide allows the base runner to get to the base quicker than any other slide. The disadvantage of the headfirst slide is that it takes longer for the runner to come to her feet and continue on to the next base. I do not recommend sliding headfirst into a tag play at home when the catcher is blocking the plate or when attempting to break up a double play. The slide is not a dive or a leap, but rather should appear as if the runner were gliding on the top of water. Her arms should be stretched forward with a slight bend in the elbows, and her head

Figure 9.3 Figure four slide.

Figure 9.4 Pop-up slide: (*a*) sliding with the weight on the bent lower leg, and (*b*) straightening the extended leg to stand up quickly.

Figure 9.5 Go by slide.

should be up to see the base. Her legs, chest, and arms are all in one parallel plane to the ground. Contact with the ground is made with the forearms, chest, and thighs, all at the same time (see figure 9.6).

Figure 9.6 Headfirst slide.

GOING TO FIRST

After contact, the batter needs to get to full speed by her second step. Many times, a batter base runner gets thrown out at first by a step, so it is important to work on quickness out of the box. On the way to first, she should sneak a peek over her left shoulder a few steps down the line to find out if she will be rounding first or running through it. Tilting the head slightly toward the infield without slowing down will enable her to see. After picking up the path of the ball, the runner must direct her attention to the bag itself.

I instruct the base runner to make the decision about whether to check the coach before going to second or not by the position of the hit. On anything hit up the middle and over to the right-field foul line, the runner makes her own decision. On anything hit to the third-base side of the shortstop, she must look to the first-base coach. This strategy allows the runner to react on her own without losing a step. When necessary, the coach should communicate visually and vocally to the runner regarding whether she should run through the base, take a turn, or go for second.

Every sure single must be considered a possible double. The runner must make the defense stop her in her effort to get to second. Only when the defense makes the play does the runner go back to first. If a coach is going to allow the players the opportunity to make many of their base-path decisions, she must spend time discussing baserunning philosophy. Some factors the runner must concern herself with are her speed, the condition of the base path, the inning and the score of the game, the number of outs, who the hitter at the plate is, and the distance of the throw.

The quickest way to the bag is running through it. The only time we allow a batter base runner to dive into first is to avoid a tag from an errant throw.

RUNNER AT FIRST

My first thought when a runner is at first base is to steal second if we can. It is my first choice if the runner is quick and the catcher is just above average, average, or below average. By teaching the runner to leave on the pitcher's heel release from the mound and to use a headfirst or avoidance slide, I feel we can be at least 90 percent successful. After a stolen base, our chance of scoring is very high.

If we want something less risky, we consider the sacrifice bunt. As the batter squares, we want her to keep all options open. The batter needs to be able to read the defense and act accordingly. We work on four types of bunts: sacrifice, push bunt, slap, and fake slap. If the middle infielders commit early and are playing back, a slap is very effective. If the corners are aggressive and charge, the hitter should look to execute a push bunt. If the corners and middle infielders are at a regular depth, the hitter should look to fake slap and bunt or hit away. We also consider a hit-and-run in this situation if we have a good runner and contact hitter.

Fake and Delayed Steals

The fake steal will allow the coach to see how the middle infielders react when the runner makes a break for second. If the coach sees one or both of them shifting their position toward second, then they will be susceptible to the hit-and-run play. The fake steal might open up a hole for the batter if one or both of the middle infielders shift toward second.

With the delayed steal, the runner conceals her intent to steal and then breaks for the bag when the catcher throws the ball back to the pitcher or to the first baseman. The delayed steal is not a called play. The player with good game sense, quick foot speed, and quick reaction is the one who is the delayed stealer. Those designated must study the pitcher and the catcher. A pitcher who looks lazy, does not pay attention to the runner on every pitch, or gets upset with her pitching or the umpiring is a likely candidate to steal on. The catcher who gets into a routine and throws the ball back to the pitcher with very little thought of the runner is also a candidate. I want my designated stealers to think about the delayed steal as soon as they reach any base, but they must be students of the play and study the pitcher and catcher throughout the game to learn their rhythm. An aggressive catcher is also a candidate to steal on because she will try to pick off the runner at first. My runner can set up that play by appearing to be too far off the base on the leadoff, and when the catcher tries to pick her off, BOOM, she's gone.

Runner at First and a Fly Ball

Too many times we see base runners not being aggressive on fly balls to the outfield. If the outfielder drops the ball, the runner is not in a good position to advance to second and possibly third. When the ball is in the air, the runner should get well off first base (a safe lead) and focus in on the outfielder. Once the ball is caught, the runner makes eye contact with the outfielder, forcing her to throw to first. A simple rule of thumb is this: The farther the runner is from the fly ball, the farther away from first base she should be. If the ball is hit very deep and there is the possibility of a catch, the first-base coach yells "Tag" and then makes the decision to send the runner on the catch. The runner must tag up on any foul ball hit in the air and if other base runners are tagging. If the runner is tagging up, she is doing so with the intent to advance to second or to make the defense think she is by faking and drawing a throw.

GOING TO SECOND

The runner leaving first should be completely aware of where the softball is. As is the case with the runner rounding first, I want the runner to make the decision whether to slide into second, round second, or go to third. The runner should pick up the third-base coach when the ball is hit behind her or in a location where she cannot easily see it in play, for example, on

- any ball hit between right center to the right-field line,
- any ground ball hit behind the runner heading for second, or
- a hit-and-run when the ball is hit behind the runner.

The runner must pick up the coach's signal about 15 to 20 feet (4.5 to 6.0 meters) from second. I find it helpful to do one of three things to signal the runner:

- Hold both arms high in the air to tell the runner to round the bag and find the ball.
- Wave both arms in a circular pattern to bring the runner to third.
- Point at second base to let the runner know to take a turn but to stay near the base.

RUNNER AT SECOND

As soon as the runner reaches second base, she must quickly review the outs, the inning, the depth of the outfielders, and the hitter at the plate. She should check the third-base coach for a sign and continue to check after each pitch. On every pitch, the runner should take an explosive jump off the base, selling a stolen base attempt.

Second base is the "keystone": When we get a player there, we must think about scoring. Can she steal third? I think this is the easiest base to steal for the following reasons: (1) The catcher's vision and throw are blocked by the batter in the batter's box, (2) the communication between the shortstop and third baseman regarding who is covering and when is very difficult, and (3) the batter can decoy the third baseman and shortstop to confuse their coverage of third. I want to know if my runner can beat the shortstop to the base, if we can decoy the third baseman and pull her up with a fake bunt, if we can fake slap and freeze the shortstop, or if the shortstop cheats toward third.

One option is to send the runner if she can beat the shortstop to the bag and the third baseman is covering the steal. The batter stays in her normal stance until the ball is nearly to the plate. She should then attempt a fake bunt at the last second by putting her bat over the ball as it crosses the strike zone. This will pull the third baseman in by a few steps, and the base runner can beat the shortstop to third.

Another option, if we are going to steal and the shortstop is cheating toward third, is to have the batter square to bunt to draw in the third baseman, and then pull back, swing, and

Timely base stealing creates offensive options and keeps pressure on the defense.

miss. This will freeze the shortstop, and the footrace to third is on. If the shortstop knows better than to freeze, she will try to cover third and may overcommit. This is the time to hit the ball on the ground to the shortstop area because she will not be there; she is breaking to cover third. This is our slap-and-steal or our hit-and-run play.

Runner at Second and a Fly Ball

When a runner on second base is reacting to a fly ball, she must quickly decide whether or not to tag. Most of the time the decision will have to be made by the runner, but there are some general rules I teach. They are as follows:

• Tag up on any foul fly ball. If there is any doubt about the ball being fair or foul, treat it as being fair. If the ball is caught in foul territory, the runner will make the decision about advancing to third. Tag on a ball that the right fielder must move toward the line or go back to catch.

• Tag up on all deep fly balls that are catchable in the outfield. Don't tag on second when there is any chance the ball will not be caught.

• On a fly ball where the outfielder has a play on the runner going to third, make every effort to get to third on the catch. However, with one out, a runner should be more conservative because we do not want to make the third out at third base. If the runner decides she cannot tag and advance, she should get as far away from second as she can and still be able to return to the base if the outfielder makes a throw to second. If there is a possibility that the outfielder will not make the catch, the runner should never be tagging at the base.

• With runners at both second and third or first, second, and third, if a routine fly ball is hit to the outfield, runners should tag if there is a chance the runner on third can score on the catch. On a throw to the plate, the runner on second will tag and advance to third. If the outfielder making the catch has no play on the runner from third, it is the decision of the runner on second whether to attempt to advance to third. If the runner on second sees that the runner on third is not going to tag on a catch, she must come down the base path toward third as far as possible (and still be able to return to second if the play is made there).

Runner at Second and a Ground Ball

This represents one of the biggest decisions the runner must make, and we spend a lot of time giving the runners the opportunity to tune their instincts. Here are some general rules to follow when there are less than two outs and the runner is not forced to advance.

- If the ball is hit behind the runner after her primary lead, she should be able to advance to third.
- If the ball is hit in front of the runner after her primary lead, she must stay balanced and advance only after the throw is made to first. This delayed advancement is made only if the runner knows she can beat the return throw to third.
- On a ground ball going toward the shortstop, if the runner can get over the ball and put it behind her, she can continue to third. The runner's speed, the jump she gets, and the defensive ability of the shortstop must be taken into consideration on a ball hit in the area of the shortstop.
- When the runner has to go to third because of a force play, I encourage her to run directly toward the third baseman's glove or the shortstop's glove if the shortstop is covering third.

GOING TO THIRD

The runner leaving second base is responsible for her actions until signaled to by the third-base coach. I like to move out of the coach's box toward the plate so that I can make good eye contact with the runner rounding third, give myself a little more time to decide what I want the runner to do, and, if necessary, give myself time to change my mind. If the ball is in front of the runner as she approaches third, she can use her own judgment on whether or not to advance to the plate.

With a ball hit behind the runner, the third-base coach will be making all of the decisions on advancing to the plate, rounding the base and holding, or stopping at third. The runner should always think about scoring as she heads toward third, and then she can make the adjustment if held up. I use the following signs for the runner approaching third:

- Waving one arm in a circular motion—I definitely want the runner to score.
- Holding both arms high in the air—I am telling the runner I do not want her to score. I want her to aggressively round the base and then to find the ball as she continues with a shuffle step toward the plate. The runner needs to locate the ball after contacting third and now is responsible for the next decision.
- Yelling "Back"—I use this command when the runner has aggressively rounded the base and is heading for the plate. I yell "Back" and that conveys to the runner to immediately stop and return to third. The runner must be prepared to dive back.
- Getting down on one knee and bringing both arms down toward the ground—I want the runner to slide; there is going to be a play made at third. The runner is responsible for finding the ball if it gets by the third baseman.

RUNNER AT THIRD

Once the runner reaches third, she must review the game situation, such as the outs, score, and inning. I review with the runner what I want her to do on various ground balls, fly balls, and passed balls. She must check for signs each time she returns to the base.

Her lead should take her a step and a dive away from the bag in foul territory. She should not turn her back away from the ball as she is heading back to the bag unless there is a throw to the bag. If there is a play, the quickest way back to the bag is in foul territory away from the reach of the third baseman.

I always tell the runner it is her call on a passed ball or wild pitch. By this, I mean if she has a good lead and is leaning toward the plate and sees the ball get by the catcher, she decides whether she can beat the play to the plate.

As soon as I can, I tell the runner to stay on the bag on a fly and to take off on a fly blooper. I also let her know when to go on a ground ball in the slot, score on an error, or go on an instinct ground ball. An instinct ground ball is a ground ball that the runner believes she can score on, taking into consideration her speed, the speed of the ground ball, and the depth of the defense. With a fly blooper I say, "Get off the bag, get off the bag," and we score when the ball hits the ground. When a ground ball is hit in the slot (the area between the corners and the pitcher), I want the runner to score. When there's an error, I coach my runners to read the play and try to score. In the final analysis, they use their instincts, and they would score on a ground ball that pulls the corners way out of position or on a play in which the corners go down on the ground to field the ball. They may also be able to score on the throw from the third baseman to the first baseman.

The on-deck hitter is the coach of the runner trying to score. As soon as the ball is hit, she must position herself near the backstop on the first-base side of the plate, in a direct line with the runner. She gives the same signs as the third-base coach: arms up and yelling "Up, up, up" or getting down on one knee and motioning with both hands to the ground and yelling "Hit it." Once she informs the runner to slide, the runner must stay with the signal even though the play might not develop. The on-deck hitter must be sure she is not too close to the plate where she might be struck by the ball.

Runner at Third and a Fly Ball

On every ball hit in the air, I want my runners to respond by heading back to the bag with the intention of tagging. Once she is at the bag and evaluates the hit, then one of the following scenarios will occur:

• **Foul ball**—I want my runners to tag up on any foul ball hit in the air. If there is any doubt about whether the ball might be fair, they should treat it as fair. I will make the decision on whether to score or not. It will depend on the game situation or the depth of the ball. I will say, "We're going to go" if I want them to score, or "Not going to go, draw the throw." When they're drawing the throw, I want them to go a safe distance down the line, keep balanced, and watch the throw coming to the plate. If the ball gets by the catcher, they must read the play and decide to score or return to third.

• **Routine or deep fly**—The same cues are given as in the previous situation. I want the runner watching the ball and leaving exactly as the ball touches the outfielder's glove. I will send the runner if the fielder is moving either back or laterally on a routine fly ball.

• **Short fly ball**—If the ball is too short to tag and score, then the runner will "get off the bag." The runner's instincts should tell her if the ball will not be caught.

Runner at Third and a Ground Ball

When there is the possibility of a ground ball with less than two outs, I will tell the runner my options prior to the ball being pitched. Depending on the situation, I tell them any one of the following:

• Not going to go on a ground ball but draw the throw.

• Going on a ground ball in the slot.

• Going on any ground ball anywhere (if there is another runner on second).

• Instinct ground ball (she will attempt to score if she sees an error, if she gets a great jump on the ground ball, or on a slow ground ball).

Runners at Second and Third

With runners at second and third, we are going to send the runner to the plate on any ground ball to the infield. The runner at second must get to third on the ground ball, and the batter base runner, after reaching first, must quickly locate the ball and possibly get to second. The runner on third will be going on any ground ball anywhere. By sending the runner to the plate, this forces the infielders to field the ball and make a good throw under a lot of pressure, and the catcher must execute a good tag. If the runner is out at the plate, the worst that can happen is that we will have runners at first and third.

Suicide and Safety Squeeze

There are two types of bunts that attempt to score the runner from third: the safety and the suicide squeeze. On the safety squeeze, the runner does not go until the ball is obviously going down toward the ground. This necessitates the runner waiting a split second to be sure the pitch was not missed or popped up. I do not like to use the safety squeeze because I feel that the delay reduces our chances of scoring the runner.

The suicide is a play to call only with the batters whose bat control you trust. In the suicide squeeze, the runner is going on the pitch as if she were stealing home. An alert base runner will be able to detect a called pitchout by the catcher and retreat back to third. I like to use the squeeze when the corners are playing a little deep and we have less than two outs, with a solid bunter at the plate and an above average base runner.

The Big Bunter

We recently had a big, new secret weapon. We were a little short on pinch hitters, but the one we did have was six feet three inches tall and intimidating. The best part was that we would bring her in the game with a runner at third. The opponents would see her and try to size her up. We would have her take the first pitch as if she were going to hit. Then on the next pitch we would put on the squeeze play. We were over 90 percent successful with this play. Her size said big, but her touch was soft and accurate and scored runs.

Suicide Hit-and-Run

The suicide hit-and-run is another play with the runner on third going on the pitch. The batter must execute a ground ball. This is a great play against a team that overplays a possible bunt or keeps their middle infielders slightly deep. The pressure is on the batter to put the ball on the ground.

SPECIAL PLAYS

We do not have trick plays in our offense. But there are times when the bats will go cold and we must create runs or manufacture an offense. The score, inning, batter, and base runner are all factors that will be considered when determining which of these plays to use.

Communication between coach and baserunner, whether verbal or through signals and body language, can create extra bases and, ultimately, more runs.

First and Third   This is a play that often trades an out for a run. I send the runner from first to second at a full-speed run with her eyes keying the ball, selling a straight steal but stopping about 20 feet (6 meters) from second. She will stop in a balanced position to see where the ball is. If the ball is at second, I want her to quickly retreat and get into a rundown. If the ball has been cut off or was not thrown to second, she will have the opportunity to continue to second. For the runner on third, I call one of three plays: not going to go, but draw the throw; going on the throw "down" toward second; or going on the throw "through" to second.

On the first play, the runner on third gets a big jump, forcing the catcher to pay attention to her and letting the runner steal second. On the second play, the runner on third is going to the plate on the catcher's throw down toward second. The only question the runner on third has to ask is, "Is the ball going past the pitcher?" If the ball goes back to the pitcher, the runner on third must scramble back to avoid getting picked off at third. This should give the runner on first the opportunity to get to second easily. The third play takes the most work for the runner at third. She will attempt to score on the catcher's throw *to* second. She is looking for the ball to go "through" the pitcher and "through" the cutoff.

This has been a high-percentage play for us. The runner going to second must sell the steal and be able to stop in a balanced position. The runner on third must be familiar with the terminology and understand exactly what is expected on each of the options.

Hit-and-Run   The hit-and-run is used to try to move the runner with a chance of fooling the defense into leaving their positions too soon resulting in the runner and the batter being safe. The runner is stealing on the pitch while sneaking a peek on the way down. The hitter is to hit the ball no matter where it is pitched, and hit the ball on the ground, preferably at the position whose job it is to cover the base on the steal.

Push Bunt   On this play, the batter will push a sacrifice bunt beyond the charging corners. The right-handed batter needs to direct an inside pitch toward the shortstop and an outside pitch toward the second baseman. The left-handed batter needs to direct an inside pitch toward the second baseman and an outside pitch toward the shortstop. This is a play to advance the runner and to get the batter base runner safe at first. I find this play to be very effective with a runner on second as well as the one on first.

Sacrifice Bunt   On the sacrifice bunt, the offensive team is giving up the batter in order to advance a runner or runners. The ball must not be fielded by the catcher, and it should be bunted toward the baselines on the ground. The batter must make sure the pitch is a strike when the bunt is on. When the runner is advancing to third, I prefer to have the bunt directed toward the third baseman. If the batter makes the third baseman field the ball, the batter has done her job, as long as it is a soft bunt. A bunt down the first-base line will work just as well if the first baseman is not left-handed, as long as it is well placed and away from the catcher.

Slap and Steal   The slap and steal is very tough on the middle infielders, because it forces them to cover two bases at the same time. The shortstop must both cover second on a steal and field the ground ball. The second baseman must cover first on a possible bunt or cover second on a ground ball double play from the left side of the infield. On the slap and steal, the runner goes on the pitch, and the batter shows a bunt but then slaps the ball on the ground toward the shortstop position. This is a play that can advance the runner and possibly have the batter safe at first.

Bunt and Steal   The bunt and steal is a play where the team can advance the runner two bases on a bunted ball. In this play, the batter is instructed to drop a bunt toward the third baseman, forcing her to field it. If the runner starts at first base, she will go to second on the bunt and steal third on the infielder's throw to first. This is an instinctive play where the runner rounds second and picks up the action at third. If the third baseman has fielded the bunt, the runner will have a good chance to get to third before the pitcher, catcher, or left fielder can cover the bag.

OFFENSIVE DECISIONS

I did some unusual research at a recent women's College World Series. I studied nine offensive situations and kept track of the decisions that coaches made as well as the outcomes of those offensive plays. The results for each situation were as follows:

• **Runner on first base and no outs**—This situation occurred 50 times. The bunt was successful (meaning it moved the runner) 63 percent of the time, and the runner eventually scored 15 percent of the time. The slap moved the runner 17 percent of the time, but these runners never scored. The swing successfully moved the runner 38 percent of the time, and the runner scored 8 percent of the time. The steal was tried 4 times and succeeded twice; these runners did not score.

• **Runner on first base and one out**—This situation occurred 40 times. The bunt was tried 4 times and moved the runner every time. It was successful 100 percent of the time. The runner eventually scored 25 percent of the time. The slap was successful 33 percent of the time, and the runner scored 33 percent of the time. The coach selected the swing 29 of 40 times. It moved the runner 28 percent of the time, and these runners eventually scored 14 percent of the time. The steal again came in at 50 percent success, but again these runners did not score.

- **Runner on first base and two outs**—This situation occurred 55 times. The bunt and slap were not chosen. The swing was used 46 times, and it successfully moved the runner 33 percent of the time; the runner eventually scored 9 percent of the time. The steal was successful 67 percent of the time, but again these runners did not score.

- **Runner on second base and no outs**—This situation occurred 14 times. The bunt was used 3 times, and 3 times the runner got to third base; however, they never scored. The slap was tried twice, and the runner was not advanced. The swing was tried 6 times, and the runner got to third base only once (that runner eventually scored). The steal was tried 3 times, but the runners never made it to third or the plate.

- **Runner on second base and one out**—This situation occurred 44 times. Neither the bunt nor the steal was tried. The slap was tried twice and succeeded once (that runner did not score). The swing was tried 42 times and succeeded 40 percent of the time. These runners eventually scored 6 times or 14 percent of the time.

- **Runner on second base and two outs**—This situation occurred 56 times. No bunts were tried. Two slaps were tried—neither moved the runner. The swing moved the runner 33 percent of the time, and 17 percent of the runners that started on second eventually scored. The steal was tried twice, and it succeeded once (that runner scored).

- **Runner on third base and no outs**—This situation never occurred in the 12 games, looking at both the home and the visiting teams.

- **Runner on third base and one out**—This situation occurred 18 times. Neither the bunt nor the slap was employed. The swing was successful 47 percent of the time. When the swing was used, the runner scored 35 percent of the time. (Note that if the play selected was a swing and the batter walked, I called it a success.) A squeeze was used once, and that runner did not score.

- **Runner on third base and two outs**—This situation occurred 34 times, and the swing was used every time. The swing moved the runner 38 percent of the time, and they scored 24 percent of the time.

There are many offensive decisions the coach has to make. What information does the coach use to make those decisions? Knowing your personnel and trusting your instincts will allow you to draw your own conclusions. You can do your own research by watching games and charting the outcomes of the coaching decisions.

SIGNS AND SIGNALS

I am the coach in the third-base coaching box, and I initiate all offensive signals. It is the hitter's responsibility to pick up the third-base coach after every pitch for a possible sign. All base runners pick up the signals from the third-base coach right after the pitcher has received the ball back from the catcher. The hitter usually looks at me before the base runner does, which gives me a chance to establish eye contact with the hitter and then with the runner before flashing signs. This way I can give one quick set of signs to both players.

If a player needs to have the signs repeated, she gives the repeat sign by circling her hands in front of her body. When calling for the suicide squeeze bunt, I have the batter give a sign back and the runner acknowledge the sign to verify that all parties know the squeeze is on. Our signals are learned and practiced as often as possible. We have signals for the following:

- Suicide squeeze
- Slap or push bunt
- Sacrifice bunt or base hit bunt
- Bunt and steal
- Steal
- Slap and steal
- Repeat play
- Take off or clear
- Take
- Fake bunt and slap
- Swing and miss
- Hit-and-run

I give an indicator first and then the signal. For example, touching my head is the indicator, and the sign that follows is the one to execute. If the play is still on for the next pitch, I will give the repeat play sign. We also have a "take off" signal to tell all parties the play is off. You can also create a "close" signal to indicate the play is on; without the "close," nothing is on. You can be creative with your signals, but you should keep them simple. Clear signals are essential for good communication between players and coaches.

BASERUNNING DRILLS

The following baserunning drills will help the athlete improve mechanics and increase running speed. When these skills and actions are practiced, they will help in increasing explosive power off the base while increasing the aggressiveness of the base runner.

All Bases

Purpose: To improve the mechanics of baserunning and player conditioning.

Procedure: Athletes are lined up at home plate. A coach is in the third-base coaching box, and a coach is in the first-base coaching box. The runner sprints to first base and jogs to home plate. She repeats this one time. The runner sprints to second and continues to round the bases by jogging to home plate. She repeats this two times. The runner sprints to third and jogs to home plate, repeating three times. Then the runner sprints from home to home.

Coach Communication

Purpose: To familiarize the player with the coach's verbal cues and to improve the player's reaction to those cues.

Procedure: The team is divided into two groups. One of the groups is in a line at home plate, and the other is in a line at second base. One coach is at first, and one coach is at third. On a signal given by one of the coaches, the first person in each line runs to the base ahead of her. The runner looks to pick up the coach's physical and verbal cues on whether to stay at that base, advance, or any other baserunning situations. When both runners have finished their route, the next two runners will begin when given the signal. This sequence continues for as long as desired.

Independent Runner

Purpose: To experience gamelike baserunning situations at three different bases.

Procedure: All defensive positions are filled. There are base runners at home, first, and third. A coach is at home plate with a ball, and the pitcher is on the mound with a ball. The pitcher pitches the ball to the catcher, the runners get their jumps, and when the ball hits the strike zone, the coach hits a ball into the field of play (fungo hit). The runners react accordingly. The defense can be instructed to make a play on any one of the runners. Each runner plays as if she is the only runner on the field.

Turns and Slides

Purpose: To work on turns at first base and various slides into second.

Procedure: Place half your runners at first and half your runners at the plate. The runners at first are lined up single file one step beyond first. Once the runner from home hits first base for the turn, the runner at first takes off toward second. This forces the runner going to first to make a sharp turn to avoid getting in the way of the other runner. The runner from first sprints to second as if she is stealing, and once near the base, she works on a chosen slide. The batter base runner stops a third of the way to second base and dives back into first.

Variation: Put runners at all bags and work on different slides and turns going to every bag.

CHAPTER 10   DEFENSIVE FUNDAMENTALS

Games are won because the defense prevents runs from scoring. The game can be won with one run if your team's defense has held or prevented the opponent from scoring. Where the offense strives to create runs, the defense tries to thwart that creativity by making great plays of its own. The offense is full of schemes. That is why the defense must be polished and tight; it must be the one thing a team does correctly 95 percent of the time. In this chapter, we will look at what it takes to play each position on the field. Because of the importance of pitching, chapter 13 is committed to the teaching of that position.

It takes a combination of hitting, pitching, and defense to win a ball game. In hitting, players are successful 3 or 4 times out of 10 at best, so they will be failing 60 to 70 percent of the time. However, in defense, the team is striving for a success ratio of over 95 percent. Thus, defense must be a team's constant strength. Defense and pitching are the two elements the team can control. Softball and baseball are the only sports where a team is on defense when they have the ball. It is true that offense wins games, but defense wins championships!

THROWING MECHANICS

Throwing is an area that must not be undercoached, and it is vital for the health and safety of the athlete and the success of the team. Even at the Division I level, coaches teach throwing skills all year long and throughout their players' careers. We make sure our players know how to grip the ball to their advantage and move their bodies into the most efficient position to throw, and we teach a proper release to get maximum speed and accuracy.

- **Grip**—The player should grip the seams of the ball with three fingers across the seams and the thumb opposite the middle finger (see figure 10.1). The ball should be raised off the palm, and there should be an equal distance between each finger.

- **Star position**—The ball is brought back behind the head with the ball pointing down; the elbow is parallel to the ground with the upper and lower arm at a right angle. The wrist is limp. An infielder will point her elbow at the target whereas the outfielder will point her glove. The player positions her body sideways and is ready to drive off the back leg. Rotation begins with the hips and back leg while the elbow leads the ball forward (see figure 10.2).

- **Release**—The upper arm should remain parallel to the ground while the wrist snaps back, placing the ball facing up just above the head (see figure 10.3). The thrower then pulls the arm through and releases with the ball rolling off the fingertips for a backspin. I teach a very complete follow-through with the throwing arm crossing the body and making contact with the opposite thigh, as shown in figure 10.4.

Figure 10.1   Gripping the ball for the throw.

Figure 10.2   The star position.

Figure 10.3   The release.

Figure 10.4   Completing the throw with a full follow-through.

During our team's warm-ups, similar position players throw with each other—that is, pitchers with pitchers, corners together, middle infielders together, and outfielders together. They are paired together because they make similar throws, and it is easier for the coaches to evaluate them. In the off-season, we spend a lot of time working on throwing mechanics and arm strengthening. We begin every practice with a 12-minute throwing program broken into four segments. For the first 3 minutes, the players are about 45 feet (13.7 meters) apart and work on a full range of motion. For the next 3 minutes, the players are about 60 feet (18.3 meters) apart and work toward a strong throw to a target. For the next 3 minutes, the players drop back to 75 feet (22.8 meters) and continue the full range of motion with a smooth delivery and complete follow-through. The last 3 minutes may take the players to 90 feet (27.4 meters) apart or to 60 feet again, depending on the time in the season. (Early in the season, we will have them return to 60 feet.) During these 12 minutes, I work with each athlete, correcting form and technique. At the end of the throwing progression, the players finish with three throwing drills:

- **Right Leg Drive**—Player A kneels on her glove leg with the glove shoulder pointing at the target. Player B, who has a ball, stands and drives off her back leg with one step (no shuffle) and throws to player A. When player A receives the ball, she repeats the same technique by driving off her back leg and throwing to player B. Ideally, both players should be accurate with their throws so each can receive the ball on her knee and not have to move to catch the ball. It will eventually become a quicker throwing drill while also allowing players to work on a quick release of the ball.

- **Left Leg Drive**—The athlete kneels on her throwing leg. If she is a right-hander, she holds the ball in her glove on the ground next to her left foot. If she is a left-hander, she holds it next to her right foot. She quickly brings the ball to her ear, drives up with her left leg, lands on a loaded right leg turned sideways, steps, and throws. This is a "crow hop" or power hop simulation. This is beneficial for all players, but specifically for outfielders.

- **Hops**—The athletes hop three times on their throwing leg and drive hard off of that leg

to work on generating force through their back leg. They should do this drill on a cue from the coach so that no one is rushed through the drill.

During the season, our team will not continue with drills that involve breakdowns on the knees, but we will still spend a significant amount of time on throwing warm-ups.

POSITIONAL FUNDAMENTALS

When determining who plays and who does not play, you must understand what skills are required at each position in order to make the puzzle of your team fit together. What follows is a breakdown of the skills and performance each position requires.

Catchers

The coach must not overlook the catching position. The catcher plays one of the most important positions on the field and needs just as much work as all of the other specialty positions. Specific drills should be incorporated every day to help the catcher develop a strong arm, quick release, quick feet, and mental and physical toughness that breeds confidence with a take-charge attitude. The role of catcher requires many parts: physical skills, team leadership qualities, and the ability to be an emotional companion to the pitcher. All defensive plays initiate from the catcher.

The catcher has more jobs on the field than any other player. These jobs include giving signals, receiving the ball, blocking bad pitches, throwing to bases, picking off runners, calling plays, handling force and tag plays at the plate, catching pop-ups, and fielding bunts. The following list describes these skills in more detail:

- **Basic stance**—In the basic catching stance, the feet should be slightly farther than shoulder-width apart with the toes pointing slightly out. The body weight should be balanced. The body should form an L with the shoulders over the top of the knees and not hunched over. The right foot (for a right-handed catcher) should be one to two inches (2.5 to 5.0 centimeters) behind the left foot, and the body weight should be distributed over the inside of the feet. With a runner on base, the right foot should be three to four inches (7.6 to 10.0 centimeters) behind the left foot, and more weight should be shifted to the balls of the feet to allow for a quicker throw. The glove is semi-extended in front of the body, with the bare hand making a loose fist behind the right knee when no one is on base, and behind the glove in an extremely relaxed position when there is a runner on base (see figure 10.5).

Figure 10.5 Catcher ready to receive the pitch.

• **Giving signals**—When giving signals, the catcher assumes a narrowed stance with her trunk up and her head facing the pitcher. The right-handed catcher can rest her left forearm on her left thigh with the wrist held up at the top of the knee. Her glove rests gently along the knee with the pocket facing the other knee in order to hide the signals from the opposing coach at third base. The throwing arm rests gently on the hip, and the hand drops tight and close to the body to give signals.

• **Receiving the pitch**—The catcher must catch the ball firmly with the arms and hands away from the body and allow the ball to come to her with a relaxed, semi-extended glove. Upon contact with the glove, framing the pitch is a technique used to keep a borderline pitch within the strike zone. On an inside pitch, the right-handed catcher catches the left side of the ball and drops the glove (with the wrist only) in toward the zone. To frame a high strike, the receiver catches the top of the ball and drops her glove toward the zone. For an outside pitch, the receiver catches the right side of the ball and quickly turns her wrist down and in toward the zone in a counterclockwise motion. On a low pitch, the catcher simply picks the ball up and in toward her body. When the ball is just out of the strike zone, the catcher needs to receive the pitch centered in front of her body by using a simple shifting technique. The catcher moves her hips, legs, and arms but not her feet.

• **Blocking**—It is imperative for a catcher to keep the ball in front of her when it is thrown in the dirt. For a ball thrown in front, the glove immediately needs to drop to the ground with her hand behind it, her chin should tuck, and her trunk should angle over the ball (see figure 10.6).

Figure 10.6 Keeping the ball in front of the body using the blocking position.

For a ball to the catcher's left, the glove moves to the ball; the hips, knees, and feet shift around the ball; the chin tucks; the trunk angles over the top of the ball; and the body faces the inside of the plate. For a pitch thrown in the dirt to the right, the catcher shifts her entire body around the outside of the ball, facing the outside of the plate.

- **Communication**—The catcher is in a great position on the field for calling the base that throws need to go to. She can see the whole field in front of her. Whether the ball is coming from the outfield or the infield, she must be loud and confident with her direction, yelling "One, one" and so forth. Her communication is also vital on cutoff and relay plays. For example, if she wants the throw to the plate to be cut off, she would yell, "Cut two" or "Cut three."

- **Force plays at the plate**—In a force play with a chance of a double play at first, the catcher needs to position herself about one or two feet (30.4 to 60.9 centimeters) behind the plate, facing the fielder, and provide a clear target. Once the ball is thrown, the catcher moves forward and steps across the plate with her left foot and drags the right foot across the plate. As the foot drags, she should jump pivot to face first base and make a throw. On a force play with no chance of a double play, she would position herself as a first baseman would, with her body facing directly toward the fielder and with the ball of her right foot located at the middle front corner of the plate. She should provide a clear target by holding both arms in the air and calling for the ball. If there are runners at other bases, she should fake the throw to first base, possibly allowing her a chance to pick off the runner.

- **Tag plays at the plate**—Before the ball gets to the plate, the catcher needs to position herself with her left heel just off the plate toward third base and her toes pointing toward third base to avoid injury to the knee. She must have a wide and stable base to prevent the runner from "taking her out." Once the catcher has the ball, she reaches straight down into the tag with both hands while dropping her right knee to block the plate. If the runner slides around the tag, the catcher's body should continue with the glove on the ground, and at that point the left knee could drop as well. She must not reach out to

make the tag, because that will leave too much room to sneak around the tag and will also put the catcher in a less balanced position to brace for a tag.

- **Catching pop-ups**—Generally, with a right-handed batter, a popped-up inside pitch will move to the catcher's left, and an outside pitch will move to the catcher's right. She should remove her mask and hold it in her right hand while quickly scanning the sky. As soon as the catcher finds the ball, she should toss the mask in the opposite direction, away from the ball (see figure 10.7a). I want the catcher to be on the balls of her feet and to catch every pop-up with two hands at eye level, with the fingers pointing up (see figure 10.7b). She should catch with her back to the infield whenever possible due to the spin of the ball rotating back toward the infield.

- **Fielding bunts**—As figure 10.8, a through c, shows, the catcher should spring out quickly and throw the mask in the opposite direction from where the ball is. She should field the ball with her chest right over the ball, the ball centered between her feet, and her body already in the direction she is going to throw. She should pick it up using a scooping motion with both glove and throwing hand down to the ball. The catcher should bend her knees to get to the ball and step in the direction of the throw. If she is lined up down the first-base line, she needs to shuffle and clear toward the infield. If the ball is down the third-base line, she needs to approach the ball with her back to the shortstop area, pivot, and throw.

- **Picking off runners**—When a pickoff is called or a runner is stealing, the catcher needs to allow the ball to take her into the throwing position instead of framing the pitch. When the ball contacts the glove, the catcher turns her body sideways to either step and throw or shuffle step toward her target. Her elbow needs to point and drive at the base. She starts low and drives to a more extended position to get maximum speed on the throw. Although I call pickoffs from the dugout, I will also give my catcher the green light to call the pickoffs at first, second, and third.

- **Pitchouts**—If you anticipate the runner stealing and call a pickoff, the catcher should call for the pitch at chest height about a foot

Figure 10.7 When catching a pop-up, the catcher first (*a*) finds the ball and throws her mask in the opposite direction, then (*b*) makes the catch with both hands.

(continued)

Figure 10.8 Catcher fielding the bunt: (*a*) scooping up the bunt, (*b*) beginning the throw, and (*c*) following through after the throw.

Figure 10.8 *(continued)*

(30.4 centimeters) off the plate and assume a target toward the outside corner of the plate. If the batter is right-handed, the catcher stays in a low position with bent knees, steps out with her right foot, catches, pivots, and throws. If the batter is left-handed, the catcher steps out to the left, swings the right foot behind, and steps in the direction of the throw.

• **Intentional walks**—To execute an intentional walk, the catcher stands up and, with confidence, reaches straight out with the right hand. When the pitcher releases the ball, the catcher must quickly bend her knees and move the left foot to the right foot spot, and then move the right foot directly out to receive the ball.

• **Wild pitches**—If the ball ends up to the first-base side of the plate, the catcher should approach the ball from the right, drop to her right knee, stay over the ball, pick up the ball, and throw from the ground. There is not enough time to lift up her body and throw over the top. If the ball gets by the catcher on the third-base side, she should approach the ball from the left, drop to her right knee, take the ball directly from the ground to her belly, and flip leading with her elbow. The less the ball spins the better, and it is important not to try to throw it hard.

Infielders

The four infielders must be united and work as a unit throughout the game. They are the only ones who throw the ball around after an out and go into the pitcher's circle to talk with the pitcher during the game. They communicate with each other about outs, speed of the runners on base, the situation, and the plays. A team is as strong as the infield unit, and there is no place for a weak player.

First Baseman

If a team has a solid first baseman, everyone else on the infield will have an easier job. A first baseman needs to give off a sense of confidence. A first baseman does for her infield what a catcher does for her pitcher. Her job is to catch everything and to make everyone's throws look good. Size is not a factor, but a first baseman needs agility, quick feet, and to have no fear.

The first baseman's stance should be a low fielding position, facing the batter, with the glove near the knee. Her weight is on the balls of her feet with her knees flexed, and her arms are extended out in front of her body. On the hit, she would drop step toward the bag while opening up to her right. She would then turn to face the throw and present the biggest target possible by having both shoulders squared toward the thrower. Her foot on the bag is opposite her glove hand, and she touches the corner of the base with her full instep. She must always anticipate a bad throw. She should stay in a relaxed and athletic position—knees bent, feet shoulder-width apart—and should not stretch until after the ball is thrown and she can judge its path.

On balls hit to her right, her range involves one step and a dive. Anything beyond that range is fielded by the second baseman. She should make an attempt at anything that is hit hard. She can call for any ground ball, but communication with the second baseman and pitcher is important so that the bag is always covered.

Second Baseman

The player assigned to play second should be a smart, consistent infielder with quick feet, good hands, and a quick release. She must have an accurate throwing arm with good range, and a keen understanding of bunt coverage. Leadership skills are vital because she has more duties than any other position on the infield.

The second baseman will possess the same physical qualities as the shortstop, with the only difference being in the strength of her arm. The stronger arm would be at shortstop because of the long throw across the infield. The second baseman covers both first and second during defensive plays.

The second baseman does not cover the bag on most stolen bases. There are a few situations where the second baseman may be the logical choice to cover on the steal, but because of possible bunt situations with a runner on first, coaches choose to have the shortstop cover the steal. If the second baseman does not cover, she positions herself to back up the throw down to second. She is also utilized to pick off runners at first and second.

Here are four different footwork patterns a second baseman may use to turn the double play at second.

1. **Right tap**—The player taps on the bag with the right foot, and then steps the left foot in the running lane (see figure 10.9). This should be used only with a slow runner at first base or a hard shot to a fielder (when the runner is not up on the second baseman).

Figure 10.9 The second baseman turning the double play: The second baseman (*a*) steps on the base with her right foot as she catches the ball, then (*b*) brings her left foot in line with first base as she throws.

2. **Left tap**—The player taps on the bag with the left foot, and then pushes back to a loaded right side, staying to the front side of the bag.

3. **Across bag**—The player's left foot strikes the bag, and the right foot plants on the ground across the bag and loaded. The loaded right leg allows the momentum of the throw to take the second baseman toward first.

4. **Over the bag**—The second baseman gets to second with a little time to spare. She will step over the bag with her right foot—heel about two inches (5 centimeters) away from the base—landing as the ball touches her glove. As she transfers the ball to the throwing hand, she drags her left foot over the base, and then plants it in a direct line toward first base.

Third Baseman

The third baseman has to be aggressive and fearless because of the nature of the hits that come her way. She must handle everything from sharply hit line drives and short hops to slow rolling bunts. The third baseman must play far enough in to retrieve bunts but a safe distance away to field hard hits. The distance she plays from the foul line is fixed to some extent by her reaction time and her ability to make a backhand catch. The third baseman must have good instincts and the ability to read the batter's intent. She must be able to respond quickly and throw with speed and accuracy from a wide variety of set and off-balance positions.

Protecting against stolen bases is a shared responsibility with the shortstop. I have the third baseman cover third on batter swings. If the batter fakes a slap bunt, the third baseman must get back.

Shortstop

The shortstop position should be assigned to your best right-handed athlete. She should have the strongest arm in the infield as well as possess great range and quick reactions. She must be a take-charge player with solid leadership skills. She must be the most consistent glove player. I am willing to sacrifice some offense at this spot if I have a player who can play this position well.

I have the shortstop cover second base on most stolen base attempts and on all first and third double steals. The shortstop will cover third on a stolen base if the batter shows bunt.

The shortstop will cover second on all force plays that are thrown from the right side of the infield, from the catcher, and from the pitcher. If a pitcher is attempting to field a batted ball to her right side, the shortstop will be in the backup position and will not cover second.

When a shortstop covers second base on a double play, her hands should be up, open, and at waist level, presenting a large target to the person with the ball. She should be verbal and approach the bag in an athletic position, expecting a bad throw. This mind-set will always make her ready in case a bad throw occurs.

The shortstop's pivot at second base for a double play will include one of three patterns, depending on the situation and the location of the other infielder making the play.

1. **Step left**—If the throw is coming from the inside of the base path (on the front side of the bag), the shortstop will step left, drag her right foot across the front side, load, and throw.

2. **Outside**—If the throw is coming from the outside of the base path (for example, a throw from the second baseman playing deep), the shortstop would receive the throw on the outside of the base. In this play, she would plant her right foot as she is making the catch, drag through the bag to the front of her left foot, load to the right leg, plant, and throw.

3. **Left tap**—When it is necessary to get the lead runner and then try to turn the double play, the shortstop can use the left tap done on the inside of the bag. She would tap with the left foot on the bag and load, push left off the bag, turn the right instep open to first base, load, and throw.

Basic Infield Plays

Some defensive plays are the same for all infielders. These include the ready position, ground balls, emergency plays, fake throws, going back on fly balls, intentional walks, and tag plays at the bases.

Ready Position

We teach an explosive ready position with the weight on the balls of the feet and the back straight. The corners have their gloves about knee high, while the middle infielders have their gloves slightly higher. The feet are squared and

Figure 10.10 Infielder in ready position.

Figure 10.11 Infielder fielding a grounder with arms in the "shovel out" position.

more than shoulder-width apart with the toes pointing toward the plate. (See figure 10.10.)

Fielding a Ground Ball

Infielders should get in front on every ground ball and only use backhands and forehands as emergency plays. When fielding a ground ball, their arms should be in an L position, and their head should stay at the same level as they move to field the ball. Both arms should look identical with a slight flex at the elbows. I want my players to field the ball away from their body, with the glove and ball underneath their forehead and their feet a little farther than shoulder-width apart; their left foot should be a few inches in front of their right, with their knees pointing out. Their hands scoop or shovel the ball out in front with the throwing hand on top of the ball (see figure 10.11). With a cradling motion, the ball is brought to the throwing position with the back of the glove up.

Emergency Plays: Forehand and Backhand

Emergency plays are ones that necessitate the fielder using only one hand to field the ball as she is moving to her left or right. I teach our players how to use these plays, but the players are told not to use them unless absolutely necessary.

• **Forehand**—The emergency forehand is used to field a ground ball to the fielder's glove side (see figure 10.12). The mark of a good infielder is being able to range to her glove side, make the pickup, and regain balance to make an on-target throw.

To field the ball on her forehand side, the right-handed infielder crosses over with her right foot in the direction of the ball, creating an angle to where she thinks she will meet the ball. The glove should be carried in a running position to get the most drive from her arms. She must stay low and run on the balls of her feet. Keeping the head down and staying in low running form will help the infielder to make a play without the ball going under the glove. After fielding the ball, she should bring the ball and glove to the release point quickly as she is turning her body in the direction of the throw. It is important that she step toward her target.

• **Backhand**—The backhand is used to field a ground ball to the throwing hand side (see figure 10.13, a-d). This play can prove very difficult unless proper mechanics are used. For the backhand, the fielder runs in the direction of the ball while pumping both arms. The infielder must become adept at cutting the ball off at the sharpest angle so that she can shorten the distance of her throw to the target. The infielder needs to cross over with her left foot while

Figure 10.12 The emergency forehand. When fielding on the forehand side, the infielder will stay low and drive for the ball, and then field the ball with the glove leg in front and with her weight on the ball of her foot.

carrying the glove low. Once she sees that her best play on the grounder will be a backhand play, she must get her body under control. She needs to bend at both the knees and the waist as she extends her glove so that the upper part of her body goes to full extension. She must be sure to keep her head steady and her eyes on the ball. The ball should be fielded about three to six inches (7.6 to 15.2 centimeters) in front of whatever foot is forward with the elbow of the glove arm slightly bent. The glove must be opened, fully exposing the entire pocket of the glove to the ball. As soon as the ball is in the glove, the infielder brings the glove up quickly

(continued)

Figure 10.13 The emergency backhand. When fielding on the backhand side, the infielder will (*a*) cross step and (*b*) stay bent at the waist as she moves to the ball with the glove opened fully.

Figure 10.13   *(continued)*   When the ball is in the glove, the fielder (*c*) takes another short step and (*d*) plants the foot for the throw.

to her throwing-side shoulder, where her bare hand grips the ball for the throw.

When fielding the ball with the left foot forward, the infielder must take another step with the right foot. As she catches the ball, she must take a short extra step with the right foot in the direction that her momentum is taking her, load, and throw.

• **Dives**—Infielders may also occasionally have to dive to stop a hard hit grounder or line

drive. The infielder will leave her feet for a ball in an emergency situation, such as when she cannot backhand or forehand the hit ball. A dive by the corner infielders is reactionary, while a dive by the middle infielders permits them more time to set an angle. For all infielders, diving to their right requires them to pivot and push off their right foot, driving their bodies horizontally with full extension of their gloves (see figure 10.14). The nonglove hand helps cushion

Figure 10.14   To make the diving catch, the third baseman drives off the foot on the side of the ball and stays low and horizontal as she reaches for the ball.

the landing. When diving to the left, the pivot and push-off occur with the left foot. In either direction, the objective is to stay low and parallel to the ground with full glove extension.

Going Back on Fly Balls

An infielder should not drift back on the fly ball; rather, she should go back full speed on any fly ball that she has to turn on so that she can get herself under control before the ball reaches the glove. As the ball hits the bat, the infielder executes a drop step. The angle of the step depends on the direction the ball has been hit. She must pump her arms and run on her toes in order to increase her quickness.

Intentional Walks

When the batter is being intentionally walked, the infielders should assume their regular positions in the infield in case the pitcher throws a pitch near the strike zone. The first baseman will move in 30 feet (9.1 meters) from the plate in case the pitched ball gets away from the catcher. The first baseman would then cover the plate. In this situation, the pitcher does not cover the plate on the passed ball because the first baseman is positioned closer to the plate and is able to get there faster.

Tag Plays at the Bases

On tag plays at bases, the infielder must concentrate on getting to the base as soon as pos-sible. As she nears the base, she must get her body under control by shortening her steps and lowering her center of gravity. Once the infielder is under control and set at the base, she must focus all of her attention on catching the ball and making the tag. As the ball is caught, both knees quickly flex. On close plays I recommend a sweep tag. This means that the infielder catches the ball and moves the glove and ball down hard to the tag area, and then pulls the glove away to sell the out. On a hook slide or a headfirst slide, the infielder must stay with the runner and keep the tag on her because there is always the chance she will overslide the base.

The footwork for the shortstop or second baseman covering second base for a steal consists of an explosive crossover step and a full-out sprint in the direction of second base. As the infielder nears the base, she must start getting her body under control by shortening her steps and lowering her center of gravity. I teach the shortstop to plant her left foot next to the front corner of the bag pointing toward first base. If the throw is on target, she should not reach out and get it; she should allow it to come to her. A thrown ball is always faster than the glove. If she sees it might take a short hop, she must "pick" the short hop. Her arm becomes like a pendulum and scoops the ball from the hop, then quickly (staying in the pendulum) comes back and makes a hard sweep tag.

The footwork for the third baseman covering third for a steal involves a drop step back with

Players should never give up on applying a tag to a runner to who might slide past the bag.

her left foot and a crossover step with her right foot as the catcher sets up to throw. She would then execute the same footwork as the middle infielders use in covering second base.

On tag plays involving a throw coming from an outfielder to second base, the footwork would be as follows: On a ball thrown from right-center field to the right-field line, the middle infielder should control the home-plate side of the base with her right foot, and her left foot should be in a direct line with the throw on the outfield side of the base. On a ball thrown from the left-field foul line to left center, the infielder would control the right-field side of the base with her left foot, and her right foot would be on the outfield side of the base in a line with the throw.

Outfielders

As the last line of defense, the outfielder has a responsibility on all batted balls, both primary and secondary roles. An outfielder always has something to do and a place to be. She must get to all batted balls quickly, she must be in the correct backup position (always expecting an overthrow), and she must keep all batted or thrown balls in front of her. Knowledge of the pitch location and the ability to anticipate where the hit may go will enable her to get a jump on the ball.

The left fielder has only one long throw to make and that is to the plate, so the left fielder should have the weakest arm. Since most hitters are right-handed, the left fielder will have fewer problems on balls that slice away from her. Other than the strength of their arms, the left and right fielders' defensive skills should be equal.

The center fielder should be the quickest since she has the most area to cover. She must be the most instinctive when reacting to the batted ball, along with being the most aggressive. She should be the all-around best defensive player of the three. I believe I can sacrifice a powerful arm for an accurate one in my center fielder, but I do not want to sacrifice speed and the ability to get a jump on the ball. The center fielder is in charge of the outfield and makes the decisions on who should catch the ball. She should have the first chance on catching every outfield ball.

The strength of the right fielder's throwing arm must be the number one consideration since she will have two long throws to make, one to third base and one to home plate. The right fielder must be an experienced outfielder because balls hit by right-handed batters will have a tendency to slice toward the foul line.

Standard Outfield Positioning

The individual outfielder's ability is probably the most important factor in positioning in the outfield. In deciding where to play the hitter at the plate, the outfielder must take into consideration her own arm strength and her ability to go left, right, up, or back. In a few cases, the coach will move the outfielder if she feels it is necessary.

If the field has a deep fence, the outfielders need to play deeper to avoid a long run to the fence if a ball gets by. If the fence is short, the outfielder can play closer to the infielders. If the foul-line fence is very close to the line, the outfielder can play a few steps away from the line.

If the infielder in front of the outfielder can go back quickly on balls, then the outfielder can play a little deeper. Similarly, if the infielder has a difficult time going back on fly balls, the outfielder can position herself a few steps in.

Ready Position

The outfielder should be in a comfortable semi-crouch stance with both arms out in front of the body and should rock forward on her toes on each pitch. She should catch fly balls above her chest just above eye level with both hands on the throwing side of the body.

Catching Balls on the Run

When running to catch a fly ball, players should pump their arms and should not hold their glove out (see figure 10.15). This will enable them to run faster. They should run on the balls of their feet. They must hustle for the fly ball and try to beat the ball to the spot where they believe it will drop. We have established drills (see chapter 11) that help the outfielder run back on fly balls without backpedaling, locate and touch the fence, and then come back to catch the ball. Communication with each other is critical; outfielders must call loudly and clearly to indicate where the other outfielder should throw the ball on plays to bases. We want our players to go all out to make the play on tough chances late in the game when it means stopping the winning or go-ahead run.

Figure 10.15 An outfielder going back for a catch.

Fielding Ground Balls

The majority of errors made by outfielders occur on ground balls. This is why it is so important for the coach to spend adequate time on proper mechanics. The outfielders must attempt to field the ground ball on the high hop or short hop so they do not get caught between hops. By taking the proper angle, the outfielder can keep the ball in front of her. There are four types of ground ball plays:

• **Down and block**—I teach the outfielder to go down on one knee and to field the ball with two hands in front of the body (see figure 10.16). This fielding style should be used to block the ground ball when there are no runners on base, when the play is made on a rough surface, when it is not a gambling situation, and when the throw after fielding will not result in a possible putout.

• **Infield style**—When a play might have to be made to the infield, the outfielder should field the ground ball as an infielder would (see figure 10.17). Outfielders must realize that this style should only be used when the ball is not hit very hard.

Figure 10.16 An outfielder blocking the ground ball.

Figure 10.17 An outfielder fielding a grounder infield style.

• **Scoop and shoot**—This style of fielding is only used in the late innings when the tying or go-ahead run is attempting to score. The ball is played in front of the glove foot in a scooping manner. Both knees must be bent to allow the upper body to get over the ball (see figure 10.18). The ball is fielded as the glove-side foot lands, and then a step is taken toward the target. The outfielder then crow hops off the throwing-side foot. If in doubt about her ability to field the ball cleanly, the outfielder should field the ball infield style. The scoop and shoot is an emergency play and should not be used unless absolutely necessary.

• **In the gap or down the line**—When two outfielders are in position to field a ground ball in the gap, the one in the best position for the throw should make the catch. When an outfielder is chasing a ball down the line, or is off balance when fielding the ball she should first take the steps necessary to get balanced and under control before attempting to throw.

Fielding Fly Balls

The proper technique for catching a routine fly ball involves the outfielder beating the ball to the spot she believes the ball will land. She should "hurry" under it and then position herself to catch it with the weight on her glove foot in order to be able to immediately drive into a power hop or crow hop. The proper position is one where she is behind the ball, her glove fingers are pointed up, and the catch is made about one foot (30.4 centimeters) above her throwing-shoulder side. The arms are away from the body and give a little on impact. Both hands are used for the catch, and she must look the ball into the glove. The outfielder should get to the fly ball or line drive quickly and should be in a position to make a strong and accurate throw.

On a ball hit over the outfielder's head, she should utilize a drop step. A drop step is a strong opening of the body in the direction the ball is hit. For example, on balls hit back over her throwing shoulder, she would open her hips and take a strong step with her right foot back toward the fence (if she is right-handed) (see figure 10.19). She should not lose sight of the

Figure 10.18 An outfielder performing a scoop and shoot.

Figure 10.19 Outfielder in full extension.

ball. She must attempt to make the catch with two hands whenever possible and to position the glove away from the body.

Diving for Balls

If the outfielder must leave her feet to catch a fly ball in front of her, she should use a bent-leg slide to keep the ball in front of her (see chapter 9). When catching a sinking line drive or soft hit, the outfielder should reach slightly for the ball. Most dive plays occur on short fly balls in front of the outfielder. It is okay to attempt these dives headfirst because the ball will not go very far behind the outfielder if it is uncatchable. With backups, outfielders can dive for almost anything. It is very risky for the side outfielders to attempt to dive after line drives toward foul territory because there is no backup.

The Outfielder's Throw

Ideally, an outfielder's throw should cover 60 percent of the throwing distance in a long relay situation. To best prepare athletes for this

skill, a structured throwing routine becomes paramount.

The outfielder should grip the ball with three fingers on the seam and throw with backspin, meaning the ball will spin off her fingers back toward her (in a clockwise direction if looking at it from the thrower's left side). This will keep the ball in the air longer, carry it farther, and keep it from tailing. A ball spinning straight back will also take a straight bounce to the fielder, making the ball easier to handle. The outfielder must close her throwing position to generate the force necessary for a long throw. This means to go from the star position to a complete shoulder and hip turn more quickly (see figures 10.20 and 10.21).

FLY BALL PRIORITY SYSTEM

Plays that can break a team are fly balls that drop between fielders when the play should

Figure 10.20 Outfielder preparing to throw.

Figure 10.21 Outfielder releasing the ball during the throw.

have been made. The communication for this play must be taught and practiced throughout the season. Here is a list of principles that I teach my players:

- Break full speed to the ball—do not drift.
- Call for the ball on its downward flight.
- Yell "Mine" when you are absolutely sure you can make the play.
- Once a fielder yells "Mine," all other players in the area call the fielder's name.
- Once a fielder yells "Mine," all other players must clear the area.
- When going for a fly ball, do not look for other fielders.
- Never command another fielder to take a fly ball.
- Just because one fielder calls for the ball does not mean that she should be allowed

to catch it. For example, an outfielder coming in on a fly ball would have the right of way, even if an infielder called for it first.

- When no communication is heard, it means no one thinks she can catch the ball. There is still the chance of a diving catch, and the fielder should yell "Mine" before the dive.

When two or more players have a play on a fly ball, one player must have priority in fielding it. Figure 10.22 is a chart we use to show the responsibilities of each position on the team, listing who does and does not have priority on a fly ball. This system takes a little practice, but when taught correctly, the danger of a collision is greatly reduced, and more balls will be caught.

Figure 10.22 Fly Ball Priority System

Position	Has priority over	Has no priority over
Pitcher	Catcher	Infielders
Catcher	No one	First and third basemen
First baseman	Pitcher and catcher	Second baseman and right fielder
Second baseman	Pitcher and first baseman	Shortstop and all outfielders
Third baseman	Pitcher, catcher, and first baseman	Shortstop and left fielder
Shortstop	Pitcher and all infielders	All outfielders
Left fielder	All infielders	Center fielder
Center fielder	All infielders and all other outfielders	No one
Right fielder	All infielders	Center fielder

CHAPTER 11 DEFENSIVE DRILLS

In this chapter, you will find drills that aid in the development of defensive skills. This chapter will describe simple and advanced individual drills. Let these drills be your formula for developing and implementing additional practice opportunities. They can be used in circuits or as stand-alone drills. This chapter also contains team drills that are both complex and advanced. Any of these drills can be done either inside or outside.

Similar to chapter 8, this chapter starts off with a drill finder. This table will help you locate specific defensive drills quickly. The drill finder is organized by defensive skill followed by the drills that include practice for that skill.

Fielding skill	Drill	Page
Angles	Two Cones Drill	135
Blocking	Catchers: Balls in the Dirt	136
Double plays	Infield to Bases	134
	Team Drills #2, #6	128, 130
Fly balls in front of the fielder	Up and Back	123
	Outfield Loop	137
	Slant	125
	Outfield to Bases	138
	Team Drills #3, #4, #7, #9	128, 129, 131, 132
Fly balls to the fielder	Outfield Loop	137
	Sprint Relay	126
	Outfield to Bases	138
	Team Drills #3, #9	128, 132
	Find the Fence	135
Fly balls over the fielder	Up and Back	123
	Grapevine	126
	Outfield Loop	137

(continued)

(continued)

SIMPLE PLAYER DRILLS

These simple drills take up very little space, and a lot of repetitions can occur in a short amount of time. The purpose of these drills is to build solid defensive fundamentals. You should use the names of the drills so the players will know what to do without requiring you to reexplain the drill each time it is performed.

Drills for Two Players

These drills are designed for two players working together. One player assists while the other performs the desired task. Many repetitions can be achieved with these types of drills.

Up and Back

Purpose: To practice footwork and glove work for balls hit over the player's head or balls dropping in front of the player.

Procedure: Partners stand 30 feet (9.1 meters) apart with one ball. One player is the worker and the other is the helper. The helper starts by throwing a shoestring-catch ball for the worker. The worker charges in, fields the ball, and throws it back. The worker then breaks back, and the helper throws a ball that the worker has to catch while running back. The worker makes the catch, throws it to the helper, and charges in. The helper continues the drill, throwing balls up and then back. Let the worker work until a certain amount of time has elapsed or until a certain number of plays have been completed, then rotate.

Partner Bucket

Purpose: To field a lot of ground balls without a throw.

Procedure: One partner has a bat and a bucket of balls. The fielder has an empty bucket nearby. The fungo hitter hits all the balls to the fielder, who fields them and puts them in the bucket. The partners then switch positions. Partners

stand at their normal fielding distance from the batter. For example, if one partner is a shortstop and one is a third baseman, the partners stand farther apart when the shortstop is fielding and closer when the third baseman is fielding.

Short Hop

Purpose: To practice fielding balls on the short hop.

Procedure: Partners stand 30 feet (9.1 meters) apart with one ball and throw one-hop ground balls to each other. The ball should be thrown in a sidearm style with the ball bouncing once close to the fielder.

Variation: Use a pitching machine set at 40 feet (12 meters) and pitch softies at fielders.

The execution of thoughtfully designed drills and the repetition of well-performed skills during practice sessions will prepare the athlete to play with confidence on game day.

Soft Hands

Purpose: To practice fielding short hops with soft hands.

Procedure: Partners wearing paddles on their hands stand 30 feet (9.1 meters) apart, and they throw one-hoppers back and forth. They need to use "soft hands" to field the ball and bring it to the cradle or heart position.

Drills for Three Players

With these drills, three athletes are involved. The drills are a little more complex than the two-player drills and may require more than one athlete to be working at the same time.

Three-Way Ground Balls

Purpose: To practice fielding ground balls off a bat.

Procedure: The fungo hitter stands next to a receiver, and the fielder positions herself at her normal fielding distance from the hitter. A bat and balls are needed. The fungo hitter hits five ground balls to the fielder, who throws to the receiver. The players rotate so the receiver becomes the hitter, the hitter becomes the fielder, and the fielder becomes the receiver.

Triangular Ground Balls

Purpose: To practice fielding emergency forehands and backhands.

Procedure: Three players stand 30 feet (9.1 meters) apart forming a box with a missing corner (see figure 11.1). One player is the fielder, and she stands next to the open corner. The other two players are throwers and stand next to each other with a ball each. The thrower opposite the open corner rolls the ball to that spot. The fielder moves over, fields the ball, and throws it back. When the fielder releases the ball, the second thrower rolls the ball to the open corner, and the fielder moves over to field it and throw it back. They continue moving the

fielder from side to side until 10 plays are made. Players switch positions so that they all have a turn at each of the three stations.

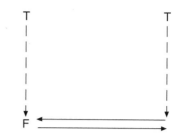

Figure 11.1 Triangular Ground Balls drill.

Drills for Four Players or More

These drills are more complex than two- or three-player drills because more athletes are involved. Coordination among the athletes, as well as spatial awareness, are now important factors. Gamelike pressure is a component of each drill.

Reaction Fielding

Purpose: To practice fielding batted balls and to eliminate a throw.

Procedure: There are four players in this drill. Partners face each other about 40 feet (12 meters) apart with two hitters in opposite corners of a square (see figure 11.2). At the same time, hitters 1 and 2 fungo hit a sharp ground ball. Fielder 1 fields the ball and tosses underhand to hitter 2, while fielder 2 fields the ball and tosses underhand to hitter 1. The hitter and fielder switch roles after a set amount of time or a certain number of hits.

Figure 11.2 Reaction Fielding drill.

Chimp and Champ

Purpose: To practice fielding batted balls in competition.

Procedure: There is one hitter with two or three fielders standing in a line about 20 feet (6 meters) from her, and a receiver is standing next to her. The hitter hits a ground ball to the first one in line, who throws it back to the receiver and then goes to the end of the line. The hitter continues hitting ground balls to the first player in line until an error is made by a fielder. The fielder who commits the error replaces the receiver, who replaces the hitter, who goes to the end of the fielding line (and everyone moves up). The object is to be at the front of the line when the drill ends.

Variation: The game can continue the next day with the players at the same places where they finished.

ADVANCED PLAYER DRILLS

The following drills focus on one player at a time, similar to the previous drills; however, now the drills become a little more challenging. There are more players involved in each of these drills, and some of the drills take more time to learn than the simple drills. Again, once the drill is learned, the coach can concentrate on teaching the skills involved.

Range

Purpose: To practice fielding forehands and backhands and to work on conditioning.

Procedure: Two fungo hitters stand diagonally opposite each other. One group of fielders stands single file facing one of the hitters, and another group of fielders forms a single-file line facing the other hitter (see figure 11.3, a-b). Fielders A and E go first.

For fielder A:

1. H1 hits a ground ball diagonally to the left.
2. Fielder A moves to the ball, fields it, and sprints toward H2.

3. Fielder A tosses the ball underhand to H2.
4. Fielder A sprints to the end of the opposite line.

For fielder E:

1. H2 hits a ground ball diagonally to the left.
2. Fielder E moves to the ball, fields it, and sprints toward H1.
3. Fielder E tosses the ball underhand to H1.
4. Fielder E sprints to the end of the opposite line.

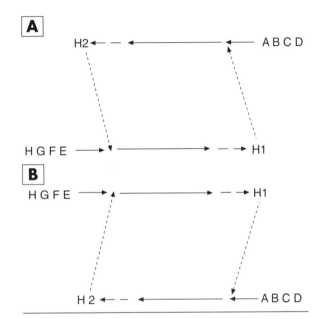

Figure 11.3 Range drill for (*a*) the backhand and (*b*) the forehand.

Slant

Purpose: To give outfielders practice at catching line drives and fly balls that tail away while in a dead sprint.

Procedure: Players line up in the center-field gap, and the coach stands with a bucket of balls on the foul line. The coach yells "Go," and a player sprints across the outfield toward second base, watching for the ball at all times. The coach then throws a variety of fly balls, grounders, and line drives just within the reach of the player. Upon catching the ball, the player tosses the ball back to the coach and starts a new line in front of second base. The next player in line takes off on command.

Grapevine

Purpose: To improve the footwork, concentration, and catching ability of all fielders while they move in both directions.

Procedure: The coach stands about 10 feet (3 meters) in front of a line of players facing her and takes the ball from the first player in line. The coach points to the right. The player turns her shoulder and hips to that side and runs in a straight line away from the coach. After about three or four steps, the coach points in the other direction. The player, using the crossover step, turns the other direction, still running in a straight line away from the coach, never losing sight of the ball (in the coach's hand). After another three or four steps, the coach points in the original direction. The player then repeats the previous crossover step and turns in the original direction. The coach then throws a fly ball in the direction of the original point, forcing the player to catch the ball by stretching over that side's shoulder. The player makes the catch and brings the ball back to the end of the line. The drill should be executed at full speed with the player in a dead sprint, and the player should change direction only when the coach makes the signal. Also, the player should never lose sight of the ball. The fly balls should be challenging and require a great deal of effort to make the catch. By the time the fielder has caught the ball, the next player in line has already set herself in the ready position.

Sprint Relay

Purpose: To condition and to practice the relay pivot and long and short throws.

Procedure: There are five players in this drill. Two players start on one end of the drill, two players start on the other end—about 80 feet (24 meters) apart—and one player starts in the center (see figure 11.4). The ball starts with F1, and each player makes a throw and follows her throw to the next position. The throw pattern is short, short, long. For example, F1 throws short to F2 and takes her place in the center of the drill. In the meantime, F4 steps up and takes F1's place. F2 throws short to F3 and takes F5's place. F3 throws long to F4 and takes her place, then F5

steps up to take F3's place. The drill starts again. Just remember to have your players follow their throws and sprint to the next spots.

Variation: The players throw fly balls or ground balls to each other.

Figure 11.4 Sprint Relay drill.

COMPLEX TEAM DRILLS

A complex drill is elaborate and utilizes five or more players at one time. The purpose of these drills is to give the players the opportunity to work together in gamelike situations. The coach needs to thoroughly explain these drills to the players. All of the drills in this section can be done outside or inside.

Three-Man Weave

Purpose: To work on receiving throws on the move, seat slides, and going back on fly balls.

Procedure: There must be three lines of players divided evenly. The drill begins with a ball in the hands of the player in the middle line. That player tosses the ball to either player next to her and then sprints behind the person she threw the ball to. The player with the ball then tosses the ball to the third player and sprints behind her, creating a continuous weave toward a point approximately 100 feet (30 meters) away. As the group gets close to the end point, coach 1 calls out a player's name. That player breaks from the weave, sprints toward coach 1, and catches a ball in a seat slide or headfirst dive. The other two players touch the end zone and take off toward the original starting point. Coach 1 then throws a fly ball that the players must compete to catch, "calling" for the ball. The one remaining player then touches the end zone and sprints back toward coach 1. Coach 2 throws a fly ball over the last player's head that she must catch. All three players then go to the end of a different line. During the weave portion of the drill, you should emphasize using tosses to each other that would be made during a rundown.

Bump Out

Purpose: To put gamelike pressure on the infielder or the outfielder.

Procedure: Players set up for any of the defensive drills in this chapter. An additional player waits off to the side of the drill. When a fielder makes a throwing or fielding error, she leaves the drill, and the player who is waiting replaces her. Every time an error is made, the fielder steps out and the waiting player steps in.

Full Field in Between With Tennis Balls

Purpose: To practice communication among all outfielders handling in-between batted balls.

Procedure: All outfielders and infielders are at their positions. A fungo hitter is at the plate with a tennis racket and tennis balls. The fungo hitter hits balls into all sections of the field. Tennis balls are caught and thrown off to the sides of the field. All fielders need to stay focused on the hitter as the hitter alternates hits to the left and right side of the field.

Blind Reaction

Purpose: To allow outfielders or infielders to work on reaction time and diving.

Procedure: There are three players in this drill. One player acts as a barrier between a player with the ball and a receiver. The player with the ball hides behind the "barrier" (so that the receiver cannot see the ball) and tosses the ball out to the receiver. The receiver can only see the ball when it passes the "barrier." When the receiver spots the ball in the air, she reacts and dives to make the catch. The balls should be tossed in a manner that requires the player to dive for the catch.

TIME-EFFICIENT DEFENSIVE PRACTICE

To assist the coach with time management, these drills involve each position working on various skills on different parts of the field. For example, the catchers might be working on a play with the pitchers as the middle infielders are working on another play. The space required is a softball field. This series can be done indoors or outdoors and can be modified to meet your individual needs. A "CO" on the illustration shows where the coach or a manager should be in the drill. Allow 10 minutes per set.

Team Drill #1

Infielders, pitchers, and catchers

Purpose: To practice tag and force plays at the plate.

Procedure: The coach at home plate sets up situations and hits all types of ground balls to the infielders and pitcher. The coach can set up every possible situation that will create a play at the plate. Catchers work on force plays and tag play mechanics. (See figure 11.5.)

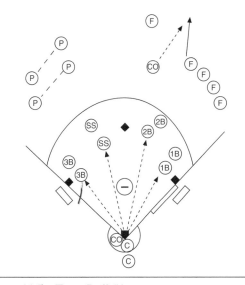

Figure 11.5 Team Drill #1.

Outfielders

Purpose: To work on communication near the fence and going back on a fly ball.

Procedure: Outfielders in right field alternate with one in right center yelling "Fence" when the other fielder is five or six strides away from it. Other outfielders are lined up about 70 feet (21.3 meters) from the fence. A manager or coach will throw a high fly ball near the fence, and the outfielders alternate going after the ball properly. The coach or manager throwing the ball is positioned about 90 feet (27.4 meters) in front of the outfielder, who is in ready position prepared to go back to the fence.

Team Drill #2

Catchers and first basemen

Purpose: To let catchers work on the mechanics of fielding all types of bunts and throwing to first base.

Procedure: Catchers (with masks on) alternate fielding bunted balls. The bunt is thrown from behind the catcher. The first baseman should simulate a bunt situation by charging toward home plate until she reads that it is the catcher's ball, and then going back to cover first base (see figure 11.6).

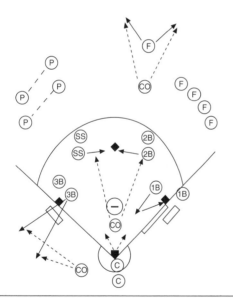

Figure 11.6 Team Drill #2.

Shortstops and second basemen

Purpose: To let middle infielders practice communicating on ground balls hit around second base.

Procedure: The coach or manager hits balls to either the shortstop or second baseman from a position about 20 feet (6 meters) from home plate to avoid interfering with catchers fielding bunts. There are no throws to first; the infielders

fake the throw. If the middle infielder wants to make an unassisted double play, she should yell, "I've got it."

Third basemen

Purpose: To work on the mechanics of fielding pop-ups around the fence area.

Procedure: The coach stands near home plate and tosses pop-ups to each fielder.

Outfielders

Purpose: To work on the mechanics of going back on fly balls.

Procedure: A coach or a manager throws balls over the outfielders' heads toward the outfield fence. The outfielder is about 70 to 90 feet (21.3 to 27.4 meters) from the coach and the same distance from the fence. The outfielder turns and goes back and finds the fence before making the catch.

Pitchers

Purpose: To work on ball spins.

Procedure: Pitchers pair up in left field and throw ball spins back and forth.

Team Drill #3

Pitchers and first basemen

Purpose: To work on communication when fielding bunts and ground balls.

Procedure: The coach hits ground balls or bunts to the first baseman or the pitcher from about five feet (152 centimeters) from home plate on the first-base side. The extra first baseman will cover first if the primary first baseman is fielding the ball or if the pitcher is fielding a bunt. This extra player is simulating the second baseman's responsibilities (see figure 11.7).

Catchers and third basemen

Purpose: To work on communication when fielding bunts, along with the mechanics of fielding a bunted ball.

Procedure: The catchers (with their masks on) alternate fielding bunted balls. The bunt is thrown from behind the catcher and goes toward the third-base side of the diamond. The

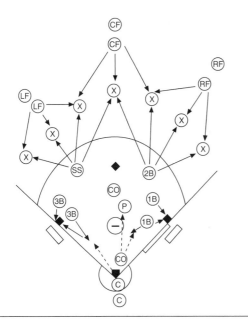

Figure 11.7 Team Drill #3.

extra third baseman covers third (this would be the responsibility of the shortstop on a real play). Balls are fielded by both the catcher and the third baseman.

Outfielders, shortstops, and second basemen

Purpose: To let outfielders work on coming in on fly balls, while the middle infielders work on going back on the same fly balls.

Procedure: A coach or manager stands between second base and the pitcher's mound and attempts to throw fly balls in the area of the outfield where two or three players will be attempting to make the play. The fielders use the fly ball priority system and communicate with each other to make the catch. The coach is throwing the ball toward the "X" on the diagram. The fly ball priority system is discussed in detail in chapter 10.

Team Drill #4

Pitchers, first basemen, second basemen, and catchers

Purpose: To work on communication when fielding ground balls and to work on backing up first base.

Procedure: The coach stands to the right side of home plate and hits ground balls from the

mound to the right side of the infield. Catchers will alternate backing up the play at first base. The first baseman may occasionally intentionally miss the ball so the catcher can check herself on backup location. Balls can also be bunted for the catcher to field (see figure 11.8).

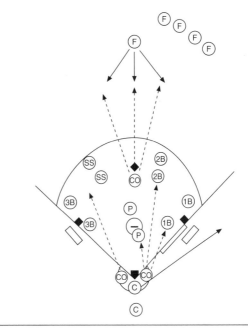

Figure 11.8 Team Drill #4.

Shortstops and third basemen

Purpose: To work on communication during situational ground balls.

Procedure: The coach is positioned on the left side of home plate and fungo hits ground balls to the left side of the infield. The coach sets up the situation: possible force play at third or runner on second not forced to advance. The coach (hitter) tries to move the third baseman to her left and the shortstop to her right. The shortstop must let the third baseman know quickly when she can make the play by saying "I've got it." The third baseman must make all the plays to her left unless the shortstop can make the play much easier. With no force play at third base, the shortstop fields the ball and completes the play as if a runner at second is breaking for third base.

Outfielders

Purpose: To practice charging ground balls with a possible play at third base or home.

Procedure: All plays are do-or-die. The manager or coach will hit balls, and the outfielders will fake the throw to either third base or home plate.

Team Drill #5

Pitchers, third basemen, shortstops, and catchers

Purpose: To work on communication on bunted balls to the third-base side of the infield.

Procedure: Simulate base runners at first and second with less than two outs. The coach throws bunted balls from behind the catchers at home plate. Catchers have masks on and call the play when the third baseman or pitcher fields the bunt. If the catcher instructs the fielder to throw to third, either the third baseman or shortstop will be at the base depending on the bunt play in effect. If the throw is to be made to first base, the fielder fakes the throw (see figure 11.9).

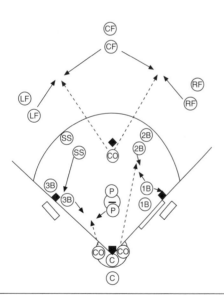

Figure 11.9 Team Drill #5.

First basemen and second basemen

Purpose: To work on situational ground balls.

Procedure: A coach hits ground balls to the right side of the infield from the right side of home plate. The coach (hitter) attempts to force the second baseman to her left and the first baseman to her right. The second baseman needs to let the first baseman know when she

can field the ball by calling the ball. The first and second basemen practice throwing to first.

Outfielders

Purpose: To work on communication on catchable balls in the gaps.

Procedure: The coach or manager throws balls from the second-base area. Outfielders have to position themselves closer than normal to each other to take into consideration that the ball is being thrown rather than batted from home plate. The outfielders should also work on their paths to the ball so that the center fielder catches the ball below the waist, and the side outfielders catch the ball above the waist, creating space between the two on the play.

Team Drill #6

Shortstops, second basemen, and pitchers

Purpose: To work on ground balls up the middle for the force play or tag play at second base.

Procedure: A coach stands in front of home plate and fungo hits ground balls for the pitcher. The pitcher fields the ball and throws to second for the force or tag. The middle infielders work on their backup responsibilities and covering the base (see figure 11.10).

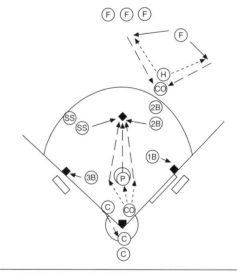

Figure 11.10 Team Drill #6.

Catchers, first basemen, and third basemen

Purpose: To work on pickoffs from the catcher to the third baseman or first baseman.

Procedure: One catcher is in front of the plate throwing to the catcher at home plate, who has her mask on. The catcher can alternate the pickoff attempt of a simulated runner at first or third base.

Outfielders

Purpose: To work on going to their right and left for ground balls.

Procedure: The manager or coach stands next to the fungo hitter in deep second-base position; the hitter hits balls to the outfielders. The outfielders are working on taking correct angles, fielding the ball properly, and throwing to the manager.

Team Drill #7

Pitchers and first basemen

Purpose: To work on pop-ups to the left of the pitcher and the right of the first baseman.

Procedure: A coach stands in front of home plate and throws pop-ups for the pitcher and first baseman (see figure 11.11).

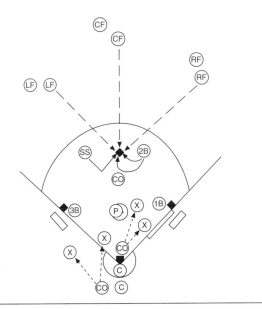

Figure 11.11 Team Drill #7.

Outfielders, second basemen, and shortstops

Purpose: To work on throwing behind the runner rounding second base on a well-hit ball.

Procedure: The coach stands between second base and the mound and hits hard line drives right at the outfielders. The second baseman and shortstop will alternate covering second base depending on where the ball is hit to the outfield. Any time the ball is not hit well, the outfielder fields it properly and fakes the throw to third base. On a well-hit ball to left, the second baseman will approach the bag from behind the runner, preparing herself to receive a throw to second base. On a well-hit ball to right, the shortstop will break from the cutoff position to second base when the ball leaves the right fielder's hand. On a well-hit ball to center, the second baseman will break to the mound side of second base and move into the base when the ball leaves the center fielder's hand. When the outfielders are in doubt about the status of the runner, they throw (fake) to third base.

Catchers and third basemen

Purpose: To work on communication when fielding pop-ups.

Procedure: The coach or manager stands behind home plate and throws to the areas designated by Xs on the diagram. Catchers must have masks on.

Team Drill #8

Catchers, shortstops, and second basemen

Purpose: To work on steals of second base and first and third double steals.

Procedure: An extra catcher delivers a ball to the catcher, and the catcher throws down to second base. The shortstop covers second base. The second baseman is in the cutoff position between the mound and second base, so she can practice cutting off the throw to second in order to hold the runner at third or throw the runner out at home (see figure 11.12).

First basemen and third basemen

Purpose: To work on fielding bunted balls and throwing to either first base or third base.

Procedure: From the left side of the batter's box, the coach throws out the bunts to either side. If the first baseman fields the ball and "One" is called, she throws the bunted ball to first base, where the other first baseman is simulating the second baseman covering the bag. If the coach yells "Three," then the first baseman fields the

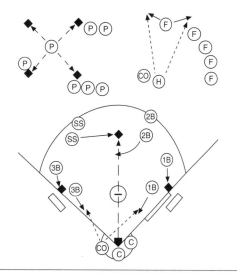

Figure 11.12 Team Drill #8.

bunt and throws to third, where the other third baseman is simulating the shortstop covering the bag. The same drill applies if the third baseman fields the bunt.

Outfielders

Purpose: To work on going back to the fence to pick up a ball and throw to the relay player.

Procedure: The fungo hitter can either hit or throw the ball to the right-field fence. A manager or coach serves as the relay player.

Pitchers

Purpose: To work on fielding ground balls and throwing to each base.

Procedure: The pitcher fields a ground ball and throws to first, second, or third base or home plate where additional pitchers are positioned. The bases are set 60 feet (18.3 meters) apart. The ball can be thrown or hit (fungo) by a pitcher with an additional player at first base.

Team Drill #9

First basemen, third basemen, and catchers

Purpose: To work on communication when fielding fly balls.

Procedure: The coach stands to the left side of home plate and tosses fly balls to the general

problem areas designated by Xs on the diagram (see figure 11.13). The catchers have their masks on.

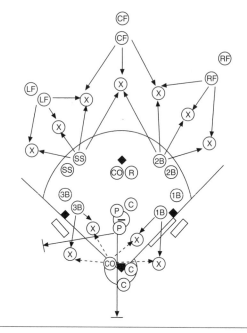

Figure 11.13 Team Drill #9.

Pitchers

Purpose: To work on getting to the proper backup position on balls hit to the outfield.

Procedure: Pitchers will alternate on the mound, faking the pitch and then reacting to the situation specified by the coach. After the pitch, the pitcher will break to the proper backup spot. For example, if there is one out, a base runner at second, and a single is hit to left field, the pitcher should break to the backstop behind home plate. With a runner on first and a base hit to right field, the pitcher should break to back up third base.

Outfielders, second basemen, and shortstops

Purpose: To work on communication when fielding fly balls.

Procedure: The coach throws fly balls to the problem areas designated by Xs on the diagram. All defensive players should use proper communication as the coach throws balls with a receiver at her side catching the return throws.

Team Drill #10

Pitchers and catchers

Purpose: To work on the pitcher covering home plate on a passed ball or wild pitch with a base runner attempting to score.

Procedure: A pitcher pitches the ball into the dirt or over the catcher's head to simulate a passed ball or wild pitch. The pitcher charges toward the plate, and the catcher charges to the ball's location. The catcher will retrieve the ball, set up properly, and throw to the pitcher covering the plate (with an imaginary base runner attempting to score). (See figure 11.14.)

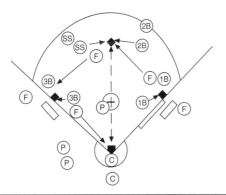

Figure 11.14 Team Drill #10.

First basemen

Purpose: To practice receiving bad throws.

Procedure: The first baseman sets up in the normal position and then breaks for the bag. From second base, the coach throws short hops, high hops, and off-target throws that will take the first baseman either left or right of the bag.

Outfielders, second basemen, shortstops, and third basemen

Purpose: To work on the tandem relay play on an extra-base hit.

Procedure: The coach fungo hits balls from behind second base to all areas of the field, forcing the outfielders to go to all areas of the fence. Once the ball is hit, and a sure double is in effect, both the shortstop and second baseman

go out for the tandem relay. The third baseman communicates where the play is to be made. The back player of the tandem will also communicate to the front player where to throw while listening to the third baseman.

INFIELD DRILLS

The following drills allow for a variety of plays and conditioning with very little standing around. They utilize more than one position and require each player to focus.

Infield Loop

Purpose: To practice fielding an assortment of ground balls (requiring different footwork positions) and throwing to different bases, as well as to work on conditioning.

Procedure: There are players at first and third, a ball in the pitching circle, and a player catching with a fungo hitter at the plate. One player works through all of the plays that follow (see figure 11.15).

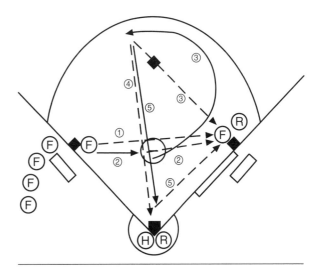

Figure 11.15 Infield Loop drill.

1. A ground ball is hit to the third baseman, who throws it to first base.
2. The player (third baseman) runs and picks up the ball in the circle and throws to first base.

3. The player then loops around second base toward the shortstop position and is hit a ground ball, which she throws to first base.

4. The player receives a ground ball at the shortstop position and throws it home.

5. The player charges the plate, and the catcher rolls a bunt, which the fielder throws to first base.

   After each player finishes, she rotates to the next clockwise position. On-deck fielders wait their turn at third.

Variation: Begin at first base and throw the first three balls to third base. Reverse the loop so the batted ball is a backhand. The bunted ball is thrown to third base.

Infield to Bases

In this drill, the outfielders are used as fungo hitters and receivers. A hitter and a receiver are on either side of home plate. Directions must be specific on which pair of hitters is hitting to which pair of infielders (middle infielders or corners) to avoid any dangerous throws to receivers.

Purpose: To have all infielders field an assortment of batted balls and throw to all four bases.

Procedure: Infielders are at their respective positions, and two fungo hitters are on opposite sides of the plate with two receivers next to them. The hitters hit four series (see figure 11.16). If there is more than one infielder per position, they alternate turns.

Series 1

1. The third baseman and first baseman work together for the play at first or third base.

2. The shortstop and second baseman work together for the play at second base.

Series 2

1. The third baseman and shortstop work together for the play at third base.

2. The second baseman and first baseman work together for the play at first base.

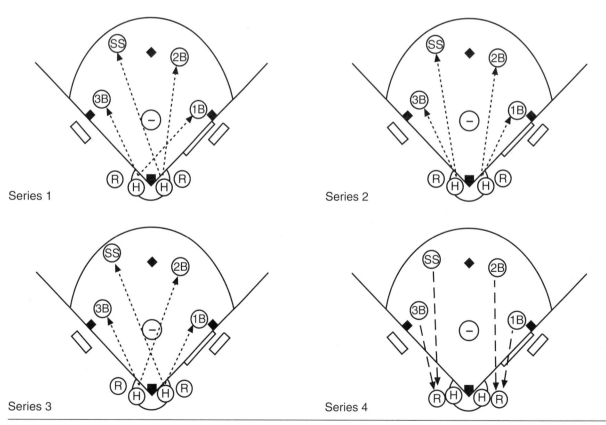

Figure 11.16 Infield to Bases drill.

Series 3

1. The third baseman and second baseman work together for the play at second and third base.
2. The shortstop and first baseman work together for the play at second and first base.

Note: In series 3, you should use only one ball on the infield at a time because both groups are making throws to second base.

Series 4

1. The first baseman and second baseman throw home.
2. The third baseman and shortstop throw home.

Infielders Work— Outfielders Run

Purpose: To put the infielders in a gamelike situation and to practice baserunning.

Procedure: The fungo hitter hits ground balls randomly around the infield, and the infielders field the balls and make the appropriate plays. The base runners run to first until all runners are at first; then they run to second until all runners are at second; and so on.

Middle Infielders

Pendulum

Purpose: To practice making tags on a runner stealing when there is a bad throw.

Procedure: The middle infielder gets in receiving position for a steal, with her left foot on the front corner of the bag and her toe pointing at first base. A partner tosses the ball so that it lands short in front of the bag. The middle infielder uses a pendulum action with her arm, transfers her weight with the pendulum but doesn't move her feet, and scoops to get the bad hop. Then she pendulums back, shifts her weight back to the bag, and puts down a hard tag in the dirt. Once practiced, this should be a smooth and quick transaction.

Two Cones Drill

Purpose: To work on a drop step that will enable the infielder to take better angles to the ball.

Procedure: Two cones are set up approximately six feet (1.8 meters) apart in the shortstop or second-base area. The middle infielder stands between and in front of the cones. A tosser rolls the ball to either side of the middle infielder performing the drill, and the fielder drop steps inside the two cones to field the ball.

Corners

Diving Drill

Purpose: To make it mandatory for the corners to stay low when diving and to give them a visual aid to help.

Procedure: The coach has a flotation device called a "noodle." She stands behind the fielder and holds the noodle waist high and about three feet (91 centimeters) to whichever side the fielder will be making the dive. A partner tosses a ball in that direction, and the fielder has to stay low and dive under the noodle to make the stop. Because the noodle is made of Styrofoam, it will not hurt if the player does not get all the way underneath.

Find the Fence

Purpose: To practice finding the fence when fielding pop-ups.

Procedure: One player either tosses or hits balls in the air near the fence and dugout, and a partner finds the fence with the glove or hand and then makes the catch.

Stationary Ball Drills for Bunts

Purpose: To simulate squeeze bunts for the corners and to enable the catcher to field squeeze tosses and execute tags. This also provides conditioning for the corners.

Procedure: Four balls are placed down the first-base line and four on the third-base line 8 to 10 feet (2.4 to 3.0 meters) from the plate. The first baseman stands approximately 5 feet (1.5 meters) from the catcher, and the third baseman stands at the third-base bag. On command, the third baseman sprints to field the stationary ball, and the first baseman sprints back to first. The third baseman flips the ball to the catcher, and the catcher puts on an imaginary tag. Then the first baseman sprints to field the stationary ball, while the third baseman sprints back to the bag. Each player will take four balls.

Catchers' Drills

Balls in the Dirt

Purpose: To teach the catcher how to move to block pitched balls in the dirt.

Procedure: A batter is in the batter's box, and a helper simulates a pitched ball to the catcher's left or right. The catcher moves laterally in position to block the ball.

Catcher Command

Purpose: To give the catcher practice in calling plays.

Procedure: This is a drill for the entire team. A catcher throws soft tosses to the coach, who hits to all positions on the field. Base runners are running gamelike starting from any base the coach specifies. As the play unfolds, the catcher calls out which base the fielder should throw it to. If an incorrect base is called by the catcher, the coach reviews the play and the necessary correction.

Fielding Bunts

Purpose: To simulate game conditions while fielding bunts down the first- and third-base lines.

Procedure: The catcher assumes her position behind the plate with full gear. One helper is at first base, one at third, and one is behind the catcher with softballs. The helper at the plate rolls a ball out for the catcher to field and throw to first or third (see figure 11.17).

Figure 11.17 Fielding Bunts drill.

Plays at the Plate

Purpose: To allow the catcher to practice catching balls that are thrown to the plate while a runner is coming at her.

Procedure: One player simulates a runner trying to score, while a helper hits ground balls toward the catcher from all sides of the field. The ground ball simulates a thrown ball to the plate. For added mental and physical toughness, a runner can run down the line with a football pad and actually run into the catcher as she is trying to make the play. This simulates actual game contact.

Pop-Ups

Purpose: To allow the catcher to work on fielding pop-ups behind her, in front of her, and to her sides.

Procedure: The catcher assumes her position at the plate (in full gear), and a helper stands behind her where the umpire would be. The helper yells "Up" and throws a pop-up to various locations in foul and fair territory. The catcher must visually locate the ball, throw her mask in the opposite direction of the ball, and then make the catch.

Quick Feet

Purpose: To help develop foot quickness for a catcher to react to passed balls, bunted balls, or balls in the dirt.

Procedure: The catcher starts in a blocking position. On command, the catcher must pop up and get into a throwing position. Repeat.

Quick Hands

Purpose: To increase the catcher's quickness from catch to release.

Procedure: The catcher kneels on the ground square to the pitcher; this isolates the catcher's upper body. A partner tosses to the catcher, who proceeds to smoothly and quickly toss the ball right back. It is helpful if a coach is kneeling next to the catcher and mimicking and verbalizing the speed she wants (for instance, "catch, release, catch release"). You can also use a stopwatch and see how many releases the catcher can get in a certain amount of time.

Stolen Bases

Purpose: To allow the catcher to practice throwing to second and third base, simulating stolen base attempts.

Procedure: With a simulated batter in the batter's box, a catcher (in full gear) receives the pitched ball and throws to second or third base.

OUTFIELD DRILLS

The following drills incorporate several plays and multiple players at once. They enhance player conditioning and communication while encouraging players to focus and to multitask. They include assorted angles, various kinds of balls off the bat, and throwing to all bases.

Outfield Loop

Purpose: To practice fielding an assortment of batted balls (requiring different footwork positions) and throwing to different bases, as well as to work on conditioning.

Procedure: Players are in left field and at second (with a ball) and third base, with a player catching and a fungo hitter at the plate. One player works through all the defensive plays that follow (see figure 11.18).

1. A ground ball is hit to the left fielder, who throws it home.
2. The left fielder runs into center field where the second baseman throws a fly ball. The player catches the fly and throws it to second base.
3. Then the player runs into right field where the second baseman throws a ground ball

toward the foul line. The player fields the ball and throws to third base.

4. Lastly, the player runs to left field where the batter hits her a ground ball, which is thrown home.

After the player completes the circuit, the outfielder becomes the catcher at home, the catcher rotates to third base, third base rotates to second base, and second base rotates to left field. Additional players are waiting their turns at the outfield position.

Outfield to Bases

Purpose: To practice fielding an assortment of batted balls and throwing to all four bases.

Procedure: All outfielders are at their positions, and a fungo hitter and a receiver are at each bag. The hitters hit four series of ground balls (see figure 11.19). Outfielders take turns in each field.

Series 1

1. The right fielder throws to first base.
2. The center fielder throws to second base.
3. The left fielder throws to third base.

Series 2

1. The right fielder throws to second base.
2. The center fielder throws to third base.
3. The left fielder throws home.

Series 3

1. The right fielder throws to third base.
2. The center fielder throws home.
3. The left fielder throws to first base.

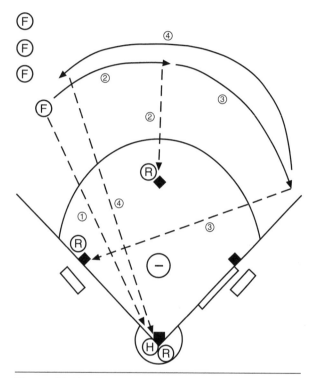

Figure 11.18 Outfield Loop drill.

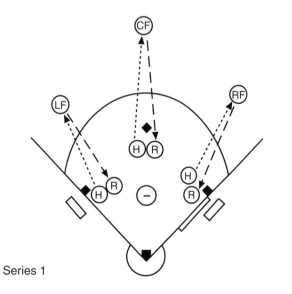

Series 1

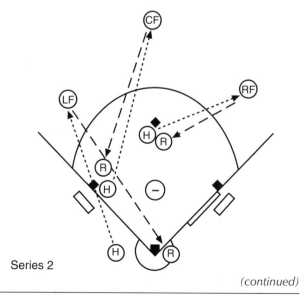

Series 2

(continued)

Figure 11.19 Outfield to Bases drill.

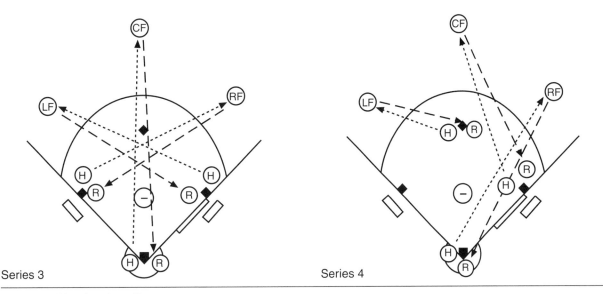

Series 3   Series 4

Figure 11.19 *(continued)*

Series 4

1. The right fielder throws home.
2. The center fielder throws to first base.
3. The left fielder throws to second base.

Outfielders Work— Infielders Run

Purpose: To put the outfielders in a gamelike situation and to practice baserunning.

Procedure: This drill requires all outfielders, all catchers, necessary infielders, and additional base runners. The outfielders are at their positions with a fungo hitter at the plate. There is a base runner at second base and one at home plate. The fungo hitter hits ground balls and fly balls randomly to the outfielders, and they make the plays to throw home. A player or coach at third tells the runner "Go" or "Back," depending on if the runner can score.

Variation: Put a runner on third base and hit fly balls.

COMPETITION AND CHALLENGE DRILLS

The following drills allow players to grow and to develop skills while engaging in some friendly competition. Fast paced and challenging, these drills offer gamelike situations in which players must work together and anticipate one another's moves.

21 Outs

Purpose: To execute 21 straight outs. This drill creates a gamelike atmosphere for the defense. This can be used for the outfield, the infield, or the entire team.

Procedure: The coach hits balls off a soft toss, and each contact is either a base hit or an out. To create more of a competitive atmosphere, if an error is made, you can stop the game and record how many outs have been made. Then it is a challenge for them to beat that number the next time. A variation of the game is to start at zero outs if an error is made and run the drill for a certain amount of time, or do not stop the drill until the team gets 21 outs in a row.

Outfield Rapid Fire

Purpose: To develop communication among outfielders and to improve individual quickness.

Procedure: Outfielders pair up and challenge each other. The coach puts aside a certain number of balls, for example, 15. The two challengers are approximately 25 feet (7.6 meters) away from the coach. The coach tosses the 15 balls in rapid-fire succession side to side, front and back. The two players communicate with each other and try not to allow any of the balls to drop. The winning pair allows the fewest balls to drop.

Ultimate Flexiball

Purpose: To work on communication skills as well as throwing and receiving.

Procedure: Make a flexiball (softie) playing field in the outfield approximately 100 feet long with buckets as end zones. There are two teams as evenly divided as possible. We like to play the freshmen and juniors versus the sophomores and seniors. Neither team uses gloves. The object of the game is to score goals by throwing the ball into the end zone for a catch. The player with the ball is only allowed to take two steps before she must throw it to a teammate. Any time the ball hits the ground, the other team gets possession. To score a goal, the ball must be thrown through the end zone, not carried through.

CHAPTER 12 DEFENSIVE STRATEGIES

Once the players have developed consistent individual fundamentals, it is time to work on plays for the entire team. In this chapter, I present specific strategies to assist you in teaching how to defend against such plays as sacrifice bunts, squeeze bunts, and double steals, along with proper field coverage on ground balls, fly balls, and base hits. If the players know where to go to back up the hit or the throw, and who should cover the bases, the end product will be an efficient defensive unit.

I stress communication throughout the defensive alignments so that players are talking to each other about coverage before the pitch is thrown. For example, when a fast runner is on first base, the middle infielders talk with each other about a possible hit-and-run or steal play. The defense will communicate with each other about outs and the batting order throughout the inning. The catcher gives signals to the pitcher and the infielders, with the middle infielders relaying the called pitch to the outfielders. The players will remind each other about the strength of the batter as well as where the batter hit the last time up. This information is shared throughout the game.

Having a consistent and fundamentally strong defense could make the difference between a win and a loss. A tight defense will minimize the number of runs the opponent will score, and this will put the team's offense in a position where the game can be won with only a limited

number of runs being scored. Offensive ability and the runs produced will win games, but a team's defense wins championships.

DEFENSIVE POSITIONING

Some of the factors that influence how players position themselves defensively include

- the inning,
- the score,
- the number of outs,
- the count on the batter,
- the field conditions,
- the batter's strength,
- the pitcher's strength,
- what pitch is coming,
- the position of the runners, and
- whether to expect a bunt.

Outfielders

Center fielders usually play closer to the plate than the side fielders do, but all outfielders must communicate with each other and the infielders regarding their positions. For example, if the center fielder is playing deep, she will tell the middle infielders that they have more territory to cover on balls hit in between the infield and the outfield. The outfielders do not need to have the same amount of space between each other, but they will often shift together based on the batter's tendencies and the strength of the pitcher. Also, outfielders need to check the wind direction and make a one-step adjustment. They should have a run-and-wait-for-the-ball mentality so that they do not have to dive or fall back when fielding.

The batter's ability will also determine an outfielder's location. Naturally, the outfielder will play the number three, four, and five hitters deeper than the rest of the lineup. For a left-handed slapper, the left fielder is closest to the plate, followed by the center fielder, with the right fielder playing the deepest. The fielder should be able to judge the spin of the pitch and the bat speed and should already be *gone* by the time the ball is hit. The fielder must read the ball off the bat and take her first step to charge toward the area where she anticipates the ball to land or roll. This is considered getting a jump on the ball. Typically, a left-handed batter will hit with more power to right field, and a right-handed batter will hit with more power to left field. In these cases, the opposite fielder can play a little shallower.

The outfielders should adjust to the count on the batter by repositioning themselves according to the count. When the pitcher is behind in the count, the outfielders should take a step back and a step to the pull side because the hitter will be geared up to hit her pitch. When the pitcher is ahead in the count, the outfielders should take a step in because the pitcher should be able to force the hitter into making weak contact.

An outfielder must review the base runners on base before each pitch. This information will allow her to make the proper throw and to anticipate steals, bunts, and pickoff plays.

The inning and the score can also dictate how deep the outfielder must play. For example, in a close ball game with a runner on third and less than two outs, the outfielder must play a little shallower so that she can throw out the runner at the plate on a fly ball. Similarly, late in the game with a two-run lead and a runner at second base, the outfielder can position herself a little deeper, because her throw will go to second

The outfielder is the final line of defense. Her initial positioning, anticipation of the batted ball, and strong throw to the desired base can and will prevent runs from scoring.

base in the attempt to keep the runner from reaching scoring position.

Infielders

The infielders also take similar considerations into account when positioning themselves. For example, the first baseman moves in toward the plate when the infield is wet and soft, when a weak but fast hitter is at bat, or in a bunt situation. The first baseman moves back when a strong, left-handed pull hitter is at bat, when there is a slow runner at the plate, or when there are two strikes on the batter.

The second baseman adjusts her position depending on the defensive situation as well. She is responsible for all batted balls (including slaps) between first and second base. The second baseman will also cover first base on bunted balls, unless the first baseman calls her off. The second baseman will cover second base on force plays from the third baseman and shortstop, and on balls hit to the right of the pitcher. On all average or slow batters, the second baseman should position herself five or six steps in back of the baseline (to give her more range on a hard-hit ball) and closer to second than to first base (so that more balls can be fielded on her forehand side than on her backhand side). If the batter is a fast right-hander, the fielder should take two steps in and two steps toward first base. If the batter is a fast left-hander, the fielder should be positioned in the base path and an equal distance from first and second. With a slow left-handed batter, the second baseman plays the standard five or six steps behind the baseline and an equal distance between the bases. With less than two outs and a runner on third, the second baseman moves into the base path.

One of the most challenging plays for the second baseman is the play with runners on first and third base. If the offense attempts to steal, the defense must prevent the run from scoring, and if possible, prevent the runner on first from getting into scoring position. In this situation, I will bring the second baseman into the cutoff position for the throw from the catcher to second base. That position is halfway between the mound and second and slightly off the line to enable the shortstop, who is covering second, to see the catcher and the ball. I instruct the second baseman to catch the ball if (1) the runner on third breaks for the plate or takes a big lead and can be picked off or (2) the throw is off target. With practice, an experienced second baseman can make these decisions herself. However, I will sometimes call the play in advance to take the decision-making factor out of her hands.

Like the first baseman, the third baseman moves in toward the plate when the infield is wet and soft, when a weak but fast hitter is at bat, when a strong, left-handed pull hitter is at bat, or in a bunt situation. The third baseman moves back when a strong, right-handed pull hitter or a slow runner is at bat, when there will be a pitchout or pickoff attempt on a runner at third base, or when there are two strikes on the batter. She will protect the line in late innings to prevent extra-base hits.

The shortstop's normal position is two or three steps behind the baseline and an equal distance between bases. With a very fast runner at the plate, she will move toward the base path.

This position decreases her range but allows her to reach the ball faster and shortens the throw to first base. The shortstop will play deeper on power hitters as well as on slow runners, and she plays closer to second when her third baseman can move well to her left. With less than two outs and a runner on third, the shortstop should move to just in front of the base path. She will adjust toward third base on an inside pitch as well as on a change-up. It is her responsibility to verbally alert the third baseman that a slow pitch is coming.

Figure 12.1 shows examples of good defensive positioning in certain defensive situations, pointing out the adjustments for the corners, middle infielders, and outfielders.

BASIC DEFENSIVE STRATEGIES

What follows are some key defensive strategies regarding bunt defense, backup position on throws and on batted balls, stolen bases and double steals, intentional walks, pickoffs, wild pitches and passed balls, rundown plays, and relay and cutoff plays.

Bunt Defense

To defend against the squeeze bunt, the defense must look for signs by the offensive team. If we suspect the squeeze, we will pitch out to try to catch the runner off third base. The corners need to watch the hands of the batter and watch for any sign she might give that she is going to squeeze.

My defense for a push bunt and a slap is to be sure the middle infielders commit toward the plate when the batter squares and hold their positions until the ball is down on the ground. The players then follow bunt procedure for coverage.

Backup Position

When any player is responsible for backing up throws from teammates, she should abide by two rules: First, allow at least 30 feet (9.1 meters) between players. This will allow for reaction time if the ball is thrown high, low, or

Figure 12.1 Defensive Positioning

Situation	Outfielders	Middle infielders	Corner infielders
Sacrifice bunt	Move in five steps	Move in two steps	Move in two steps
Slapper	Move in three steps and two steps to the right	Move into the base path	Move in one step
Runner on third and less than two outs	Move in five steps	Move in front of the base path	Move in one step
Power hitter	Take three steps back and two steps toward the power foul line	Move behind the base path	Move back one step
Ahead by three, fifth inning or later, runners in scoring position	Take three steps back	Move behind the base path	Hold normal position
Change-up	Take five steps back and two steps to the right	Move behind the base path and one step to the right	Move one step back
Curveball	Move three steps to the left	Move one step to the left	Hold normal position
Wind blowing in	Move in three steps	Move in one step	Hold normal position
Wind blowing out	Take three steps back	Take one step back	Hold normal position
Pitcher ahead in the count	Move one step in	Hold normal position	Hold normal position
Pitcher behind in the count	Take one step back and one step to the right for right-handed hitters; one back and one to the left for left-handed hitters	Hold normal position	Hold normal position

wide. The distance is important because you do not want the backup person to have a difficult play. Second, the fielder with backing up duties must sprint to the spot of the backup and then wait for the play to unfold. If she is still moving to the spot when the ball arrives, the play will become harder for her because both she and the ball will be in motion.

When the fielder is backing up the batted ball, she should also abide by two rules: First, she should react to the batted ball as if she believes the fielder will miss the ball and the backup will have to make the play. Second, she must take the deepest possible angle to the ball so that the ball does not get by her.

Stolen Bases

If the base runner attempts to steal second base, the shortstop will cover while the second baseman backs up the throw to second. If the shortstop is shading toward the line, the second baseman can cover second on the steal. It is more difficult for the second baseman to cover second than the shortstop because she must make a quarter turn to face first base.

When the base runner is stealing third, the third baseman will cover third if the batter takes the pitch, swings and misses, or fake slaps and misses. The shortstop will cover if the batter fakes a bunt.

Double Steals

An important aspect of defensive play in fast-pitch is the ability to properly defend against a double steal when runners are on first and third. It is the coach's responsibility to determine which one of the defenses to utilize. The coach needs to take into account numerous circumstances before choosing the type of play she wants the defense to execute. Those factors are as follows:

- **Number of outs**—The most likely time for an offense to run a double steal is with two outs. With less than two outs, most teams will give the batter the opportunity to score the runner on third.

- **Inning**—Late in the game, the offense will try a double steal more often with less than two outs because they can afford to lose the out to score a run.

- **Score of the game**—In almost all cases, the offense will not attempt a double steal when they are down by a few runs early in the game or down by more than one run in the last two innings. Throwing the ball through to second is always preferred in situations where the runner at third base is not of importance at the time of the double steal. If the double steal defense is done properly, a team should be able to keep the runner on third base from scoring and also make a play on the runner from first.

- **Strength of the shortstop's arm**—Along with the ability of the catcher to throw through to second base, the strength of the arm of the shortstop handling the throw to second base needs to be considered. If the shortstop cannot throw the ball well, then the defensive coach might be hesitant to call for a throw through to second when an important run is at third late in the game.

- **Hitter at the plate**—Generally, with a good hitter at the plate, the need to attempt a double steal is reduced. A weaker hitter might prompt the offensive coach to attempt some type of double steal, especially with two strikes.

- **Strength of the pitcher**—If the pitcher is dominating the opposing team's hitters, there is more of a tendency on the opposing coach's part to try to score a run off the double steal or to advance the runner from first into scoring position.

- **Count on the batter**—The best time to run a double steal play is when a good hitter is up with two strikes and two outs. With less than two outs, the offense may want to run with no strikes so that the batter might protect the runner by swinging and missing or fake a squeeze so second base goes uncovered. An ideal time is a 3-2 count with one out, enabling the runner on first to execute a straight steal.

- **Ability of the runner at first base**—The better the base runner at first base, the more likely the chance the offensive coach will attempt the straight steal. It is advisable not to throw through to second base if there is little chance of getting that out.

- **Ability of the runner at third base**—The better the base runner is at third base, the greater the chance she will break for the plate on the throw through to second. In most cases, with a poor runner at third base, the defense should throw to second.

- **Opposing team's double steal tendencies**—A coach usually has certain tendencies in regard to her offensive and defensive decisions, and this holds true for the double steal. When teams have played each other or scouted each other, each coach will know a little more about the opposing coach's philosophy. By knowing what these tendencies might be, the coach can make a better decision on the type of double steal defense to utilize.

The double steal play illustrated on page 165 is shown with two outs. With less than two outs, the same options exist, but now the middle infielders are in front of the base path. You must ensure that your middle infielders do not move laterally until the ball passes through the strike zone. If the middle infielders are moving to their cutoff positions and the batter slaps or hits the pitch, the first rule of defense is violated: Field the batted ball before covering bases.

Intentional Walks

When intentionally walking a batter, the pitcher and catcher must be sure the ball is not too close for the batter to reach out and hit, and they must make sure that the pitch is catchable. In the intentional walk, the pitcher is throwing to an invisible target because the catcher cannot set up outside of the catching box.

I will call for an intentional walk if the game is close, if first base is open, and if one of the opponent's best batters is up. If there are two outs and the above scenario is in place, it is an easier decision to intentionally walk that batter. Now with a ground ball the infielders can touch any base.

Questionable Intentional Walk

In my first year as head coach, we were playing Michigan during a tournament. It was the seventh inning, and we were winning by one run. Next up to bat was an outstanding hitter who had already gone two for two against our pitcher. She was the winning run; the tying run was on base. Not wanting her to hit in the tying run, or worse yet, give up a walk-off home run, we decided to walk her. We ended up winning that game. During the celebration afterward, a parent asked me, "Why did you intentionally walk the winning run on base?" I acted as if it was no big deal, but that is when I started to realize the impact that decision could have had! As rookie coaches, my assistant coach and I had not even thought about the consequences of intentionally walking the winning run! Fortunately, it worked out in our favor.

Pickoffs

Occasionally, the base runner will get a huge jump, and the defensive coach feels a properly executed pickoff will get her out. I like to use the play with a young runner or a pinch runner. It is also effective if the ground is not firm or when the first-base coach is not paying attention to the runner or the defense. On the pickoff at first base, I utilize two plays: the second baseman slipping behind the runner and the first baseman dropping back. In the first play, the catcher calls a pitchout, and the second baseman signals back. The second baseman then adjusts her position by taking two or three steps toward first base before the pitch signal is given. This movement must be done in a way that it

is not noticed by the runner or the first-base coach. As the pitcher begins her windup, the second baseman will sprint to first, straddle the bag, and "box out the runner." The first baseman moves in toward the catcher to decoy the runner and toward the pitcher to get out of the way of the throw.

In the second play I utilize for a pickoff at first, the catcher signals the first baseman, and as the pitch approaches the catcher, the first baseman drops back with her left foot toward first base. Her left foot should plant one foot (30 centimeters) down the line toward second so that a sweep tag lands in front of the base, not on it. A left-handed first baseman drop steps with her right foot and plants her foot with the heel against the bag.

On the pickoff at third base, two plays can also be utilized: the shortstop slipping in behind the runner or the third baseman dropping back. I will let the catcher know through a signal which play we are going to try. She will then signal to the shortstop or the third baseman. When utilizing the shortstop to pick the runner off, the play unfolds just as a pickoff would with the second baseman covering first base. If the pickoff attempt is going to the third baseman, we will not use a pitchout, but the third baseman will stay back to prepare for the hit or the catcher's throw. In both cases, the catcher must throw on the second-base side of third base to avoid throwing into the runner. The defense must be precise when running both of these plays because a miscue on the throw or catch will result in a run.

Wild Pitches and Passed Balls

On a wild pitch or a passed ball, the pitcher must sprint to the plate and station herself off the plate on the infield side. She should give the catcher a chest-high target as she calls for the ball. The catcher should throw her mask away from her route to the ball and should sprint to the ball. When picking up the ball, it is best if the catcher pushes it into the ground so a good grip is assured. The first baseman will sprint into a backup position for any overthrow from the catcher to the pitcher.

Rundown Plays

The rundown play should involve one or two throws. Any more than that and the chance of error increases. It would be even better for the fielder to make a tag on the runner without a throw. The fielder with the ball must start running under control toward the runner, forcing the runner to commit to full speed. The fielder with the ball will establish the angle of her approach on the run so that the receiver of the throw can establish a position off the line. In this way, the throw will not hit the runner, and the receiver will have an unobstructed view of the ball. The fielder with the ball should have the ball up and should *not* fake a throw; the throw should be a soft snap with the wrist. The ball should be thrown to the receiver's chest, and the receiver should step to the ball. After the throw, the fielder should veer out of the way toward the side of her throwing hand and retreat back to the original base she was covering. The coach may also choose to have her fielders follow their throw, making sure they avoid contact with the runner.

Here are some general rules for fielders to follow when the base runner is in a rundown:

- Remember that the runner is in trouble, not the defense.
- Always force the runner back to the base she came from.
- Throw the ball ahead of the runner to force her back.
- Throw the ball with moderate speed chest high.

Ideally, six players are involved: two infielders at each of the bases and two players backing up. Those involved in the rundown will gradually move in and narrow the distance or "close the gap" between the two defensive players.

Relay and Cutoff Plays

The difference between a relay and a cutoff is usually the distance involved with the throw. If the throw cannot reach the target without help, the defense uses a relay. A cutoff comes from a throw that can make it all the way, but can get "cut off" to make another play or to hold a runner.

Relay Plays

I use both the shortstop and the second baseman to relay extra hits from the outfield. If the ball gets by the outfielders in left field, the second baseman positions herself about 20 feet (6 meters) behind the shortstop. It is the second baseman's job to catch any overthrow in the air and to handle any other misplayed ball. The second baseman's relay and the shortstop's backup function exactly as the shortstop's relay and the second baseman's backup on a ball hit to right field. The first baseman can become the cutoff to home, or you can have her trail the batter rounding first and become the second baseman. The pitcher is the backup at third and home.

When the outfielder approaches a ball that has gone all the way to the fence, she will reach down to the ball, twist to pick it up, and in one motion "chuck it" in the direction of the players occupying the relay positions. No steps should be taken nor should the outfielder look for her relay. The "field awareness" of the outfielder and the verbalizing of the first relay will allow for a blind throw. This saves time and will result in the ball being caught by one of the two relays in position. The infielders should know the different arm strengths of their outfielders and should adjust accordingly—going out farther for those with weaker arms and staying closer to the infield for those with stronger arms.

Some general rules for the relay are as follows:

- On a relay play, it is assumed that the outfielder cannot get the ball to the desired base or home plate because it is too long of a throw.

- Both the shortstop and the second baseman are the relay players. The second baseman is backup to the shortstop when the ball is hit to left; the shortstop is backup on a ball hit to right.

- Since both the catcher and third baseman will have the play in front of them, they should assist the fielders by communicating where to throw. The command should be made prior to the ball reaching the glove of the relay so the relay can immediately throw the ball to the correct bag without hesitation.

- The communication must be very loud so that every defensive player can hear. The third baseman is generally closer to the fielders, and she needs to yell the play and the base at least twice.

Cutoff Plays

The first or third baseman will serve as a cutoff on balls thrown from the outfield or relayed to the plate (see figure 12.2). The cutoff player must be positioned slightly off a line from the ball to the plate about 35 to 40 feet (10.6 to 12.0 meters) from home plate. She should be positioned off the line so that she does not obstruct the view of the outfielder to the plate and the view of the catcher to the ball. She must listen for the catcher's instructions and cut the ball if the catcher yells. Before catching the ball, she should step forward on her right foot and then use that foot to pivot toward the plate. This opening of the body allows her to be in a position to quickly get rid of the ball. You may

Figure 12.2 The first baseman in cutoff position for a relay throw.

also choose to use your pitcher as the cutoff. In this instance, the first baseman becomes the backup to home.

Some rules for the cutoff are as follows:

• On a cutoff play, it is assumed that the fielder can throw the ball to the proper base or home plate. The cutoff is in line with the ball and the base.

• A cutoff player can be assisted into the proper position by the defensive player at the base or the plate. The player can help line up the cutoff with the fielder throwing the ball by instructing her to move to her right or left by the commands "Right, right" or "Left, left." This alignment should happen before the fielder releases the ball.

• The cutoff should have both arms up in the air so that she is an easy target for the outfielder or the tandem relay infielder making the throw. By anticipating where the play will be made, she will be able to better position herself for the proper play.

• The defensive player at the plate or the base will inform the cutoff if the ball should be cut or not. This should be done well in advance of the ball getting to the cutoff. If the player at the base wants the ball to be cut off, she will yell, "Cut." If there is no play or the ball is thrown off line, she should have the ball cut off.

• The fielder should throw through the chest of the cutoff. The cutoff needs to cut all throws that are off line. There should be enough time to move forward or backward to prevent getting short-hopped.

• The cutoff should always fake the catch if she is going to let the throw go through. This may keep the runner from taking an extra base.

• When the ball is coming toward the cutoff and a play is going to be made on the runner, the cutoff needs to keep the ball lined up with her glove side. The player will be in a good position to catch the ball, if commanded, and then throw the ball, all in one motion.

Setting Up Situations in Practice

In each practice, we spend at least 45 minutes on defense. We incorporate full-field practice into our schedule with other offensive and defensive drills. This occurs after we have worked on individual skills or unit skills (such as infielders and outfielders). During the preseason, we spend at least 15 minutes every day teaching defensive situations. Once games have started, our full-field defense is polished throughout the week. We also work on specific plays that have occurred during games where execution was lacking.

DEFENSIVE RESPONSIBILITIES

The number one objective for the defense is to prevent the scoring of runs and the movement of runners into scoring position. All strategy is keyed to this objective, and there are basic rules for fielders:

1. Set the defense to field the batted ball.
2. Set the defense to back up the batted ball.
3. Cover all bases.
4. Back up throws.

These four principles must be followed in this exact order. Your team cannot cover bases if they have not set the defense to field the ball and to back up the hit first. Within this basic framework, there are specific moves each defensive player should make in given situations. These defensive plays are diagrammed and explained on the following pages.

Ground Balls

The following plays cover ground balls hit to all of the infield positions. Simple plays with no one on base are presented first, followed by routine plays with runners on base.

Situation: Ground ball to the third baseman with no one on base.

Objective: The play at first. The right fielder and the catcher back up the throw to first.

Catcher: Follows the runner toward first and backs up the base.
First baseman: Covers first and takes the throw.
Second baseman: Covers second.
Third baseman: Fields the ball and throws to first.
Shortstop: Backs up the batted ball.
Left fielder: Moves toward third to back up the hit or a possible throw.
Center fielder: Backs up a possible throw to second.
Right fielder: Moves toward the foul line to pick up any overthrow.

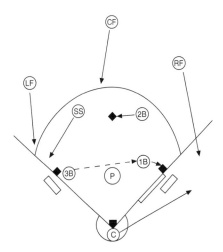

Situation: Ground ball to the second baseman with no one on base.

Objective: The play at first. The right fielder backs up the batted ball, and then the right fielder and the catcher back up the throw to first.

Catcher: Follows the runner toward first and backs up the base.
First baseman: Covers first and takes the throw.
Second baseman: Fields the ball and throws to first.
Third baseman: Covers third.
Shortstop: Covers second.
Left fielder: Moves toward center field to back up a possible throw to second.
Center fielder: Backs up the second baseman for any deflection and backs up second for a possible throw.
Right fielder: (1) Backs up the batted ball and then (2) moves to the fence for any possible overthrow of first.

Situation: Ground ball to the pitcher with a runner on first and less than two outs.

Objective: The play at second. The pitcher should know where the player covering second wants the ball. For example, if the shortstop is moving toward the bag, the pitcher would throw a lead throw to her.

Pitcher: If the ball is fielded on the pitcher's right side, she looks for the second baseman covering. If the ball is fielded on the pitcher's left side, she looks for the shortstop covering.
Catcher: Follows the batter toward first and backs up the base.
First baseman: Covers first.
Shortstop and second baseman: The player who does not cover the throw backs up the play.
Third baseman: Covers third.
Left fielder: Moves toward third to back up a possible throw.
Center fielder: Moves toward second to back up the throw.
Right fielder: Moves toward the foul line to cover any overthrow.

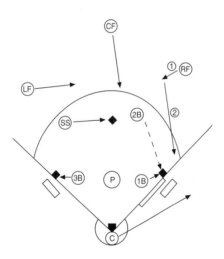

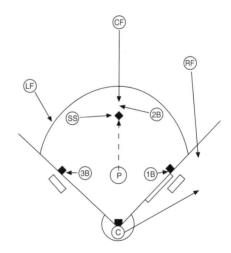

Situation: Ground ball to the first baseman with a runner on first and less than two outs.

Objective: The double play with the shortstop covering second. The first baseman should throw to second on either side of the baseline to avoid hitting the runner.

Catcher: Follows the runner toward first and backs up the base.
First baseman: Fields the ball and throws to second, then covers first for the throw from the shortstop.
Second baseman: Backs up the first baseman and is prepared to cover first if the first baseman cannot come back.
Third baseman: Covers third.
Shortstop: Covers second, takes the throw, and throws to first.
Left fielder: Backs up the throw to second.
Center fielder: Backs up the throw to second.
Right fielder: Moves toward the foul line to back up the throw to first.

Situation: Ground ball to the second baseman with a runner on first and less than two outs.

Objective: The double play with the shortstop covering second.

Catcher: Follows the runner toward first and backs up the base.
First baseman: Covers first.
Second baseman: Fields the ball and throws to second. The second baseman may also have the opportunity to tag the runner, then throw to first.
Third baseman: Covers third.
Shortstop: Covers second, takes the throw, and throws to first.
Left fielder: (1) Backs up the throw to second and then (2) backs up the possible throw to third. Moves from position 1 to position 2 when the play is completed at second.
Center and left fielders: Back up the throw to second 30 feet (9.1 meters) apart and at different angles.
Right fielder: (1) Backs up the second baseman and then (2) backs up the throw to first.

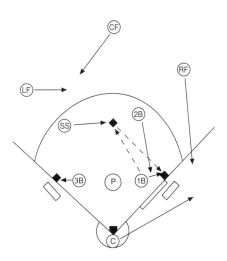

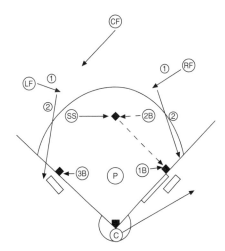

Situation: Ground ball to the shortstop with a runner on first and less than two outs.

Objective: The double play with the second baseman covering second.

Pitcher: Backs up third and moves to foul territory.
Catcher: Follows the batter toward first and backs up the base.
First baseman: Covers first and takes the second baseman's throw.
Second baseman: Covers second, takes the throw, and throws to first.
Third baseman: Covers third.
Shortstop: Fields the ball and throws to second.
Left fielder: Backs up the batted ball on an angle behind the center fielder.
Center fielder: (1) Moves to back up the hit and then (2) sprints to back up the throw from the shortstop to second base.
Right fielder: (1) Backs up the throw to second and then (2) backs up the throw to first. Moves to the secondary position as soon as the center fielder is in position to back up the throw from shortstop to second base.

Situation: Ground ball to the third baseman with a runner on first and less than two outs.

Objective: The double play with the second baseman covering second.

Pitcher: Backs up third.
Catcher: Follows the batter toward first and backs up the base.
First baseman: Covers first and takes the second baseman's throw.
Second baseman: Covers second, takes the throw, and throws to first.
Third baseman: Fields the ball and throws to second and then covers third.
Shortstop: Backs up the batted ball to third.
Left fielder: Backs up the batted ball.
Center fielder: (1) Moves to back up the hit at a deeper angle than the left fielder and then (2) sprints to back up the throw from the third baseman to second base.
Right fielder: (1) Backs up the throw to second and then (2) backs up the throw to first. Moves to the secondary position as soon as the center fielder is in position to back up the throw from the third baseman to second base.

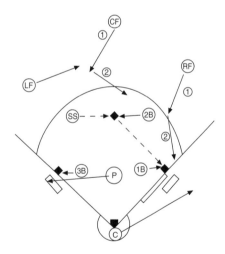

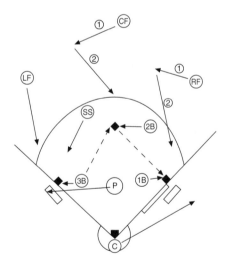

Situation: Ground ball to the shortstop with a runner on third and less than two outs.

Objective: To get the lead runner out at the plate if she goes; if not, the play at first.

Pitcher: (1) Attempts to field the ball and then (2) moves toward home plate in the event of a rundown.

Catcher: Covers home plate.

First baseman: When either the third baseman or the shortstop fields a ground ball with a runner on third (less than two outs), the first baseman moves to the "short position." She sets up to receive the throw along the foul line, about 10 to 15 feet (3.0 to 4.5 meters) in front of the bag. From here, the throw to the plate on a delay by the runner at third will be a shorter throw. The first baseman would get the batter out if there were no play at the plate.

Second baseman: Covers second.

Third baseman: First attempts to field the ball; if she doesn't field the ball, she covers third as the runner from third breaks for the plate.

Shortstop: Fields the grounder and throws home, then backs up third. If the third baseman fields the ball, the shortstop should cover third.

Outfielders: Move toward the infield and back up the base in front of them for a possible throw.

Note: With runners on first and third and less than two outs, the coach must decide whether to have the infielders try to hold the runner at third or go for the double play. Unless the runner on third is vital and there are no outs, you should instruct the pitcher, shortstop, and second baseman to go for the double play. This

defense allows the middle infielders to play deeper and reach more ground balls. The first and third basemen, because their double play throws are longer, should check the runner at third and throw home if the runner breaks or throw to second if the runner at third holds.

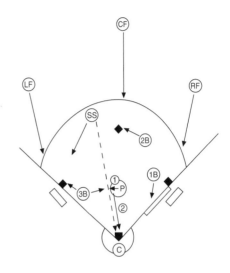

Hits

In all of the following hit situations, the play is the same regardless of the number of outs. The plays are organized beginning with singles and proceeding to extra-base hits. In the first set of plays, the objective is to prevent the batter from reaching scoring position. In the next set of plays, the defense's objective is to prevent the batter from reaching third base. The final set pertains to the play at the plate.

Situation: Long single (possible double) to left center with no one on base, with a runner on second, a runner on third, or with runners on second and third.

Objective: The play at second to prevent the batter base runner from reaching scoring position. A long throw from the outfield may require a relay.

Pitcher: Backs up second. Does not stand in the base path where she may interfere with the runner.
Catcher: Follows the runner to first in case of a rundown.
First baseman: Covers first.
Second baseman: Covers second, prepares to take the throw, and tells the shortstop whether or not to cut.
Third baseman: Covers third.
Shortstop: Moves to the outfield, in line with the outfielder and second base. Listens to the second baseman's instructions and cuts the throw or lets it go through.
Left fielder: Fields the ball, uses the shortstop as a possible relay, and throws to second.
Center fielder: Backs up the batted ball.
Right fielder: Backs up the throw to second.
Note: This play is diagrammed for a ball hit to left center. The fielders' assignments are the same for a long hit down the left-field line.

Situation: Long single (possible double) down the right-field line with no one on base, with a runner on second, a runner on third, or with runners on second and third.

Objective: The play at second to prevent the batter base runner from reaching scoring position. A long throw from the outfield may require a relay.

Pitcher: Backs up second. Does not stand in the base path where she may interfere with the runner.
Catcher: Follows the runner to first in case of a rundown.
First baseman: Covers first.
Second baseman: Moves toward the outfield, in line with the outfielder and second base. Listens to the shortstop's instructions and cuts the throw or lets it go through.
Third baseman: Covers third.
Shortstop: Covers second, prepares to take the throw, and tells the second baseman whether or not to cut.
Left fielder: Backs up the throw to third.
Center fielder: Backs up the batted ball.
Right fielder: Fields the ball, uses the second baseman as a possible relay, and throws to second.
Note: This play is diagrammed for a ball hit down the right-field line. The fielders' assignments are the same for a possible double to right center.

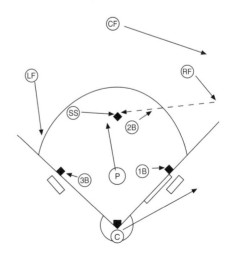

Situation: Double (possible triple) to left center with no one on base, with a runner on second, a runner on third, or with runners on second and third.

Objective: The play on the batter base runner trying to reach third. The shortstop is the relay, and the second baseman concedes the double and backs up the relay.

Pitcher: Backs up third.
Catcher: Covers home plate.
First baseman: Trails the runner to second for a possible pickoff throw from the relay player.
Second baseman: Backs up the shortstop about 20 to 30 feet (6.0 to 9.1 meters) behind her in line with third base.
Third baseman: Covers third and prepares to take the throw. Tells the shortstop or second baseman whether or not to cut the ball.
Shortstop: Moves toward the outfielder, in line with the ball and third base, so that she is able to catch the outfielder's throw in the air.
Left fielder: Fields the ball and throws to the relay.
Center fielder: Backs up the batted ball.
Right fielder: Moves toward second to back up a possible throw.
Note: The fielders' assignments are the same for a possible triple down the left-field line.

Situation: Double (possible triple) to right center with no one on base, with a runner on second, a runner on third, or with runners on second and third.

Objective: The play on the batter base runner trying to reach third. The second baseman goes to the relay position, and the shortstop backs up the relay.

Pitcher: Backs up third.
Catcher: Covers home plate.
First baseman: Trails the runner to second for a possible pickoff throw from the relay player.
Second baseman: Moves toward the outfielder, in line with the ball and third base, so that she is able to catch the outfielder's throw in the air.
Third baseman: Covers third, tells the shortstop whether or not to cut the ball, and prepares to take the throw.
Shortstop: Backs up the second baseman about 20 to 30 feet (6.0 to 9.1 meters) behind her in line with third base. Listens for the third baseman's call about cutting the ball.
Left fielder: Moves toward third to back up a possible throw.
Center fielder: Backs up the batted ball.
Right fielder: Fields the ball and, using the second baseman as a possible relay, throws to third.

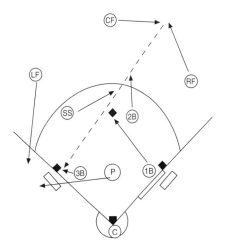

Situation: Double (possible triple) down the right-field line with no one on base, with a runner on second, a runner on third, or with runners on second and third.

Objective: The play on the batter base runner trying to reach third. The first baseman serves as the backup when the second baseman goes out for the relay.

Pitcher: Backs up third.
Catcher: Covers home plate.
First baseman: Backs up the second baseman about 20 to 30 feet (6.0 to 9.1 meters) behind her in line with third base. Instructs the second baseman on whether or not to relay the throw.
Second baseman: Moves toward the outfielder, in line with the ball and third base, so that she is able to catch the outfielder's throw in the air. Listens for the first baseman's instructions.
Third baseman: Covers third and prepares to take the relay. Tells either the first or second baseman whether or not to cut the throw.
Shortstop: Covers second for a possible pickoff throw from the second baseman.
Left fielder: Moves toward third in case of a rundown.
Center fielder: Backs up the right fielder.
Right fielder: Fields the ball and throws to the second baseman relay.

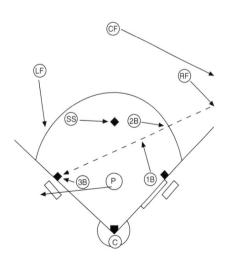

Situation: Triple (possible inside-the-park home run) to center.

Objective: The play at home plate to prevent the batter from scoring.

Pitcher: Backs up home plate.
Catcher: Covers home plate, prepares to take the throw, and instructs the first baseman whether to cut the ball.
First baseman: Moves directly in line with the second baseman and home plate about 40 feet (12 meters) from home plate. Follows the catcher's instructions to cut off the relay or let it go through.
Second baseman: Moves toward the center fielder, in line with the ball and home plate, so that she is able to catch the throw in the air. Listens for the shortstop's instructions on whether to cut the throw and throw to third or cut the throw and throw home.
Third baseman: Covers third.
Shortstop: Backs up the second baseman about 20 to 30 feet (6.0 to 9.1 meters) behind her in line with home plate. Instructs the second baseman on whether or not to relay the throw.
Left fielder: Backs up third in case of a pickoff overthrow from the first baseman or catcher.
Center fielder: Fields the ball and throws to the second baseman.
Right fielder: Backs up the hit.
Note: On hits to the right-field side of the center fielder, the second baseman is the relay. On balls to the left-field side, the shortstop becomes the relay.

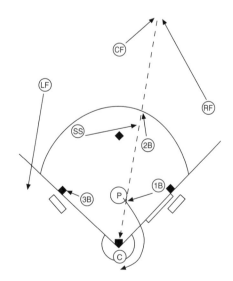

Situation: Single to right with a runner on first.

Objective: The play at third and holding the batter to a single.

Pitcher: Backs up third.
Catcher: Covers home plate.
First baseman: Covers first.
Second baseman: (1) Moves out to field the hit and then (2) repositions to cover second.
Third baseman: Covers third, prepares to take the throw, and instructs the shortstop whether or not to cut the ball.
Shortstop: Moves in line with the right fielder and third base. Follows the third baseman's instructions to cut off the throw or let it go through.
Left fielder: Moves toward third in case of an overthrow or rundown.
Center fielder: Backs up the hit.
Right fielder: Fields the ball and, using the shortstop as a possible relay, throws to third.
Note: On hits to the right-field side of the center fielder, the second baseman is the relay. On balls to the left-field side, the shortstop becomes the relay. On a single to center or left, the play is the same coverage except there would be no relay needed and the second baseman would cover second. The center and left fielders would back up the batted ball.

Situation: Long single (possible double) down the left-field line with a runner on first, with runners on first and second, runners on first and third, or with the bases loaded.

Objective: The play at second to prevent the batter base runner from reaching scoring position.

Pitcher: Backs up third or home.
Catcher: Covers home plate.
First baseman: Covers first.
Second baseman: Covers second. Instructs the shortstop whether or not to cut the throw from the left fielder.
Third baseman: Covers third.
Shortstop: Moves into the outfield, directly in line with the left fielder and second base. Listens for the second baseman's instructions. Cuts off the throw or lets it go through.
Left fielder: Fields the ball and, using the shortstop as a possible relay, throws to second.
Center fielder: Backs up the left fielder.
Right fielder: Moves toward the infield in case of an overthrow at second.
Note: The diagram for this play shows a ball hit down the left-field line. The fielders' assignments are the same for a possible double to left center with a runner on first, runners on first and second, runners on first and third, or with the bases loaded. If the batter has a chance of reaching second, the runner on first will usually make third easily.

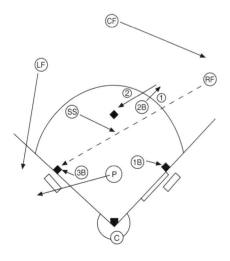

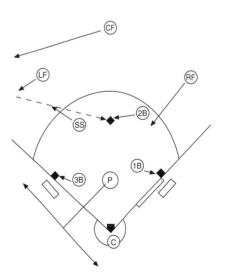

Situation: Long single (possible double) to right center with a runner on first, with runners on first and second, runners on first and third, or with the bases loaded.

Objective: The play at second to prevent the batter base runner from reaching scoring position.

Pitcher: Backs up third or home.
Catcher: Covers home plate.
First baseman: Covers first.
Second baseman: Moves into the outfield, directly in line with the right fielder and second base. Listens for the shortstop's instructions. Cuts off the throw or lets it go through.
Third baseman: Covers third.
Shortstop: Covers second, prepares to take the throw, and instructs the second baseman whether or not to cut it off.
Left fielder: Moves toward the infield in case of an overthrow at second.
Center fielder: Backs up the right fielder.
Right fielder: Fields the ball and, using the second baseman as a possible relay, throws to second.
Note: The diagram for this play shows a ball hit to right center. The fielders' assignments are the same for a possible double to left center with a runner on first, runners on first and second, runners on first and third, or with the bases loaded. If the batter has a chance of reaching second, the runner on first will usually make third easily.

Situation: Double (possible triple) to left center with a runner on first, with runners on first and second, runners on first and third, or with the bases loaded.

Objective: The play at the plate or the play at third.

Pitcher: Moves outside the third-base line, close to home plate. Backs up third or home, depending on the play.
Catcher: Covers home plate. If the relay comes toward the plate, the catcher prepares to take it and instructs the first baseman whether or not to cut it off.
First baseman: Moves near the pitcher's mound, directly in line with the shortstop and home plate. Follows the catcher's instructions to cut off the relay or let it go through.
Second baseman: Backs up the shortstop about 20 to 30 feet (6.0 to 9.1 meters) behind her in line with home plate. Instructs the shortstop on where to relay the throw or to just cut it off.
Third baseman: Covers third and takes the relay if it comes there.
Shortstop: Moves into the outfield, directly in line with the left fielder and home plate. Listens for the second baseman's instructions. Relays the throw either to the plate (using the first baseman as a guide) or to third, or just cuts off the throw.
Left fielder: Fields the ball and throws toward the middle infielders.
Center fielder: Backs up the left fielder.
Right fielder: Covers second.
Note: In this play, there is a relay player and a cutoff player.

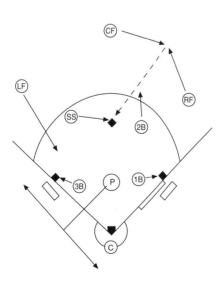

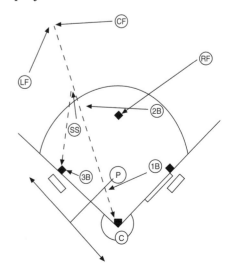

Situation: Double (possible triple) down the left-field line with a runner on first, with runners on first and second, runners on first and third, or with the bases loaded.

Objective: The play at the plate or the play at third.

Pitcher: Backs up third and home.
Catcher: Covers home plate. If the relay comes toward the plate, the catcher prepares to take it and instructs the first baseman whether or not to cut it off.
First baseman: Moves near the pitcher's mound, directly in line with the shortstop and home plate. Follows the catcher's instructions to cut off the relay or let it go through.
Second baseman: Covers second.
Third baseman: Serves a dual role: (1) backs up the relay and (2) covers third and takes the relay if it comes there. Both occur at the base.
Shortstop: Moves out into the outfield, directly in line with the left fielder and home plate. Listens for the third baseman's instructions. Relays the throw either to home plate (using the first baseman as a guide) or to third, or just cuts off the throw.
Left fielder: Fields the ball and throws to the shortstop.
Center fielder: Backs up the left fielder.
Right fielder: Backs up a possible throw to second.
Note: In this play, there is a relay player and a cutoff player.

Situation: Double (possible triple) to right center with a runner on first, with runners on first and second, runners on first and third, or with the bases loaded.

Objective: The play at the plate or the play at third.

Pitcher: Backs up third and home.
Catcher: Covers home plate. If the relay comes toward the plate, the catcher prepares to take it and instructs the first baseman whether or not to cut it off.
First baseman: Moves near the pitcher's mound, directly in line with the second baseman and home plate. Follows the catcher's instructions to cut off the relay or let it go through.
Second baseman: Moves into the outfield, directly in line with the right fielder and home plate. Listens for the shortstop's instructions. Relays the throw either to the plate (using the first baseman as a guide) or to third, or just cuts off the throw.
Third baseman: Covers third and takes the relay if it comes there.
Shortstop: Backs up the second baseman about 20 to 30 feet (6.0 to 9.1 meters) behind her in line with the throw to third. Instructs the second baseman on where to relay the throw or to just cut it off.
Left fielder: Backs up third in line with the first baseman in case the relay to the plate is cut off and the throw goes to third.
Center fielder: Backs up the right fielder.
Right fielder: Fields the ball and throws to the second baseman.
Note: In this play, there is a relay player and a cutoff player.

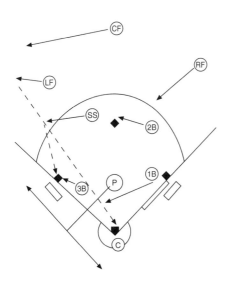

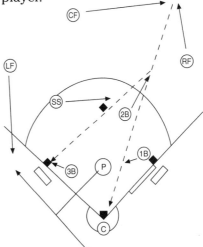

Situation: Double (possible triple) down the right-field line with a runner on first, with runners on first and second, runners on first and third, or with the bases loaded.

Objective: The play at the plate or the play at third.

Pitcher: Backs up third and home.
Catcher: Covers home plate. If the relay comes toward the plate, the catcher prepares to take it and instructs the first baseman whether or not to cut it off.
First baseman: Moves near the pitcher's mound, directly in line with the second baseman and home plate. Follows the catcher's instructions to cut off the relay or let it go through.
Second baseman: Moves out into the outfield, directly in line with the right fielder and home plate. Listens for the shortstop's instructions. Relays the throw either to the plate (using the first baseman as a guide) or to third, or just cuts off the throw.
Third baseman: Covers third and takes the relay if it comes there.
Shortstop: Backs up the second baseman about 20 to 30 feet (6.0 to 9.1 meters) behind her in line with the plate. Instructs the second baseman on where to relay the throw or to just cut it off.
Left fielder: Backs up third in line with the first baseman in case the relay to the plate is cut off and the throw goes to third.
Center fielder: Backs up the right fielder.
Right fielder: Fields the ball and throws to the second baseman.
Note: In this play, there is a relay player and a cutoff player.

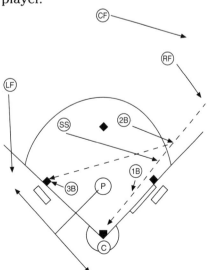

Situation: Single to left with a runner on second, or with runners on first and second, runners on second and third, or with the bases loaded.

Objective: The play at the plate and holding the batter to a single.

Pitcher: Backs up home plate.
Catcher: Covers home plate. If the throw comes toward the plate, the catcher prepares to take it and instructs the third baseman whether or not to cut it.
First baseman: Covers first.
Second baseman: Covers second and takes the throw if it comes there. It may come from the left fielder, the third baseman, or the catcher.
Third baseman: Moves near the pitcher's mound, directly in line with the left fielder and home plate. Follows the catcher's instructions to cut off the throw or let it go through.
Shortstop: Covers third.
Left fielder: Fields the ball and throws to the plate.
Center fielder: Backs up the batted ball.
Right fielder: Moves toward the infield in case of an overthrow at second.
Note: Players should not let the tying run get into scoring position at second base by throwing to the plate when the runner is likely to score or has held up at third.

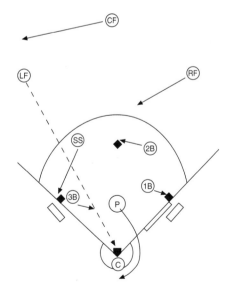

Situation: Single to center with a runner on second, or with runners on second and third.

Objective: The play at the plate and holding the batter to a single.

Pitcher: Backs up home plate.
Catcher: Covers home plate. If the throw comes toward the plate, the catcher prepares to take it and instructs the first baseman whether or not to cut it off.
First baseman: Moves near the pitcher's mound, directly in line with the center fielder and home plate. Follows the catcher's instructions to cut off the throw or let it go through.
Second baseman: Covers first.
Third baseman: Covers third.
Shortstop: Covers second and takes the throw if it comes there. It may come from the center fielder, the first baseman, or the catcher.
Left and right fielders: Back up the batted ball.
Center fielder: Fields the ball and throws to the plate.
Note: Players should not let the tying run get into scoring position at second base by throwing to the plate when the runner is likely to score or has held up at third.

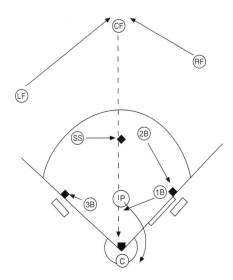

Situation: Single to right with a runner on second, or with runners on first and second, runners on second and third, or with the bases loaded.

Objective: The play at the plate and holding the batter to a single.

Pitcher: Backs up home plate.
Catcher: Covers home plate. If the throw comes toward the plate, the catcher prepares to take it and instructs the first baseman whether or not to cut it.
First baseman: Moves near the pitcher's mound, directly in line with the right fielder and home plate. Follows the catcher's instructions to cut off the throw or let it go through.
Second baseman: Covers first after the throw has been made to the plate.
Third baseman: Covers third.
Shortstop: Covers second and takes the throw if it comes there. It may come from the right fielder, the first baseman, or the catcher.
Left fielder: Moves toward the infield in case of an overthrow or rundown.
Center fielder: Backs up the batted ball.
Right fielder: Fields the ball and throws to the plate.
Note: Players should not let the tying run get into scoring position at second base by throwing to the plate when the runner is likely to score or has held up at third base.

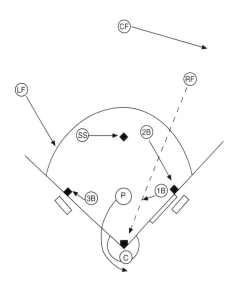

Fly Balls

On all fly balls to the outfield with a runner on third, the first baseman is the cutoff for all throws to the plate. The play will be the same when there are no outs and one out.

Situation: Possible sacrifice fly to the outfield with a runner on third.

Objective: The play at the plate.

Pitcher: Backs up home plate.
Catcher: Covers home plate and prepares to take the throw. When the throw comes toward the plate, the catcher instructs the first baseman whether or not to cut it off.
First baseman: Moves near the pitcher's mound, directly in line with the outfielder and home plate. Follows the catcher's instructions to cut off the throw or let it go through.
Second baseman: Covers first.
Third baseman: Covers third.
Shortstop: Covers second.
Left fielder: Backs up center field, third base, or catches the ball and throws home.
Center fielder: Backs up the batted ball or catches the ball and throws home.
Right fielder: Backs up center field or catches the ball and throws home.
Note: The location of the ball determines which outfielder fields it. In the diagram, the center fielder makes the catch.

Situation: Possible sacrifice fly to left with runners on first and third.

Objective: The play at the plate and holding the other runner at first.

Pitcher: Backs up home plate.
Catcher: Covers home plate and prepares to take the throw. When the throw comes toward the plate, the catcher instructs the first baseman whether or not to cut it off.
First baseman: Moves near the pitcher's mound, directly in line with the left fielder and home plate. Follows the catcher's instructions to cut off the throw or let it go through. If the first baseman cuts the throw because there is no play at home, she can hold the runner at first.
Second baseman: Covers first.
Third baseman: Covers third.
Shortstop: Covers second.
Left fielder: Catches the ball and throws home, or if there is no play at home, throws to second.
Center fielder: Backs up the batted ball.
Right fielder: Moves toward the infield in case of a rundown or an overthrow at second.
Note: An accurate throw and a properly positioned cutoff player will keep the runner on first from moving to second. On a sacrifice fly to right or center with runners on first and third, the defense is the same.

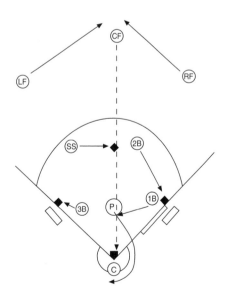

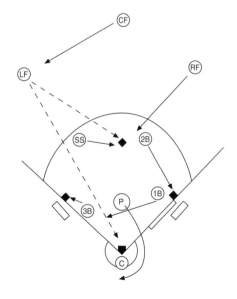

Situation: Possible sacrifice fly to center with runners on second and third, or with the bases loaded.

Objective: The play at the plate or the play at third.

Pitcher: Backs up home plate or possibly third base.
Catcher: Covers home plate and prepares to take the throw. Instructs the first baseman whether or not to cut off the throw.
First baseman: Moves near the pitcher's mound, directly in line with the center fielder and home plate. Following the catcher's instructions, the first baseman cuts off the throw to hold the runner or lets it go through.
Second baseman: Covers first.
Third baseman: Covers third.
Shortstop: Covers second.
Left and right fielders: Back up the batted ball.
Center fielder: Catches the ball and throws home, or if there is no play at home, throws to third.
Note: An accurate throw and a properly positioned cutoff player will keep the runner on second from moving to third.

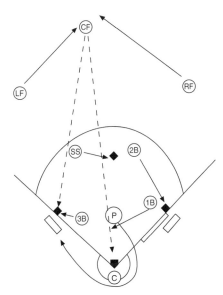

Situation: Possible sacrifice fly to right with runners on second and third, or with the bases loaded.

Objective: The play at the plate or the play at third.

Pitcher: Backs up home plate or possibly third base.
Catcher: Covers home plate and prepares to take the throw. Instructs the first baseman whether or not to cut off the throw.
First baseman: Moves near the pitcher's mound, directly in line with the right fielder and home plate. Follows the catcher's instructions to cut off the throw or let it go through.
Second baseman: Covers first.
Third baseman: Covers third. If the throw comes toward third, the third baseman prepares to take it and instructs the shortstop whether or not to cut it off.
Shortstop: (1) Moves directly in line between the right fielder and third base. Follows the third baseman's instructions to cut off the throw or let it go through. (2) Covers second.
Left fielder: Moves toward third in case of a rundown or overthrow.
Center fielder: Backs up the batted ball.
Right fielder: Catches the ball and throws home, or if there is no play at home, throws to third.
Note: An accurate throw and a properly positioned cutoff player will keep the runner on second from moving to third. On a possible sacrifice fly to left with runners on second and third, the defense would remain the same.

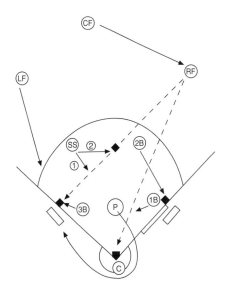

Sacrifice Bunts

On sacrifice bunts, the catcher calls the play when she is not fielding the ball. When she is fielding the ball, the shortstop calls the play.

Situation: Sacrifice bunt with a runner on first.

Objective: A force play at second or the sure out at first. The infielders would make a play on the base runner going to first if they have the opportunity to get her out.

Pitcher: Breaks toward the plate after delivering the pitch. If she fields the bunt, she follows the catcher's instructions and throws to second or to first.
Catcher: If possible, fields the bunt and makes the play—either to second or to first—or instructs the infielder who picks up the bunt where to throw. Covers third if the third baseman fields the ball.
First baseman: Breaks in and covers the area between the foul line and the mound. If she fields the bunt, she follows the catcher's instructions and throws to second or first.
Second baseman: Covers first.
Third baseman: Breaks in and covers the area between the foul line and the mound. If she fields the bunt, she follows the catcher's instructions and throws to second or first.
Shortstop: Covers second.
Left fielder: Moves toward the infield in case of a throw to third (she is in the backup position).
Center fielder: Backs up second.
Right fielder: Backs up the throw to first.

Situation: Sacrifice bunt with runners on first and second.

Objective: A force play at third or the sure out at first.

Pitcher: Breaks toward the plate after delivering the pitch. If she fields the bunt, she follows the catcher's instructions and throws to third or to first.
Catcher: If possible, fields the bunt and makes the play—either to third or to first—or instructs the infielder who picks up the bunt where to throw.
First baseman: Breaks in and covers the area between the foul line and the mound. If she fields the bunt, she follows the catcher's instructions and throws to third or to first.
Second baseman: Covers first.
Third baseman: Breaks in and covers the area between the foul line and the mound. If she fields the bunt, she follows the catcher's instructions and throws to third or to first.
Shortstop: Covers third.
Left fielder: Moves toward the infield in case of a throw to third (she is in the backup position).
Center fielder: Covers second.
Right fielder: Backs up the throw to first.

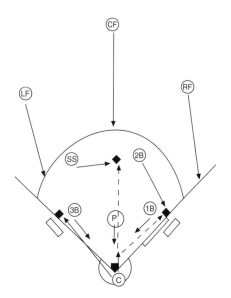

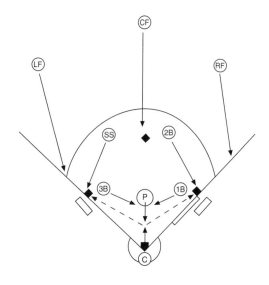

Double Steals

Situation: Double steal with runners on first and third.

Objective: To get an out and prevent the run from scoring.

Pitcher: Delivers the pitch, moves off the line of the throw to second, and if there is a rundown with the runner at third, backs up the catcher.
Catcher: Receives the pitch, looks at the runner on third to freeze her, throws down to second, and prepares to cover the plate and receive the throw from the infielder.
First baseman: (1) Moves to defend against the bunt and then (2) moves to cover first in case of a rundown.
Second baseman: Moves into the cutoff position an equal distance from the mound and second, just slightly off the catcher's throwing line to second base. She has three options: (1) Decoy the runner at third by making a fake attempt to catch the ball and letting the throw go through; (2) Catch the ball and either throw to the shortstop covering second or make a play on the runner at third; (3) Catch the ball if the throw from the catcher is wide.
Third baseman: (1) Moves to defend against the bunt and then (2) moves to cover third in case

the throw comes there from the catcher or the second baseman.
Shortstop: Covers second.
Left fielder: Backs up the throw to third from the catcher or the second baseman.
Center fielder: Backs up the throw to second and is ready for a possible rundown.
Right fielder: Breaks for first as soon as the catcher receives the pitch and the runner breaks for second to help on a possible rundown between first and second.

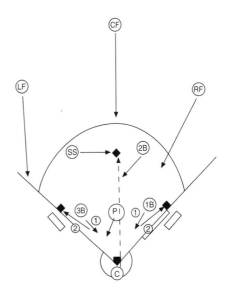

CHAPTER 13

PITCHING FUNDAMENTALS

There is a direct relationship between the effectiveness of the pitcher and the outcome of a game. That alone shows the responsibilities put on the shoulders of a pitcher. The pitcher spends countless hours practicing both the mental and physical parts of pitching so that when she takes the mound, she is in control. The tone of the game is set by the pitcher.

I look for several different attributes in a pitcher. I like to see one who runs to the circle as if she cannot wait to get out there. I want her to show poise and confidence on the mound. After all, the pitcher controls a great deal of the game and has a large responsibility—she is the only player who touches the ball every pitch. Her poise and choice of emotions on the mound will help set the tone of the game. Pitchers need to have strong personalities and resilience to overcome a momentary failure.

Problem	Drill	Page
FASTBALL		
High throwing shoulder	Knee Drill, Ball on Ground	178
	Knee Drill, Ball Under Leg	178
	Under Rope or Band	182
	Multicircle Path	179
	Mirror Drill	179
Crunching	Two Step	182
	Mirror Drill	179
Bowling	Walk-Throughs	182
	Two Step	182
	Mirror Drill	179
Weak leg drive	Speed Drill	180
	Sprinter Drill	182

(continued)

(continued)

Problem	Drill	Page
FASTBALL *(continued)*		
Throwing arm not in a straight circle	Multicircle Path	179
	Mirror Drill	179
Timing	Walk-Throughs	182
	Two Step	182
Improper posture and weight shift	One-Legged Drill	179
	Two Step	182
Glove off power line	Glove Slap	178
CHANGE-UP		
Weak leg drive	Speed Drill	180
	Sprinter Drill	182
Arch in the path of the ball	Under Rope or Band	182
DROP BALL		
Crunching	Two Step	182
	Mirror Drill	179
Lack of wrist snap	Drop Ball Drill	177
No leg drive	Two Step	182
Improper body angle	One-Legged Drill	179
	Two Step	182
Incorrect spin	Spinner	181
	Ball on Wooden Dowel	177
Improper posture and weight shift	One-Legged Drill	179
	Two Step	182
RISE BALL		
High throwing shoulder	Knee Drill, Ball on Ground	178
	Knee Drill, Ball Under Leg	178
	Under Rope or Band	182
	Multicircle Path	179
Crunching	Two Step	182
Lack of wrist snap	Rise Ball Drill	180
Incorrect spin	Spinner	181
	Ball on Wooden Dowel	177
Improper body angle	One-Legged Drill	179
	Fall Back	177
Close of hips	Fall Back	177
Improper posture and weight shift	One-Legged Drill	179
	Two Step	182

Problem	Drill	Page
CURVEBALL		
Timing	Walk-Throughs	182
	Two Step	182
Incorrect spin	Spinner	181
	Ball on Wooden Dowel	177
Body lead	Two-Knee Drill	178
	Mirror Drill	179
Improper posture and weight shift	One-Legged Drill	179
	Two Step	182
SCREWBALL		
Timing	Walk-Throughs	182
	Two Step	182
Improper posture and weight shift	One-Legged Drill	179
	Two Step	182
Incorrect spin	Spinner	181
	Ball on Wooden Dowel	177

PITCHING PLAN

Coaches' pitching plans and strategies have changed throughout the last couple of years in response to the changes in the sport of fastpitch. There have been more hits and higher earned run averages because of the development of the athlete, high-tech bats, and a new core in the college ball. With these changes in the offense, coaches have had to make adjustments on the mound. In addition, in most programs around the country, there has been an increase in the number of pitchers on staff, and this has also changed the strategy of the game.

You must have a plan for attacking each batter, but you also need to adjust as the at-bat unfolds. For instance, the pitch called may not go where it was intended to go, or the batter may not swing at a pitch that the pitcher intended her to swing at. When deciding what your pitcher should throw to a specific batter, you can get hints from the batter's warm-up swings, previous at-bats, and how she handles the bat and her body once she is in the box. See figure 13.1 for a pitching chart containing suggestions about which pitches are best against batters with specific characteristics. To create strike-

outs, ground balls, and pop-ups, your pitchers should use a constant mix of pitches that are in, out, up, down, fast, and off speed. The main goal is to throw off the batter's timing.

I want our pitchers to have great control of three pitches, one being an off-speed pitch. Many pitchers throw with an average command of four or more pitches and never quite get control of the game. A common progression for learning pitches would be to learn the fastball, change-up, then drop ball. After that, pitchers usually choose between the rise, curve, or screwball. A pitcher should learn mechanics first, then speed, and then control.

I do not call the pitches during a game unless a catcher needs the help. As a coach on the bench, it is difficult to tell the exact location where the pitch was thrown—and therefore difficult to call the next pitch. Also, you do not want your catcher to be a puppet behind the plate. She needs to be in the game completely and in charge of the whole field. Calling the game on her own may give her the mental edge she needs to have that authority. On the other hand, a young catcher may need a little stress taken off to be able to handle her other duties, such as receiving the pitch and calling the correct

Figure 13.1 Pitching Chart

Stance and characteristics	Optimal pitch(es)
Up in front of the box	Rise ball, fastest pitch, change-up
In back of the box	Drop ball, breaking ball
Crowding the plate	Rise ball or fastball high in or out, inside curve or screwball, drop inside, rise inside
Off the plate	Drop outside, curveball or fastball outside
Closed stride	Inside rise, inside drop
Open stride	Outside drop, outside curve
Hands held close to the body	Rise ball or fastball high inside or out, drop inside
Hands above the strike zone	Drop ball or low fastball in or out
Long stride	Rise ball or fastball high in or out, change-up
Hitch	Rise ball or fastball high in or out, change-up or off-speed pitch
Lunges	Curveball or fastball outside, change-up or off-speed pitch
Sweep swing	Inside curve or screwball, rise ball in or out
Big swing	Change-up
Game situations	**Pitch selection**
Runner on first, bunt situation	Rise ball or fastball high in or out, inside
Runner on second, right-handed batter	Drop inside or low fastball inside
Runner on second, left-handed batter	Drop outside or low fastball outside
Runner on third, right-handed batter, squeeze is on	Rise, pitchout, drop inside, or low fastball
Runner on third, left-handed batter	Drop ball or low fastball outside
Suspected squeeze or suicide bunt, hit-and run, slap and steal, or bunt and steal	Pitchout
Slapper	Outside change, rise inside, drop ball or low fastball outside, inside curve or screwball
Aggressive batter	Off-speed pitch, change-up
Pull hitter	Drop outside, curveball or fastball outside, change-up or off-speed pitch inside

bag. Either way, you should work with your battery and review situations so that everyone is on the same page regarding how to pitch in a given situation.

MECHANICS

Pitching style is very individual. You should allow your pitchers to create their own style. However, be sure to teach them the following pitching fundamentals, which must be consistent among all pitchers in order for them to be successful.

• **Power line**—To create an efficient throwing pattern, a pitcher should throw on a power line or in a line of force. The best way to teach the power line technique is to put down tape (or draw a line) from the middle of the rubber to home plate, and then observe as the pitcher goes through her pitching motion. The motion should begin and finish on the tape. If the stride foot and glove hand do not start and finish on the power line, she will create an inefficient motion toward first or third instead of toward the catcher.

• **Leg drive and stride**—Leg drive is one of the most common deficiencies in young pitchers. The back leg needs to drive out and off from the mound. It should be mobile and move with the body. The body should come up and over the toe of the back leg, and the toe should bear no weight through the drive. If the push-off foot completely turns (to 90 degrees), there will be a hesitation in motion, and this will kill the back leg power. The push-off foot would have to turn again, creating a break in the motion. If the back foot stays anchored (or pivots to 90 degrees), the stride is limited; this may promote injury to the drive knee. The knee of the drive leg, or back leg, should be directed toward the catcher. The front leg should remain flexed all the way through the pitch. The back foot glides off the rubber to maintain the same distance from the front foot no matter how long or short the pitcher's stride is. An effective way to add strength to the leg drive is to use a harness to resist and assist as the pitcher is driving off the mound.

• **Arm motion**—In the windup, the arm must start loose. There should be a natural arm circle, relaxed on the way up and accelerated on the

During practice, a pitcher should rehearse driving off the rubber efficiently. Her drive foot should push up and over the toe, becoming mobile with her body.

way down. The pitcher should have a slightly bent arm that extends through release. The follow-through should yield a loose arm out and away from the body, with the wrist turned and the fingers dangling. The glove arm must stay on the power line or it will create a left-to-right motion that works against the pitcher.

When the pitcher's body performs with all its parts working together as an engine, it will produce the most efficient pitching style for the desired pitch and speed. You want your pitchers to be able to throw accurately, throw fast, and throw for a considerable amount of time. For these things to occur, the pitcher must work on her motion daily to keep it efficient and to give her body time to learn through muscle memory.

The following are descriptions of the mechanics for six different pitches. Although each pitcher has her own style, mechanics should be consistent from pitcher to pitcher for optimal performance.

Fastball

In the fastball grip, the ball should feel sturdy and comfortable in the pitcher's fingers. The middle finger rests on the seam, and the thumb is on the seam directly across from the middle finger. The pitcher may use a two-seam (horseshoe) or four-seam (C) rotation grip (see figure 13.2). The ball must rest in the fingers of the pitcher's hand, not deep in the hand. If the ball is deep in the hand, it will not allow for a good wrist snap or a fast-spinning rotation.

Figure 13.2 Fastball four-seam rotation grip.

At foot-to-ground contact, the body is in an upright position. If 12:00 is above the pitcher's head and 6:00 is the ground, her glove should be at 3:00, pointing at the catcher, and her throwing hand should be between 10:00 and 12:00, pointing toward second base. The weight should be on the front leg through release.

When throwing the ball high in or high out, the pitcher should adjust the step just left or right of the power line—perhaps half an inch (1.2 centimeters)—and release farther out in front of her body. When throwing low in or low out, the pitcher again adjusts her foot on the power line and then releases sooner than she would on a higher pitch.

As the hand reaches the bottom of the arc, the wrist should be cocked back with the heel of the hand leading to the catcher. Upon release, the wrist and fingers should snap through the ball. The last finger to leave the seam should be the middle finger. The pitch is thrown with a follow-through out and away from the body. To aid in wrist snap, your pitchers can use a 16-inch (40.6-centimeter) softball during their warm-ups and a weighted ball to develop strength.

Change-Up

The change-up is one of the most important pitches in a pitcher's repertoire. It can be deadly when the change-up is thrown to look the same as the pitcher's other pitches, but then approaches the strike zone at a speed about 15 miles (24 kilometers) per hour slower than the batter expected. The objective of the change-up is to catch the batter off balance. To ensure this, the pitcher tries to throw the pitch with little change in her motion and keeps the grip hidden in the glove until the motion begins. There are many ways to throw this pitch, including the backhand flip change, knuckleball change, and shove. The following describes the backhand flip.

The advantage of the backhand flip change-up is that the ball is held like a fastball so the batter cannot see a difference in the pitcher's grip. The windup is the same as a fastball until the pitcher's arm reaches just before the hip. At that time, the hand flips completely around so the back of the hand is facing the catcher. Once the arm passes the hip, the hand should just open to allow the ball to pop out (see figure 13.3).

Figure 13.3 Flip change-up release.

A common problem with the change-up is a pitcher reducing her arm speed to try to slow the ball down. To help with this, you can use speed drills that involve alternating a fastball with a change-up during the drill. Allowing the pitcher to see the difference on video can also be an effective way to correct this problem.

Drop Ball

There are two basic types of drop balls: (1) a peel drop, which involves "peeling" the ball off the fingers similar to a fastball but with a shorter stride and with the body angled toward the catcher, and (2) a turnover drop, which involves turning over the wrist (similar to turning a door handle at the pitcher's side) to create the downspin. The following describes a turnover drop.

The spin created by different grips of the turnover drop pitch can be either a two-seam (horseshoe) or four-seam (C) spin. The first common grip is a split finger with the first finger on the side of a seam and the middle finger on the side of the next seam (see figure 13.4). The thumb can rest directly under the ball or off to the side. The other common grip is the index and middle finger right next to each other, pushing against a seam. The thumb should rest on the same side of the ball as the fingers.

As the pitcher drives off the mound, the body once again comes up and over the toes. The stride should remain strong, but the step should be a bit shorter than the step when throwing a fastball. At foot-to-ground contact, the body needs to be over the top of the stride leg in a lean (not a bend) toward the catcher. The pitcher should have her hand underneath the ball with

the fingers pointing away from the body as her arm nears her hip during the arm circle.

The pitcher begins the rollover, or turnover, of the hand when it passes her hip. The release of the pitch should be from top to bottom, creating a downspin or topspin. The body drives through the front leg. At the end of the pitch, the pitcher should follow through down and loose (see figure 13.5).

Figure 13.5 Drop ball finish.

Rise Ball

The rise ball may be the most difficult pitch to learn. Many pitchers who claim to have a rise ball actually only throw a high fastball because they are lacking the most important factor of the pitch—a backward spin. Once the spin is mastered, the pitcher can work on strength and speed of the wrist and forearm to generate power through the pitch.

There are two common grips for the rise ball: (1) digging the index finger into the ball and (2) curving the index finger so that it is split apart from the middle finger. The objective of these grips is to get the ball spinning in

Figure 13.4 Drop ball two-seam grip.

a backward rotation so that when the air hits the seams, the seams push off the air and the ball rises. The C grip or the horseshoe grip will work with either of these finger positions. (See figure 13.6.)

At foot-to-ground contact, the body should be angled back away from the catcher, and the upper body should be in a slight lean to the throwing side. The hips should stay behind the front leg, and the shoulder should stay behind the hips. The glove arm must remain on the power line.

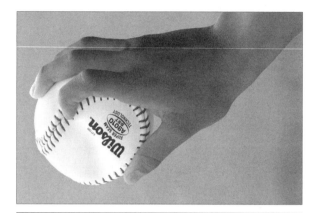

Figure 13.6 Rise ball grip.

Two different release techniques are used when throwing a rise ball: the cupping technique and the wrist-cocking technique. During the cupping technique, the wrist cups slightly during the arc, and at release, the hand just slides underneath and past the ball. In the cocking technique, the wrist bends back through the arc. When the hand reaches the bottom of the arc, the fingers should be on top of the ball with the palm facing outward away from the body. At release, the wrist makes a full snap down and around the ball. On release in both techniques, the elbow should be the same distance away from the plate as the hand. I tell my pitchers to lead with their elbow. If the elbow is farther from the plate, the hand will turn inward and cause the ball to corkscrew instead of spin backward. The hips should not fully close on the rise ball, and the throwing shoulder should remain slightly lower than the glove-side shoulder. Closing the shoulders will cause the elbow to go to a more comfortable position toward the rear of the circle so that it is farther from the

plate than the hand (corkscrew). The pitcher's posture should remain angled away from the catcher, with her weight back behind the stride leg. (See figure 13.7.)

Figure 13.7 Rise ball release.

Curveball

A curveball must attain a flat, horizontal spin for it to break suddenly and aggressively. Without the spin, the ball will just float to an outside part of the strike zone, a pitch that is fairly easy to hit.

The curveball grip can be the same as for the rise ball, except the index finger pulls around the ball instead of down and the fingers should be facing up. The ball must remain in the fingertips, which all pull around the ball.

To throw the curveball, the pitcher's body should be tilted in the direction of the desired ball movement at foot-to-ground contact. The foot should be positioned slightly across the power line. The shoulders should stay back at release. Upon release, the body can fall in the direction of the lean.

The release point for the curve is a later release than for the other pitches, occurring in front of the body just as the hand crosses the hip. At release, the hand should be under the ball with fingers pointing up. The fingers then pull around the ball. A twist of the trunk is not necessary; the wrist snap is the key. (See figure 13.8.) An effective way for a pitcher to practice the curveball is to kneel on both knees at a 45-degree angle to the catcher. This isolates the upper body and allows the pitcher to work on the spin without being concerned about the movement of the lower body.

Figure 13.8 Curveball release.

Screwball

The grip for the screwball varies from pitcher to pitcher. I suggest having your pitchers try all kinds of grips until they find one that will yield the correct spin. One option is for the pitcher to put the index finger or middle finger along the narrow seam (for a two-seam rotation) or the wide seams (for a four-seam rotation). If the pitcher chooses her middle finger, the index finger should be right next to it. Another option is for the pitcher to use the same grip that she uses on the rise ball.

To release the ball on the correct angle to the plate, the stride foot must land to the left of the power line for a right-hander. This allows the ball to start at a more severe angle to the plate and finish on the front inside corner. If the pitcher does not create the angle, the ball will finish too far inside. At foot-to-ground contact, the body should be in a lean toward the direction the pitcher wants the ball to go, with her weight over the front foot. If the pitcher feels as if she will fall to her right, she is probably in the correct position.

At the bottom of the arc, the arm and wrist will have an inside-out approach to the release. The pitcher can concentrate on bringing her hand *in* to the glove knee and then start a twisting motion of the hand, moving it *out* away from her body. The ball should come off her index finger or middle finger (depending on which one she chooses to put on a seam), and if she is right-handed, the ball will spin clockwise. Because of the lean and the body weight transfer, after the release of the ball, the pitcher's body will inevitably fall to the right. (See figure 13.9.)

PITCHERS' DAILY ROUTINE

Even though there are no standard pitch counts, there are a few general guidelines to follow. Younger pitchers can generally throw 50 to 100 pitches three or four times per week. Once the pitcher's stamina increases, she can practice longer and throw more pitches. Coaches must spend a lot of time working on spins and mechanics with younger pitchers. I would suggest beginning each practice with spin work. The more the pitchers understand the spins and physics behind the pitches, the more they can become their own best teachers. After the spin work is complete, the pitchers can move back to behind the mound and begin throwing lightly underhand until loose. Once they are loose, the pitchers can begin throwing their pitches hard.

Figure 13.9 Screwball release.

Older pitchers can throw between 100 and 200 pitches five or six times a week. Their routine should also incorporate spin drills, but the intensity and length of the workout will increase. After a warm-up that involves pitching from a long distance, they will begin working from the mound on the designated pitch or pitches. Our pitchers' routines also include the use of weighted, light, and 16-inch (40.6-centimeter) softballs. These are very effective aids in the development of a correct, strong, and quick snap of the wrist. I try to end practice with speed drills and a run.

The quality of a pitching practice is more important than the length or frequency. Do not

allow a pitcher to continue to throw a pitch if her technique is wrong. Help her to break it down, work on the spin and mechanics of the pitch, and gradually work back up to full speed. On the flip side, the more a pitcher practices at slow speeds, the more the body remembers that speed. You should plan your practices so that they include a good mix of mechanics work, full speed and distance work, and speed drills. Figure 13.10 presents a plan that can guide you over the course of a season.

PITCHING DRILLS

In this section, I present several different pitching drills (and, in some cases, variations for those drills). Some drills are for specific pitches while others can apply to all pitches. In my program, we set aside specific time for the pitchers to work on these drills during practice. I suggest that if a pitcher requests more time to throw, you give it to her, but make sure that your pitchers get time to do their position-specific drills.

Figure 13.10 Seasonal Focus for Pitching Practice

Off-season	Preseason	In-season
Very little live pitching	Speed training	Target practice
Drills, drills, drills	Target practice	Speed training
Conditioning and weight training with emphasis on the core, rotator cuff, legs, triceps, and forearms	Pitch movement	Conditioning and weight training
	Refining spins	Spin work
	Refining motions	
Speed training	Counts and live pitching	
Pitch learning and spin work	Mental training	
Changes in motion (for example, trying to correct a crow hop)	Conditioning and weight training	
Videotaping		
Mental training—broad scope		

Ball on Wooden Dowel

Purpose: To aid the pitcher in identifying and throwing with the correct spin.

Procedure: Drill a hole through the middle of a ball. Place a wooden dowel through the hole. A coach or partner holds the dowel, while the pitcher (in release position) spins the ball around it.

Rise: For a rise ball spin, the dowel should start and remain parallel to the ground, pointing at the third baseman. The hand action should be a snap in the clockwise direction for a right-hander.
Drop: For a drop ball, the dowel should start and remain parallel to the ground, pointing at the third baseman. The hand action should be a snap in the counterclockwise direction for a right-hander.
Curve: For a curveball, the dowel should start and remain perpendicular to the ground, with the long end—the end without the ball—pointing to the sky.
Screw: For the screwball, the dowel should start and remain parallel to the ground, pointing at the catcher.

Drop Ball Drill

Purpose: To reinforce the correct mechanics for a drop ball (getting on top of the ball and snapping it into the ground).

Procedure: The pitcher has a bucket of 30 balls (they can be softies). She stands approximately three feet (91 centimeters) away from a catch net, tarp, fence, or experienced catcher. The pitcher goes through her pitching motion and exaggerates her release of the drop ball by snapping it directly into the ground, trying to achieve a high bounce into the net. Let each pitcher throw three buckets of balls.

Fall Back

Purpose: To assist the pitcher in keeping her hips open and weight back through the release of the rise ball.

Procedure: The pitcher goes through her motion for a rise ball, and after release, she falls straight back and catches her body with her drag foot. Her position should be facing the third baseman.

Glove Slap

Purpose: To help the pitcher keep her glove on the power line.

Procedure: A player or coach stands with a glove on the power line in front of the pitcher. The pitcher goes through her motion, and on the way down, she slaps the glove with her own glove (see figure 13.11).

Figure 13.11   Glove Slap drill.

Two-Knee Drill

Purpose: To work on upper body mechanics and spin for the curveball.

Procedure: The pitcher kneels on both knees at a 45-degree angle to her catcher. The pitcher works on the spin from release position and keeps the body behind the wrist snap. Add arm circle.

Knee Drill, Ball on Ground

Purpose: To work on relaxing the pitching motion (the shoulder specifically) and keeping the throwing shoulder from rising higher than the glove shoulder.

Procedure: The pitcher kneels on her throwing-side knee. The ball is placed on the ground right next to her knee. The pitcher starts with her hand in front of the ball, goes through a smooth pitching arc with her arm (without any extra motion), and slaps the ball to a partner or net. If her shoulder rises, she will not be able to reach the ball with her fingers. (See figure 13.12.)

Variation: Knee Drill, Ball Under Leg. The pitcher kneels on her throwing-side knee. Her body is turned sideways with the outside of her stride leg facing the catcher. With a smooth delivery, she pitches the ball under the stride leg (left leg if the pitcher is right-handed) to a catcher or net.

Figure 13.12   Knee drill, ball on ground.

Mirror Drill

Purpose: To teach the body muscle memory of the proper mechanics.

Procedure: The pitcher will need her glove (for balance purposes) and a full-length mirror. She stands four to five feet (121 to 152 centimeters) from the mirror. The pitcher goes through the proper pitching motion at a slow speed while watching and evaluating her performance in the mirror. Each pitch should be performed 20 to 30 times to help the body learn the motion.

One-Legged Drill

Purpose: To help the pitcher learn proper weight shift over the front foot for different pitches.

Procedure for drop ball: With her back foot off the ground, and all her weight on the front foot, the pitcher throws a drop ball from the K position without the step.

Procedure for rise ball: With her front foot off the ground, and all her weight on the back leg, the pitcher proceeds to spin a rise ball from the K position without the step, trying to maintain balance.

Procedure for screwball: With her back foot off the ground, all her weight on her front foot, and her body in a lean to the right (for a right-hander), the pitcher practices the release of the screwball from the K position. Remember that the pitcher should fall in the direction of the break.

Multicircle Path

Purpose: To work on a smooth arm circle throughout the pitching motion.

Procedure: The pitcher stands in the K position, or foot-to-ground contact position (see figure 13.13), and delivers five loose and fast arm circles toward the direction of her catcher. On the sixth circle, she releases the pitch. The sixth arm circle should feel the same to the pitcher as the ones without the release.

Figure 13.13 Foot-to-ground contact, or K position, in the pitching motion.

Rise Ball Drill

Purpose: To reinforce the correct mechanics for a rise ball (getting under the ball, using backspin, using a long arm, keeping the body angled away from the catcher).

Procedure: Partners stand six feet (1.8 meters) apart with one ball. The pitcher stands in the K position, with her back heel off the ground and her body angled back behind and under the ball. She finishes her pitching motion while working on her rise ball technique. She wants to be sure to keep her hand cocked and to get backward rotation on the ball. The player receiving the ball should be squatting to allow the pitcher to get in the habit of throwing to the correct zone.

Variation: The pitcher gets down on her right knee with her left leg extending out (or in the case of a left-handed pitcher, her right leg). Her hips should be open, and her pitching arm should be straight up. From here, her arm should come down and pass her hips, and then her release occurs (see figure 13.14). This variation isolates the snap so the focus is on correct spin.

Speed Drill

Purpose: To work on developing pitch speed by working the legs and arms.

Procedure: Set aside a certain number of balls you will be using with the pitcher that day (for example, you may want to start with 10). The pitcher should start approximately 50 feet (15.2 meters) away from her catcher. The drill starts upon the toss of the ball from a partner to the pitcher. The pitcher walks into the pitch, drives, throws to a target, and then sprints back to the starting spot while the tosser is feeding her ball number two. The drill continues until all the balls have been pitched. The objective is to get through the specified number of balls as quickly and powerfully as she can using her legs to drive out as far as she can.

Variation: Pick an allotted time and see how many pitches she can throw.

Figure 13.14 Rise Ball drill.

Spinner

Purpose: To aid the pitcher in identifying and throwing the correct spin.

Procedure: A "Spinner" is a pitching tool (developed by Cheri Kempf at Club K) that is the same weight and diameter as a softball but is in the shape of a hockey puck. For all pitches, the Spinner is received by a catcher. It is meant to be used just as a softball, but this creates a visual tool for those learning the spin.

Rise ball: Upon correct release, the Spinner should have a straight up-and-down spin. (See figure 13.15.)

Drop ball: The pitcher kneels on her throwing-side leg, and the Spinner is placed (on end) on the ground next to the pitcher's leg. The pitcher should start with her hand on the top of the Spinner and roll it to a catcher to achieve the correct topspin. It can also be pitched down to the ground. With correct spin, the Spinner will bounce and spin straight to the catcher.

Curveball: With correct spin, the Spinner will rotate from left to right parallel to the ground. (See figure 13.16.) It can also be performed overhead.

Screwball: With correct spin, the Spinner will rotate clockwise with the flat surface of the Spinner facing the pitcher.

Figure 13.15   Rise ball with Spinner at release.

Figure 13.16   Curveball with Spinner at release.

Sprinter Drill

Purpose: To improve and strengthen the pitcher's leg drive.

Procedure: The pitcher should start with her feet on the mound but in a sprinter's position (as if in the starting block). Her body should be bent over her front leg with her chest almost touching the knee. The pitcher's knees are bent, and her hands are dangling next to the ground. Place a mark for reference near where the edge of a pitching circle would be. On command, the pitcher must drive out and try to reach this reference point, pushing up and over her toe and allowing her push-off leg and foot to glide behind her. (The up-and-over-the-toe motion is the action a person takes while walking.) At foot-to-ground contact, she is to hold this position and evaluate. (See figure 13.17.)

Figure 13.17 Sprinter drill start.

Under Rope or Band

Purpose: To work on a smooth pitch delivery and keep the shoulder in the correct position.

Procedure: String an elastic band or rope across the delivery area in front of the pitcher at about thigh height. The pitcher must deliver the pitch under the rope, keeping her shoulder from coming up during the delivery. This is particularly good for practicing the rise ball.

Up and Over Toe

Purpose: To help prevent a 90-degree turn of the pitcher's drive foot resulting in a crow hop and reduced power. This drill helps improve the pitcher's drive off the mound.

Procedure: This drill is done without release of the ball to keep the focus on the legs, not on the target or speed. The pitcher performs her pitching motion, coming up and over the toe in a smooth drag and driving under control off the mound to a specified point on the ground. This motion is the motion a person uses while walking. As she gets better at it, she will add more power, speed, and distance.

Walk-Throughs

Purpose: To promote a smooth pitch delivery.

Procedure: The pitcher is positioned about 50 feet (15.2 meters) away from the catcher. The pitcher begins walking toward the catcher. She takes approximately three steps before she steps into her pitching motion and delivers the ball to the catcher with leg drive but without breaking stride. The pitcher wants the ball to reach the catcher at a certain spot. She can use this drill to work on all of her pitches.

Two Step

Purpose: To help pitchers learn how to land in the correct foot-to-ground contact position.

Procedure: At three-quarters speed, the pitcher begins the pitch and then stops at foot-to-ground contact. The coach helps the pitcher evaluate her body position for the specific pitch being worked on. If it is incorrect, the pitcher makes the adjustment and then finishes the pitch.

MENTAL APPROACH

Coaches should not use a cookie-cutter mental approach with their pitchers, because everyone is different and will respond differently when faced with a challenge. Pitchers have an advantage because a great batter is one who gets a hit 4 out of 10 times, and the majority of the batters they face will not be that successful. The pitcher will be successful at forcing the batter to commit an out over 60 percent of the time. Knowing these facts helps the pitcher feel a little more at ease and definitely more confident.

I talk to the pitchers about being committed to the pitches they throw. If they believe a pitch is not right for a certain situation or if they feel a pitch is not working well, they are probably right. Because they are not committed to the pitch, it will most likely fail. To be successful, they must first believe they can be.

The advice I give the most is that the pitchers must remember that they do not have control of what goes on around them. If it is cold or rainy, or the fans are heckling them, or even if the shortstop has dropped two balls, they cannot control these things. The best thing the pitchers can do is control how *they* respond to what is going on around them. I tell them to shrink their focus to just their catcher and the task at hand. They should try to focus on throwing one pitch at a time. If they can bring their focus into that tunnel, they will be in control of the one thing that they can control—their performance.

A pitcher needs to expect to pitch every game so that mentally she will be ready to go. But our pitchers do not know for sure who is pitching until game day. At the beginning of warm-ups, we let our entire pitching staff know who is starting and who will be in relief and in what order. It is then up to the pitching staff to get themselves physically and mentally ready to go.

I want my relief pitchers to be ready at any pitch of the game. It is up to them to prepare so that all I have to do is look in the bull pen and they are ready to come in. They do understand, however, that as the game unfolds, our plan might change.

One of the most important things that our pitchers do to prepare both mentally and physically is running. Running offers much more than just physical benefits (conditioning) and has made our pitchers mentally tough. We put aside time for them to run in practice and also encourage them to run on their own. Running strengthens their legs and builds their endurance. It is as much mental as it is physical. If the pitcher can see the way her mind can control her performance, she will have more control over her game.

OTHER PITCHING CONSIDERATIONS

Besides the typical things that coaches work on with the pitchers (such as mechanics, fielding, game situations, and conditioning), there are other considerations that need to be addressed. Coaches must spend time addressing what kind of workout a pitcher needs the day before a game, how to prepare for the unexpected, and how to deal with failure.

Day Before a Game

Every pitcher on staff needs to assume she will pitch in the game the next day. With this in mind, most pitchers would want to do some kind of workout the day before a game. They use this practice time to iron out some of the kinks they have discovered in previous practices. Most pitchers prefer to use this time for working one on one with a catcher in the bull pen or with the pitching coach. They might also do some light throwing and ball spins and possibly a few drills. We make an effort to ensure that all of our pitchers have worked with each one of our catchers. This is important so that everyone is familiar with each other's style.

To determine the proper workout for the day before a game, you must communicate with your pitchers and ask them what they are comfortable with. You need to accommodate those needs so that when game time comes your pitchers feel they are prepared.

Expecting the Unexpected

Although routines are important to pitchers for daily practices and game warm-ups, you must prepare your pitchers to handle the adversities the game may bring. For example, a pitcher needs to practice pitching in the rain, warming up in a hurry, and dealing with a poor umpire. We try to incorporate as many different situations as we can in practice so a pitcher can keep her poise on the mound when the "unexpected" comes into play.

Learning From Failure

College coaches recruit pitchers who have been successful in high school or travel ball. These players have learned their style and technique through many years of pitching. They have been doing it "their way" for many years. A college pitching coach must be careful how much she tries to change her freshmen pitchers. If a coach urges a pitcher to change something and the pitcher fails, it becomes the "coach's fault." If a coach allows a pitcher to fail her own way, the pitcher learns a great deal from that and may be more receptive to learning new things.

Tell your pitchers that they are not expected to do it all. No pitcher will be on her game every day. When you take a pitcher out of a game, she should not take it personally. Remind your pitchers that when it is not their day, you will give another pitcher a chance to make it "her day" on the mound.

CHAPTER 14 PREPARING FOR GAMES

I want my team to have the best chance to win every game we play. I prepare my players by teaching and honing individual and team skills, and when the time comes, we put that preparation to the test against our opponent. But to give our team an additional advantage, I want us to know as much as we can about that opponent when we walk on the field.

My staff and I prepare a scouting report to study the other team's offense, defense, and pitching. In this chapter, I will discuss the preparation of scouting charts as well as pregame practices and preparing for games.

SCOUT YOUR OPPONENTS

I like to go into every game having an idea of how the other team stacks up against us. This information gives me some idea of how to prepare and what we need to focus on to win the game. The main questions I have about the opponent are as follows: What kind of pitcher do they have? What type of hitting team are they? Who is their best hitter? Has anyone shut her down and, if so, how? Does their catcher have a good arm? What is the steal percentage against her? Who has the most steals on the team? What kind of offense do they run? If I have this information to share with the team, I feel comfortable that we know our opponent a little better.

I believe in scouting and feel it serves its purpose with our team. However, there are times when it is appropriate to share such information with the team and other times when it is not. For example, if I know we are facing a great pitcher who has yet to lose a game or has a huge number of strikeouts, I might save that information for the end of the game. I save it because I want my players to focus on us, not on the opponent. The focus for the game should be on your own team's efforts and how your team will win, not on the efforts of the opponents. Too much information about the other team can distort this focus, make the game too much about the opponent, and become a distraction.

Offense One of our best-kept scouting reports is our pitching cards. The purpose of the pitching card is to assist the pitcher, catcher, and coach in calling the game. If, for example, we face a team whose number four batter cannot hit a drop ball, we will record this on the card. When she is up to bat, we can look at her card and know her weakness. We save all our cards for future games against the opponent. These cards are the size of a four-by-six-inch note card, and they help us keep track of who pitched against whom and how the batter performed against that pitcher. They also provide good feedback on the batter's weaknesses and strengths (see figure 14.1). With the scouting report in mind, we will structure our defensive practice to represent the true lineup we will be facing.

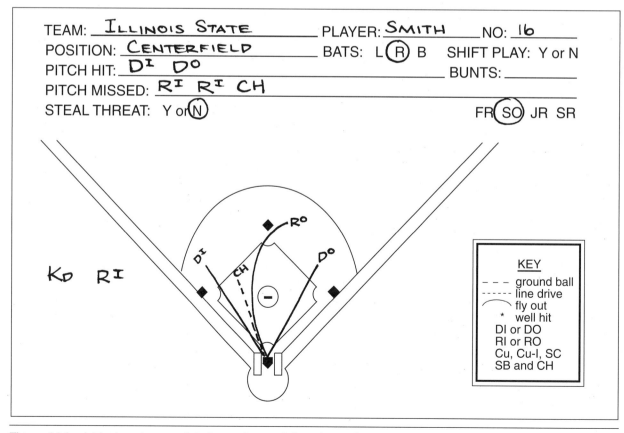

Figure 14.1 A blank and a completed scouting card that charts the opposing batter.

The card is designed to make it easy to read and easy to keep. When filling out the card, we draw lines for where the ball goes, using a dashed line for a ground ball, a dotted line for a line drive, and an arched line for a pop fly. We also initial by the line to identify the type of pitch that was thrown. So, if the hitter hit a pop fly off an inside drop ball, we initial the arched line with a DI for drop inside. We keep track of who threw what by using different colored pens for each pitcher, because one pitcher's drop ball might be different from another's. The more specific you can keep the card, the better it will serve your purpose. Players who are not playing in that game can help assistant coaches update these cards.

When going into a game against a team that we have not yet faced, we will try to find a time to watch them play. During this time, we will write what we see in each batter on the back of the card. Using the back of the card makes the information easily accessible during our game with that team. It also helps prevent us from getting the information confused with how the batter did against our own pitchers.

I would highly recommend charting your pitches and the opponent's batters if you have the staff or the time. Pitching cards, if kept correctly, are one of our best scouting tools.

Defense   When we are watching our upcoming opponents play another team, we take advantage of this opportunity to keep a defensive scouting chart on them (see figure 14.2). This chart helps us keep track of who is strongest in her position and how we can offensively take advantage of a weak link.

Pitching   We also keep scouting records on our opposing teams' pitchers. We want to know what their best pitches are and what pitches they might throw in certain situations. We record how fast the pitchers are and who the best pitcher on the team is. See figure 14.3 for a sample of that card.

Getting the Information   I like to utilize several methods to obtain scouting information about future opponents. We call other coaches, study scouting reports, and watch live or videotaped games.

- **Verbal input**—We often talk with other coaches and knowledgeable softball fans about our future opponents. We rely first on the observations of other coaches. Networking with other coaches can create an excellent sharing cycle. Several times we have received phone calls from teams wanting to know how other teams looked when we played them previously that year, and several times we have called or spoken with other coaches at tournaments to ask about some of our opponents.

- **Written input**—Discussing the opponent with other coaches helps create relationships with different schools, and we can then ask them for some scouting information about teams we are preparing to face. We will then go to our scouting forms, pitching cards, and defensive chart, and relay the information we have learned to our team.

- **Visual input**—Before heading into a big game, we usually like to see our opponent play. If circumstances do not allow this, we will call one of the teams we share information with and ask if they have played the team we need information on. If they have, we will find out if they videotaped the game.

TEAM TRAVEL

A few days before the travel date for an away game, I provide the team with a trip itinerary outlining all dates, times, estimated times of arrival and departure, and housing information. This enables the players to record the information in their handbook and to share the travel plans with their parents and fans.

The players are assigned an equipment responsibility for all away games. They are responsible for picking up the equipment, packing it, and making sure it arrives where it is needed. This way no one can assume someone else took care of it.

I think traveling together as a team is one of the most rewarding times for the players and the coaches. Not only do we get to play in different stadiums or fields, but we also get to see new cities and experience different cultures. We normally travel by bus and encourage the players to arrive 15 minutes before the scheduled departure. This gives them time to get all of their gear aboard and find their seats without feeling rushed. I want the athletes to hustle but

Figure 14.2 Sample Defensive and Offensive Chart

Date _____   Team _____

Opponent or scouting (circle one)   Weather conditions _____

Defense

	Number	Arm strength	Range	Speed	Up/back	*Comments
Pitcher						
Catcher						
First base						
Second base						
Shortstop						
Third base						
Left field						
Center field						
Right field						

*Rookie, out of position, chokes, lacks lateral movement, cheats on steals, doesn't back up throw, and so on.

Offense

Signs and signals _____

Steals? (player, number, count, outs) _____

Drag bunters? _____

never to "rush" on game day. Rushing causes the athlete to panic and worry, which is not conducive to top-level play.

Before we board the bus, the entire travel party meets outside and forms a send-off circle. We join hands and a spokesperson for the group reminds everyone of the importance of leaving their worries outside the circle and to gain strength from the circle. The spokesperson can add anything else, such as a prayer for safety and good health for all participants. I lead the send-off circle for the first and last trips of the

season, and the captains, team members, and assistant coaches have the opportunity to lead the rest.

Before the send-off circle starts, we ask the players to mentally review their travel checklists to be sure they brought everything necessary. The most important items are spikes, gloves, socks, stirrups, all uniform parts, undershirts, and sliders. Anything else we feel we can do without.

When traveling, we eat three hours before game time and strive for proper nutrition

Figure 14.3 Pitching and Special Defense Chart

Date _____ Opponent _____ Location _____ Weather _____

Who is their number one pitcher? _____

Who pitched against us? _____

Speed: Fast _____ Above average _____ Average _____ Below average _____

Types of pitches: Rise _____ Drop _____ Curve _____ Change-up _____ Screwball _____

"Go to" pitch: Rise _____ Drop _____ Curve _____ Change-up _____ Screwball _____

Primary location: Up _____ Down _____ Inside _____ Outside _____

Tendencies? _____

Patterns? _____

What does pitcher throw when:

Ahead in the count? _____

Behind in the count? _____

First pitch? _____

Full count? _____

How do they defend first and third? _____

Weaknesses in their steal defense? _____

Can we steal third? Yes _____ No _____

Weaknesses in their bunt coverage? _____

Defensive strength? _____

Defensive weakness? _____

throughout the trip. We also have fruit and peanut butter and jelly sandwiches in the dugout for all doubleheaders. On the bus, we provide water bottles and fruit juices.

When we return from our trip, we empty the bus, check it over, put away equipment and luggage, and then meet back at the bus. We join hands again for any quick announcements and reminders needed, and then we wish each other a good night. The circle dissolves and everyone heads home. We make sure everyone has a ride home, especially if it is dark outside.

PREGAME WARM-UP

It is important to maintain team continuity before the game. You can use the following sample game day warm-up plan to help create a pregame routine. This warm-up will take 63 minutes from the start of the warm-up to the beginning of the game.

Pregame warm-up

10 minutes 5-minute run, 5-minute partner stretch

10 minutes	Partner throw
20 minutes	Batting practice—pitchers and catchers go first (all players do 10 sprints during batting practice)
7 minutes	Defensive minidrills (see chapter 11)
10 minutes	Infield/outfield shuttle ground balls
2 minutes	Captains' meeting (all players meet for goal setting)
4 minutes	Final focus points

PREGAME MOTIVATION

Every player has her own individual way of motivating herself before a game. However, game day itself is the best source of motivation. Any competitor practices for the thrill of the game. Being able to put that uniform on brings an energy level that no coach can generate through words. A player's game day routine of superstitious preparations, locker room hoopla, music, or quiet time is crucial to pregame motivation. Providing them with some time before the game to prepare individually is probably the best thing you can do.

The team may have traditions to look forward to or even a yearly theme they have decided upon that may motivate them. One year each player decorated a softball. During every game, we displayed them all with a "team" ball in the middle. Our theme that year was "take care of the ball." Helping your team explore possible themes can be fun for them and helpful to the overall motivation.

Some athletes rely on their coaches to motivate them before a game. Here are a few suggestions to help motivate those athletes:

• Make it a priority to prepare your team in practice for each game, and make your players believe that they are prepared. A reminder of the improvements and the successes the team has had in practice is a great boost to the players' morale.

• Suggest to your players that they "play for someone." That person can be a parent, friend, coach, or a religious deity. Furthermore, providing an opportunity to "show off" for their chosen person can bring a player's ego and energy up a notch.

• Stay positive and in good spirits. This will keep your athletes loose, because players feed on the mood of the coach. Be aware and sensitive to that.

• Give individual pep talks. This can be very effective with particular athletes. It means a lot to a player if a coach makes the effort to acknowledge her strengths.

Lastly, if you have established a foundation of inspiration for your student-athletes on and off the field, they will naturally be motivated for each contest. The excitement of the competition should provide the athletes with the motivation they need to perform to their capabilities.

The Circle

After one pregame practice, I asked the team to sit in a circle. I then went to each athlete and talked about her individual contributions to the team. This was a time for teammates to recognize and hear how everybody gives to our mission. As I talked to individual athletes, I could see other athletes nodding, agreeing, and smiling at their teammate. When I finished, they often responded with "Good job" or "Way to be." This helped the individual feel that her effort was noticed and respected. When I finished with all the teammates and coaches, I talked about the team as a whole. I focused on our strengths and how we had done one thing better than any other team in the past—hustled. I reiterated how this great quality would help make our weaknesses less apparent and strengthen our strong points. I purposely left out averages and percentages and talked more about effort and accomplishments. When we left the room, I knew I was looking at a winning ball team. They all glowed with pride and esteem—two attributes that would help them be successful on the ball field.

Underdog Versus Favorite

We try to get our players to view every opponent as human and of equal ability to us. We don't want them to think, *UCLA—they're great!*

A few minutes of self-preparation before each game provides a calming effect and a boost to motivation.

Instead, we want them to work hard to be everybody else's UCLA. The athletes are aware of the talent pool and what teams are ranked and so on. I do not need to remind them. When we go into any game, I want my team to feel it is a big game. Every opponent, every game, every time your team hits the dirt, there is something to learn and to gain from the competition. I have seen my best teams lose to teams I thought we would beat the day after my teams played a ranked team and won. Fastpitch softball is a game of "any given day"—that is, on any given day, any team can lose to or beat another. I believe the underdogs win because of their lack of expectation. If they do not expect to win or lose, they can focus more on playing the game. Thus, I do not want to make a giant or an elf of any of our opponents. I simply want my team to do the things they have practiced and do

them right. If this happens, each game will be a success.

Big Games

Every big game brings something to the ball field that your team should work on overcoming all year—pressure. If you can create pressure situations in practice, your athletes will perform better under pressure in the game. This may seem very logical, but it is difficult to produce the pressure of a conference championship at 6:30 on a winter morning in the gym. The coaching staff must get creative to produce competitions, awards, winning incentives, and losing consequences that will help put pressure into the practice and help the athletes develop a workable system to deal with it. The practice needs to be hard so that the game is easy.

A Gift to the Parents

We were playing in a conference title game, and it was televised on Sports Channel. It was the "if necessary" game in a double-elimination tournament. Our pitcher, Mindy Dessert, was a fifth-year senior who had battled back through injury to earn the opportunity to pitch, and subsequently win, this very important game. Mindy's dad was very sick that year and did not make it to the game. My mom, an avid fan as well, was also unable to attend.

We won the game against Northern Illinois University, and Mindy and I celebrated with a hug on the mound. I said to her, "Now our parents get to see this great victory." We both had tears in our eyes as we realized the gift we were about to give. I called up my mom, told her we had won, and told her it would be televised the next day. She invited her brothers and sisters over to watch. She fixed lunch as they all watched the game. They kept asking her who won, and all she would say was, "You'll have to wait and see."

Mindy's dad watched it that day as well and videotaped it. We heard that he played the videotape for every visitor who came into his house that month.

HANDLING GAME SITUATIONS

As a coach, you must think about game situations ahead of time. This includes everything from how you handle yourself on the field to how you pick your lineup. The game is the reason the players compete and put their talents to the test. Coaches and players want to be prepared for the challenge so that, win or lose, they know that they performed at their very best. In this chapter, I will provide some statistics to help you determine the most effective batting order for your team. I will discuss the coach's and the players' conduct. I have also included some information about game duties as well as game day responsibilities. The main focus of this chapter is on some of the game situations, both normal and unique, that a coach will have to deal with.

LINEUP CONSIDERATIONS

There are hundreds of choices a coach can make when determining her team's lineup. Deciding which choices are the best is the art of coaching. The choices you make are based on your philosophy, but they are complicated because of the ever-changing dynamics involved. These dynamics might include what the players did the game before, the chemistry of the lineup, or the opponent. The starting lineup should generally be determined in off-season and preseason practice, allowing for adjustments as the season progresses. There are three questions you must ask yourself when creating a solid lineup: Who are the 10 best players? What is your defensive lineup based on these 10? What is your offensive lineup based on your defensive positioning?

Through objective and subjective evaluation during preseason practice, the coach will begin to form thoughts and opinions regarding the top players on the squad. Every team will have three tiers of players. The first tier is made up of six or seven players who clearly earn the respect to be in the starting lineup. These are the core or "black-and-white" starters. The second tier contains players "on the bubble" who have made the team by virtue of either offensive or defensive strengths. They form the "gray" area of the squad. The third tier is made up of role players only. Role players are those who have specific strengths the team might need throughout the course of the game, such as pinch hitters, pinch runners, and bull pen catchers.

The final three or four players that make up the starting lineup will be pulled from the "gray" area. When selecting the remaining members of the lineup, the coach will first need to consider who could possibly hurt the team if in the lineup. These players will then be eliminated from the second tier. From the remaining pool, the coach decides which players will help the team the most. Do they have the strengths the team needs? Will they bring leadership? Will they bring game instincts? Communication skills?

Now that you have determined your best 10 players, how will you fill your nine defensive positions? I believe the key positions are pitcher, catcher, and middle infielders. These are positions that require the strongest skills because these players handle the ball more often than those at other positions. Next, you need to decide on the corners, then the center fielder, and finally the left and right fielders. A coach must determine the defensive lineup to accommodate the overall team strength, not the strengths of individual players.

Once the defensive positions have been selected, you must decide on the batting order. To do this, you should consider a number of factors. For example, the leadoff hitter must have the ability to get on base, have enough speed to avoid the double play or to go to third base on a single to right or right center, and not have so much power that she would be more useful in the middle of the order. Therefore, good pitch selection, discipline, and a high on-base percentage are all important for the leadoff hitter; this applies to both the first batter in the lineup and the hitter who has to lead off after the first inning. I conducted a 75-game study and determined the number of times that each position in the batting order led off an inning:

Position	Led off an inning
First	68 (not including 75 leadoffs in first inning)
Second	31
Third	47
Fourth	65
Fifth	55
Sixth	62
Seventh	43
Eighth	56
Ninth	44

After the leadoff batter, the number four hitter started the most innings, with the sixth position a close third. What this research tells me is that the number one and four batters should be very much alike in terms of their attributes for leading off an inning.

The number two hitter in the lineup should be a good contact hitter since a strikeout cannot advance a runner to scoring position. She should have the ability to hit the ball to the right side of the infield. This hitter must have the discipline to look for a pitch in the hitting zone that she can drive to the area of the infield that will provide the best chance to stay out of a double play. Power is not essential here. The number two position will rarely lead off an inning according to my 75-game study.

You Be the Star

I had a pitching staff one year that consisted of a senior and a freshman pitcher. Neither one dominated, yet they both got the job done. This should have been the senior's year to shine. In her previous years, she had to follow one of our best pitchers, but now it was her opportunity to lead. Our defense was solid and our bats were hot, so even without a dominating pitcher, our spring was blooming into a great season. Our doubleheaders were being shared by the two pitchers: Usually the senior pitched the first game and the freshman the second. The majority of the time, if the senior won, the freshman won as well, and if the senior lost, the freshman lost, too.

One day we were playing the University of Iowa, and the senior lost the first game 3-2. I knew we had another shot, and I needed someone to go out and take charge. I knew right away that this could be our freshman pitcher's moment to shine. It is difficult sometimes, as a freshman, to take charge, but I went to her anyway. I talked with her a little about her pitches and then I told her to go out there and be "the star." She looked at me and smiled. She knew that this was a great opportunity for her to prove herself, and she replied, "Okay, Coach." The next thing I knew, we were in the bottom of the seventh and up 1-0. She pitched from within herself and played the game pitch by pitch. We defeated Iowa, and she had proven to her team that she could be a leader.

What position is up most often with people on base? Here are the results of a study of a 19-game fall season, showing the number of times each batting order position came up with runners on base:

Position	Runners on base
First	27
Second	35
Third	37
Fourth	41
Fifth	38
Sixth	36
Seventh	37
Eighth	26
Ninth	28

As coaches have suspected, the number four position comes to the plate with the most opportunities for advancing runners on base. The number five spot is right behind, followed by the third and seventh positions.

The number three hitter should be the hitter who you feel is the best overall hitter on your team. In every game, this batter will be up in the first inning, sometimes with runners on base. This should be your most consistent hitter, someone who is the toughest to get out with few hitting weaknesses.

The number four, or cleanup, batter should be a clutch hitter with power. Her slugging percentage will be lower than that of the number three hitter, generally as a result of her lower batting average.

The fifth spot may be occupied by a power hitter with a lower batting average and on-base average than the two hitters ahead of her. Number six may be the same kind of hitter as number five, only not quite as proficient.

Players who are starters by virtue of their defensive ability, and who may be your two weakest hitters, usually fill the seventh and eighth positions. The ninth batter shares the characteristics of the leadoff batter. The seventh batter shares the characteristics of the second, but the seventh batter produces figures that are worse than the second batter. On an especially good hitting team, a batter who hits a lot of long balls but has a low batting average and does not draw many walks might fill the seventh spot.

The Home Run Hug

We were competing in the conference tournament against Indiana State University, and the game was very tight. In the bottom of the seventh, with the bases loaded, two outs, and a full count on their batter, I thought our pitcher had just thrown strike three. However, the umpire called, "Ball four." That walked in a run, giving us a one-run lead with the bases still loaded. The next batter hit an RBI single to center field to tie the game, but the winning run was thrown out at the plate!

As I walked out of the dugout to go to the third-base coaching box, I asked the umpire, "Where was that pitch?" He just stared straight at me, and I asked him again. He continued to stare at me, so the third time I said, "Was it high, low, inside, or outside?" He finally said that it was low. I said, "You're guessing—you don't know where it was." By now he was so puzzled he pointed to the sky and quietly said, "You're out of here." I thought if I just kept walking to the coaching box he would change his mind, but no, he turned and said he had thrown me out of the game. I couldn't believe it—all I had done was ask a question.

I walked back to the dugout, and our starting pitcher and the first batter of the inning were standing in the door. I told them I had just been kicked out of the game. They both stared at the umpire and said, "Don't worry about it, Coach. We'll take care of it."

Having never been kicked out of a game before, I didn't know where I could be, and I sure did not want to miss the exciting conclusion of this one. The dugout was huge, so I stood down at the end of it, right across from first base.

The eighth inning started with our cleanup batter at the plate. On the first pitch, she sent the ball flying over the left-center field fence. Home run! She rounded the bases and met her teammates at home plate. She walked into the dugout, gave me a huge hug, and said, "That one's for you, Coach!" It was a wonderful feeling to be greeted in that manner and to feel important in the dugout. We went on to hold them in the bottom of the eighth inning for the victory, but we did not stop there. We swept through the conference championship undefeated and earned a bid to the NCAA national championship.

CONDUCT DURING THE GAME

No one is bigger than the game. Individual egos need to be managed in such a way that the attention of the audience is not on the individual but on the game as a whole. This can be accomplished when the coaches and players set a behavior standard that is beyond question. It is okay to get excited and show emotion, but not to disrespect the umpire, the opponent, or the game.

Coach's Conduct

The game is the time to coach the *game*, not the skill. For example, when the batter is on deck or in the batter's box, this is not the time to correct her swing. At this critical time, the batter needs to be reminded to focus and hit the ball. You should remain focused as well. Let yourself see each play, out, or inning through as you anticipate future decisions.

I believe that a coach should never criticize or embarrass a player in public. Refrain from yelling at an athlete during the game or in front of others. Players do not want to disappoint with their performance, and it is a serious flaw in a coach to belittle players by yelling at them. There may be times when you need to raise your voice, but these times are at practice. I also have a rule to never use profanity during a game, whether speaking to the players, the umpire, or the fans. It looks awful, sounds awful, and is degrading to those you address, to your team, and to what you represent.

As a coach, you must also show respect for the umpires. I have the greatest respect for umpires and for the difficult job they have; they must make split-second decisions on balls and athletes moving with great force and speed.

Your conduct during the game must be exemplary. Remember that you represent yourself, your team, your school, and your family. Your players will look to you and follow your example during the contest. If you cannot keep your composure, it will be difficult for your team to keep theirs. If you lose your temper, your team may do the same. Stay focused on the game and on the challenges at hand, and work to set the

Your Underwear Is Showing

In a highly charged game against the University of Missouri, the plate umpire and I were in a heated discussion. I sensed I was going to get kicked out, so I walked around behind him on the way to the third-base coaching box. I noticed that his ball bag had pulled his trousers down and that about four inches of the top of his underwear was showing.

I stopped arguing, kept walking, changed and softened my tone, and said over my shoulder, "Your underwear's showing." His right arm shot out and up, ready to eject me, as he yelled, "What? You're . . . " At the same time, he sensed something and reached back with his left hand and felt the back of his underwear. Meekly he said, "Oh." Down came the arm, and I stayed in the game. Only rarely in a season can you win an argument with an umpire.

best possible example for your players and your supporters.

Player Conduct

I expect my athletes to always behave proudly on and off the field. When on the field, they are representing the university and enjoying the privilege of playing Division I softball. But sometimes game situations will challenge their composure. For example, what happens if the umpire does not call certain parts of the strike zone? The pitcher should be prepared to handle and adjust to an uncontrollable situation.

Differences of opinion about balls and strikes can be stressful for the umpire as well. The pitcher and catcher should not get emotional in their actions or their looks because no one wants to be embarrassed, including the umpire. If the pitcher has a question about a call, she should have her catcher ask the umpire. The catcher and the umpire must develop a relationship each game, and it is quite permissible for the catcher to ask the umpire questions. Players will never win the umpire's favor by being disrespectful, but they might win his favor by approaching him with respect. We ask the same from our athletes on the bench, that when they

A catcher should establish a relationship with the umpire from the first pitch. Mutual respect between the two will create an atmosphere of cooperation.

disagree with a call, they do not question the umpire but respect the decision.

GAME PLAN ADJUSTMENTS

Coaches must take full advantage of an opposing team's weaknesses on both offense and defense. During the game, a coach needs to constantly evaluate the opponent and must change the game strategy accordingly. The reentry rule presents numerous opportunities for player substitution, including pitching changes, defensive changes, and pinch runners and hitters.

Pitching Changes

What happens if one or more of the pitcher's pitches are not working? During the course of the game, sometimes a pitch will not work, but the pitcher cannot give up on it. The pitcher should try to establish all her pitches during the warm-ups, even if she finds that one pitch is not working. If the pitcher has no movement on her pitches, you should have her work on location. In a like manner, if she is having problems hitting her location, you should have her work on ball movement. To make adjustments during the game, the pitcher should throw between innings with a catcher, working on location and spin. Do not let the pitcher give up on a certain pitch, because it may come around later in the game. If the pitcher is having trouble finding the strike zone, the catcher can move her target, or the pitcher can change her focus points.

Changing the pitcher in the middle of a game is one of the toughest decisions a coach will have to make. There have been times when I hung with a pitcher who was struggling and we got the win, and there have been just as many times when I made the decision to take the pitcher out, and we sealed the victory. There is not a textbook answer, but the pitcher and catcher can help you make the call. The catcher can potentially be your best reference on the pitcher's effectiveness. The pitcher can give some feedback on her confidence level. Knowing when to put in a relief pitcher or stay with the one on the mound is a gut instinct. If you have any doubt about your pitcher, make the change!

Defensive Changes

If a player has made two errors in the game, I may take her aside and talk with her one on one. I try to find out if she will be all right staying in the game or if she is having a hard time focusing on the task at hand. If I have to remove a defensive player, I want to make as few changes as possible. If I can keep players in the position they know the best, they are more likely to excel. There are times when I will make defensive changes near the end of a game to strengthen our defense.

A Substitution Nightmare

It is fun to think about the times when we found our opponent's weakness and snatched the win away by forcing the play. In one game in particular, we did just that. We were down 3-0 going into the sixth inning. Our leadoff batter beat out a bunt and stole second. On the steal, she slid into their shortstop, who twisted her ankle and was forced to leave the game. Their next best shortstop was playing second base, so they moved her over. They moved their third baseman to second base and put in a new third baseman. Three people were out of their starting positions—the shortstop, the second baseman, and the third baseman. We saw this as a crucial opportunity for a comeback, and we took advantage of it. We laid down bunt after bunt in the direction of their new third baseman. She had trouble getting to the ball and made some bad throwing decisions. Needless to say, they lost the game. We might have hit one ball out of the infield that troubled inning. The final score was 4-3. This is a great example of how you can capitalize on your opponent's weaknesses.

Pinch Hitters and Runners

There will be times when pinch hitters or runners can win a game for you. For example, a perfect opportunity for a pinch hitter is when a runner is on third, there is one out, and the batter due up is a weak ground ball hitter. The desired result is that your pinch hitter comes in and hits the long fly ball needed to score the runner at third. You can then reenter the fielder. It is important to keep in mind that pinch-hitting is one of the most difficult jobs for a player called from the bench. She has a one-time opportunity to put the ball in play. The pinch hitter needs to hit 1.000 every game. She does not get to try to go two for four or three for four. Use pinch hitters early in the game to get ahead or to add a run to cut into your opponent's lead. Enter the pinch runner early in the inning so that she has more than one out in which to score.

TIME-OUTS

The coach gets one trip to the mound each inning. Most of the time, you will not need to use each time-out, but there are times when you should. The most obvious is when the pitcher is having problems and you either want to talk with her or make a pitching change. You might also go to the mound when your defense has made a series of bad plays. You want to take the time to get them to relax and break the negative rhythm. Just as you might go to the mound to break a negative rhythm, you might also go if the opponents are in a positive rhythm.

Your trip should give your team a moment to get themselves together. You want to make sure you are not breaking a good rhythm for your team, so don't make an unnecessary trip. If your pitcher says she is okay, you should give her the benefit of the doubt and let her try to pull herself out of any jam before you take her out. The pitcher and catcher can call a time-out and meet on the mound without you using your trip. Let them try that first if it is not a crucial situation.

Your conversations at the mound should help relax your players or refocus them. This is not a time for yelling; all eyes are on you. Find words of encouragement, or if the players just need a breather, tell a joke. It is amazing how a smile can change the tone of the game.

If you use an offensive conference to talk to a batter, be sure you use few words and make eye contact. I have found that this is the most intense time for a player, and when you look into her eyes, you will see focus and concentration. Do not use this time to teach her how to bat or to explain a technique, but remind her of the exact needs of the team in this situation.

GAME DUTIES

Beyond the obvious game-playing duties of the starting lineup, all other players and personnel will have responsibilities throughout the game. Some of these responsibilities include chart keeping, trying to figure out the opponents' signals, making sure runners touch all the bases, game filming, communicating that runners are stealing, warming up the outfielders between innings, and getting water and snacks for the coaches. During the game, all nonstarters are expected to sprint to the foul-line fence and back each inning. Possible pinch hitters swing a bat every inning when we are on offense, and additional defensive players play catch at least once in the first half of the game. If a player is not in the lineup, she must be preparing mentally and physically to get in the game.

Coaches are in both coaching boxes when we are on offense, and when we are on defense, the assistant coach is charting each batter. The pitching cards used for this can be seen on page 189. During the game, I take notes on aspects of the game that I feel can help teach the game better. These may be on great defensive plays or mental errors that occurred. We will review these notes with the team after the game. With these notes, I can evaluate our strengths and weaknesses as well as design future practices.

POSTGAME PROCEDURES

I like to be consistent in my expectations of everyone after the game. We follow a prescribed course of action after each game:

1. During our postgame meeting, we have each player sit in a specific place for the game discussion. For example, the pitchers and catchers who played in that game sit in the front, the infielders sit together, and the outfielders sit together. The players who did not play or who played as pinch runners or pinch hitters are together behind everyone else. In this way, I can make eye contact with each player during the discussion, and I know where to look for each individual.

2. In the meeting, I review the highlights of the pitching summary: hits, walks, how the pitcher did in tough or crucial situations, and the contribution of the catcher. Next, I cover our offensive performance—key hits, runs batted in, game-winning hits—and highlight situation hitting, such as crucial bunts, hit-and-runs, and so on. I then review sparkling defensive plays and any outstanding hustle performances.

3. Next, I review situations we can learn from in the game and mistakes we made as coaches, as a team, or as individual players. This is an important teaching opportunity; this is where necessary learning takes place. What did we do wrong and how can we learn from our mistakes?

4. After the postgame meeting with the team, the coaches meet to select an offensive and defensive player of the game. These selections are announced at the next team meeting.

Winning With Class

After a win, a team should enjoy their success. I remember losing one game 15-0 and hearing the winning coach berate her team for various mistakes they made in the game. I could not help but wonder what the team needed to do to be able to enjoy the completed game. Surely in that 15-run romp there was something for our opponents to view as positive.

I believe a coach should keep everything positive. Following a win, you should let the players enjoy the fruits of their labor. The team should keep a win in perspective, but there is fun in playing and in being successful. Point out to the team all the things they did to be successful, and remind them that it will take hard work to stay successful.

Following our games, we always eat together and invite friends, parents, and families to join us. This is an important bonding time, and it also gives the team a longer time together to enjoy the victory. After a win, it is great to see everyone smiling!

Sportsmanship is an important ingredient of the game. Winning with class and losing with dignity both promote a healthy team environment.

Losing With Dignity

A peak teaching opportunity follows a loss. A loss provides immediate feedback for the coach and player alike. For example, if your catcher overthrows third base trying to pick off the runner and the runner scores, the catcher learns this is a risky play, especially late in the game. There are times in defeat when the players have given a winning effort, and it is vital for the coach to acknowledge that effort. After the loss, help the athletes maintain a positive attitude that will carry them into the upcoming games and practices.

The coaches should also learn from the loss. In the example of the catcher overthrowing third base, if the coach called the play, she learns the same lesson the catcher learned. Sometimes our opponent outplays us, sometimes they out-coach us, and sometimes we do not execute well enough to earn the victory. Be sure to point out the differences. Handle the loss with dignity, and fire up your players for the next contest. Every coach must set the tone for the next game and the next practice in the most positive way possible. After each game, I make it a point to walk through the dugout and acknowledge the effort that each individual athlete gave.

After a loss, all the players are going to be disappointed. Disappointment can be very emotional. Always address the emotion first and then the technique. Try to defuse the intensity of any emotion by telling the athlete swept up in it that you read her loud and clear. If you can acknowledge her feelings (for example, by saying, "I know it's frustrating/upsetting/embarrassing . . . "), it will be music to her ears. That tells her that she has been heard. The next thing to do is to remind the athlete of her options. Do this by giving her cues for refocusing on the job, fast, before she decides to continue being angry, embarrassed, or whatever her emotion is. It's difficult for a person to go on being swept overboard by any emotion if she is being called on to do something—anything—else.

After a loss, help your players lift their heads up. Set the tone for a positive attitude, one that states, "We will be back, stronger than today." Athletes are very resilient, but it is often the coach who can lift the spirit of a discouraged player. Let them know you believe in them and that you care about the way they are feeling. Stay positive and your team will respond!

CHAPTER 16 EVALUATING YOUR PLAYERS

This chapter emphasizes the importance of evaluating players fairly. It explains how accurate preseason evaluations, as well as continuing evaluations during the season, can help the coach make better coaching decisions.

PRESEASON EVALUATION

Preseason evaluation involves a combination of tryouts, practice, videotaping, and player self-evaluation. Understanding that there are constant changes in the quality of play of each individual, you must have a good grasp of where your team is when practices begin.

Tryouts

Tryouts are conducted on the first day of practice. These are held for any athletes who are interested in walking on to our team. My goal is to be sure that every player who either does not make it through tryouts or is cut from the program before the first game feels as though she was evaluated fairly. The player should feel that her lack of success on the field was due to her inability to perform the necessary skills that would enable her to be a contributing member of the team. Figure 16.1 is an example of a tryout

chart I use to select players. I rate them on a 1 to 5 scale for each of the skills and then add the scores together. To get additional opinions and increase your objectivity, you can also invite other coaches to watch the tryouts and to score the athletes.

After the tryout session, we meet individually with each athlete and go over her evaluation form. We discuss what the form reveals and either tell her she has made the team or discuss why she did not. I feel it is best that we talk with the athletes face to face rather than having them find the results posted. This gives them the opportunity to ask about what they need to work on if they would like to try out again.

Evaluation During Practices

When we are three weeks away from our first game, we begin to chart various offensive situations and defensive tests. These results are posted for the next day's practice so that everyone can review her individual performance, along with seeing how she "measures up" to her teammates. For example, every other Monday, Wednesday, and Friday during the preseason, we chart 10 swings off the pitching machine. We call this home run derby. The athlete earns three points if she hits a line drive to the opposite field, two points for a line drive (not to the opposite field), one point for a ground ball, and

Figure 16.1   Tryout Evaluation Form

- Take 2 laps, stretch, and do warm-up throws.

Ground balls   5   4   3   2   1
- Field 10 ground balls; 5 at SS and 5 at 2B—throw to 1B.

Fly balls   5   4   3   2   1
- Catch 10 fly balls; 5 in LF and 5 in RF—throw to 3B.

Throwing   5   4   3   2   1
- Evaluated during warm-up and when throwing to 1B and 3B during fielding and catching drills.

Hitting   5   4   3   2   1
- Swing at 10 pitches off of a machine.

Speed   1_____ 2_____ 3_____ AVG: _____
- Sprint from 1B to 2B 3 times—average the times.
- Group race; place 1st, 2nd, and 3rd overall.

Pitching   5   4   3   2   1
- Throw to catchers to demonstrate speed, accuracy, and movement of pitches.

Catching   5   4   3   2   1
- Catch pitches to demonstrate position and consistency.
- Throw to 2B 3 times, average the times (from the time the pitch hits the catcher's mitt until the ball hits the shortstop's glove at second base).   1_____ 2_____ 3_____ AVG: _____

zero points for a swing and miss, foul ball, or pop-up. We do this in a batting cage, and we incorporate this test within a circuit.

Another method we use to evaluate the players during practice is to chart game plays off a pitching machine. We record "well hits" as we go through games. Every time the athlete hits the ball "well," she receives a point, and we divide her total by the total number of her at-bats. We also chart defensive skills. For example, we will give a scorecard to a group of three infielders, and they hit 50 ground balls to each other. A fungo hitter hits ground balls to a fielder, who scores a point when she fields the ball and throws it to the receiver. We do this objective test weekly and add the results for a total.

During practices, I look for the players who can execute drills with pressure on, such as defensive players who can make the plays with live base runners. The more drills we can do that simulate game play and game situations, the stronger our individual players will be. The clutch player will stand out day in and day out, while others may do outstanding work on a more sporadic basis.

Videotape

We use the video camera as another coach. We tape hitting, pitching, and defense during practice to show what needs to be improved as well as what our players are doing well. We purchase one videotape for each player and use that tape at all of the player's recording sessions. There is a chance of overkill and videotaping doing more damage than good. For example, focusing too much on what the player is doing wrong could affect her confidence. Used carefully, however, the videotape can teach a player a lot about her performance.

During the preseason, we film and view each hitter. We show them what they are doing well and a few things they could do better. Later on, perhaps after the first couple of tournaments, we film them swinging again to point out their improvements. We film our pitchers during practice at least once a week. As part of the practice, we show the pitchers their films following the taping at a TV-VCR unit in the facility. We film our defensive players once a week in circuit work or in game play, then view it in another station.

We film all of our games during the season so that we can be accurate with our statistics and so that the athletes can see themselves perform. We watch the recordings together as a team to review general play and to increase understanding of the game as well as individual performance. Players are also encouraged to meet with a coach to view their own performances during the game. It is so true that "a picture is worth a thousand words."

Player Evaluation System

Two weeks before the start of the season, we utilize a player evaluation system where all players and coaches are given the opportunity to evaluate each player on the team. I want this procedure to be democratic, and I also want to know what my players' opinions are of each player at each position.

It is my obligation to each player to evaluate her performance as a potential team member and as a contributing factor to the team's success. Subjective criteria is involved in evaluations, but the evaluation process will be better if you use as much objective data as possible. Subjective criteria involves opinion, such as a coach's instinct about a performance, while objective criteria involves tangibles such as a hitting chart kept at practices. Each player should be familiar with the methods used in the evaluation, since this evaluation will determine the amount of playing time she can expect during the season. As the evaluations take place,

the players will be able to see the results, and we want them to feel that they can discuss the evaluation with any of the coaches involved.

At the evaluation session, I explain to the entire team the reasons behind allowing them to evaluate each other, along with what criteria they should use in making their decisions. I do not have them rank themselves until the final evaluation takes place before the opening of the regular season. They put their names on the forms so that the coaches know how each player ranked the team position by position. I tell the athletes not to use this evaluation as a personality contest, but rather, to base their evaluations on their estimation of each individual's worth to the team. They can use their observations over past seasons and during the preseason as well to form their opinions.

I ask the players and the coaches to work independently of each other and to contemplate the evaluation. A sample form is shown in figure 16.2. When filling out the position part of the evaluation form, each player selects the best and the runner-up at the defensive positions. This allows each position player to see how she is evaluated against the other players at her position; then she can look at another part of the form to see how she stands with the other hitters.

When the evaluation forms are returned, the players are listed by their overall ranking. On this overall listing, the total points next to their ranking reflects the totals of the rankings—the fewer the points, the higher the ranking. For instance, in the following sample, Cheri was ranked the number one pitcher with a total of three points. One point is given for a first-place ranking, two points for a second-place ranking, three points for a third-place ranking, and four points for a fourth.

		Coaches			Total
Pitchers	**Ranking**	**#1**	**#2**	**#3**	**points**
Cheri	1	1	1	1	3
Karenmarie	2	2	2	3	7
Annette	3	3	4	2	9
Kim	4	4	3	4	11

The hitters' evaluations and the defensive positions' evaluations by the coaches are presented in the same way as the preceding chart. For the hitters' evaluations, each rank is

Figure 16.2   Sample Player and Coach Evaluation Form

Instructions: Place your name on the line below, and rank each player in terms of worth to the team. For example, the player you feel brings the most worth to the team would receive a rank of #1. Do not include yourself in this evaluation.

Name: _____

Pitchers	Rank	Hitters	Rank
Annette	1. _____	Amber	1. _____
Cheri	2. _____	Angie	2. _____
Karenmarie	3. _____	Britt	3. _____
Kim	4. _____	Clarisa	4. _____
		Dani	5. _____
		Emily	6. _____
		Erin	7. _____
		Jen	8. _____
		Jess	9. _____
		Julie	10. _____
		Katie	11. _____
		Kelly	12. _____
		Maureen	13. _____
		Sheila	14. _____
		Stephanie	15. _____
		Tiffany	16. _____

Position	Defensive player	Rank
Catcher	_____	1. _____
	_____	2. _____
First base	_____	1. _____
	_____	2. _____
Second base	_____	1. _____
	_____	2. _____
Shortstop	_____	1. _____
	_____	2. _____
Third base	_____	1. _____
	_____	2. _____
Left field	_____	1. _____
	_____	2. _____
Center field	_____	1. _____
	_____	2. _____
Right field	_____	1. _____
	_____	2. _____
DH	_____	1. _____
	_____	2. _____

also given its point value. For example, a hitter ranked second six times, third four times, and first one time would have a total of 25. If your team uses designated players to hit for the pitchers, the pitchers may be left off the hitting evaluations. An example of the hitters' evaluation by the players would look like this:

Hitters' Evaluations by Players

Hitters	Ranking	Points
Jess	1	47
Emily	2	63
Erin	3	75
Sheila	4	81
Amber	5	123
Dani	6	148
Clarisa	7	187
Maureen	8	203
Angie	9	234
Jen	10	251
Julie	11	275
Kelly	12	300
Tiffany	13	313
Britt	14	356
Stephanie	15	378
Katie	16	400

In the final player evaluations two weeks before the start of the season, each player is allowed to place herself where she thinks she belongs compared with other players at her position.

Starting Lineup Survey

On the final evaluations prior to the first game, I will give all of the coaches and players an actual lineup card to name their starting lineup. Everyone will pick the actual order of the lineup and positions. The following chart is an example of how this information can be provided to the players and the coaches.

In the following example, there are three coaches voting. The number that follows the player's name means she received that many votes to be in the starting lineup. The number in parentheses is the most popular spot that was picked for her in the lineup. If there is only one

Teammate evaluation can help a player see her own strengths and weaknesses compared to other players in her position.

number in parentheses, it means that two or more coaches indicated this spot in the lineup. For example, Jess received all three coaches' votes, and the three and four in the parentheses means she was selected to bat either third or fourth.

Player	Lineup
Maureen	3 (7)
Clarisa	3 (2 & 8)
Jen	0
Julie	0
Erin	3 (4)
Kelly	1
Angie	2 (9)
Jess	3 (3 & 4)
Stephanie	0
Dani	3 (8)
Sheila	3 (5 & 6)

The coach evaluates hitting, throwing, and fielding during practices to help create a starting lineup.

Using the Results

Of the preseason evaluation methods, we give more weight to practice evaluations done by the coaches than to the self-evaluations done by the players. We receive valuable information from the self- and practice evaluations, but ultimately, what happens on the field day in and day out plays into the final decision. After the coaching staff has decided who the 9 or 10 starters will be, we meet each athlete individually in the office and discuss what her role will be for the start of the season.

It can be very difficult for the high school star to come to college and find out that many of her new teammates are better than she is. To ease this situation, the coach should tell each athlete what her role on the team is prior to the start of the season. This gives the athlete a clear picture of what is expected of her, along with areas she needs to improve on to get into the game.

The basic question is, Who plays and who doesn't? When comparing two players at second base, how do you determine who starts at second base and who doesn't? The answer is based on practice observations, defensive and offensive charts, video study evaluations, and game performance. The coach weighs all of these factors in deciding who gets onto the field and who sits on the bench. This procedure should be in constant flux until one player clearly beats out the other.

Choosing a starting lineup is a difficult task. I feel that all my athletes bring something great to the game. When it comes time to decide who will start in what position, I struggle with some of my decisions. I always want to play the 9 or 10 athletes who want it most, the ones with the greatest hearts. Yet I know there will always be some athletes who outshine others with pure, raw talent. It comes down to an athlete who plays ball as she would run a business. Her play is a career investment for her. Her work ethic stands out on the field. Every coach would like to think that all her athletes love the game as she does, but that is not always the case. Some athletes express their love of the game differently, and as a coach, you need to recognize that.

Regardless of whether a player is a starter or nonstarter, you should make it a point to treat all of your players equally. For example, I do not give my starters more time in the batting cage, and they are not the only ones given the opportunity to hit live pitching. In the preseason, each athlete receives equal treatment. However, as we get closer to games, there may be times when the starters are on the field longer in gamelike situations.

GAME PERFORMANCE EVALUATION

During the game, we keep a defensive chart of assists, putouts, and errors, as well as a defensive chart of important plays and an offensive chart that documents execution of plays. We will use this information to evaluate the players after every game throughout the season. We also use this information to help us evaluate where we have our athletes playing and where they are in the lineup.

During the game, our manager keeps a score book that has the rest of the information we need for postgame evaluation. The manager records an asterisk "*" in the batter's box for a well hit (well-hit ball). The scorekeeper also records the usual information, such as how the batter was put out, where the batter hit, and so on. From the asterisks in the score book, we can figure a well-hit average that is an important indicator of that player's performance.

After each game, we give awards to an offensive player and a defensive player of the game (sometimes there are more than one of each). We determine the best offensive player by the most important hits in the game. We also consider her number of well hits. The best defensive player is determined by the most important defensive plays as well as the most consistent defensive work. All of these athletes receive decals that they can put on their softball awards board. We also give a most valuable player award for the athlete who had the greatest impact in each tournament we played in.

CHAPTER 17 EVALUATING YOUR PROGRAM

An evaluation helps the program by letting those who are part of it see what they do well and where they can make improvements. You should be aware of not only the changes you may need to make, but also what aspects of your program are successful so that you can continue to utilize them.

EVALUATION STRATEGY

Before the season begins, you should consult with your players and create a mission statement. This is important because the mission statement lays out the road that you wish to travel. It provides a vision and a blueprint of the season's goals and gives the team direction for their first steps into a winning year.

Mission Statement

In the beginning of our season, we get together as a team and create a mission. Then before every game we will review and talk about our mission statement. At the end of the season, we meet again as a team to review our mission and see if we accomplished it. If we did, we discuss how; if we did not, we examine why. The mission usually consists of 10 major goals that we write on large signs and post in our locker room, weight room, gymnasium, and dugout all season long. At the last team meeting of the year, when we go through each goal of the mission statement, we talk about how we can better our mission and have greater success in achieving it. The following is a sample softball mission statement:

1. Be confident—show no fear or doubt.
2. Respect the game, your coaches, and your teammates.
3. Develop consistency—play at the end of the season with the same excitement, energy, and intensity as you do in the beginning.
4. Want to be in every game—live out the season to its fullest: NEVER SAY DIE!
5. Communicate and listen.
6. Give meaningful compliments to each other.
7. Become a family—get to know your teammates.
8. Bring something positive to every practice. Make every practice count—improve daily.
9. Bring a strong work ethic to your athletic and academic classroom.
10. Keep softball fun—remember why you play the game.

One of the major goals in the Westerwinds' mission statement is that the team becomes a family. Here, the hitter's joy in lifting the homerun out of the park is shared by her teammates.

Meeting With Players

I hold one-on-one player meetings before the season begins to formulate goals and get feedback from each player. In these meetings, I get many of the ideas that go into our mission statement for the year. This individual meeting gives the athlete the chance to speak freely about her goals and team goals, and it enables me to help the athlete set her individual mission and to formulate that into the team mission.

Senior Input

I make the seniors my priority. More than any other class, they have weathered the good times and the bad times, along with committing their careers to our university and the softball program. The four-year athletes are the ones who have truly given a lot to me in many ways, and I want to be sure their final season is one of

fond memories and no regrets. During the preseason prior to the start of their last season, the seniors and the coaches meet. I let them know how valuable they have been and will continue to be during their final "hurrah." I want them to know that their input is vital, and I want to hear from them about anything regarding the program and the success of the team. It is our goal, together, to make their last year their very best. Any and all suggestions will be honored, if at all possible. After all, the seniors are what we are all about: successful and memorable careers.

Meeting With Assistant Coaches

I give each of my assistants certain responsibilities that they can carry out without too much intervention from me. Based on their personal

The Last Hurrah

I had a four-year starter named Kimiko Chambers who was a terrific athlete. But during her senior year, her class schedule took her away from numerous practices. This caused me to wonder if her last year was as important to her as it was to me. Did she want the most out of it? At our one-on-one meeting, each player is asked to bring in her individual and team goals so that we can discuss them about a month before games begin. It was then that I asked Kimiko about her softball dream. Her eyes sparkled, and she smiled and said, "I want to experience going to nationals and regionals and to earn that conference title. I want this to be my 'last hurrah.'" I realized then the tremendous importance Kimiko placed on her last season and that she wanted to pile in the good memories to carry through her lifetime.

Shortly after that session, I met with the seniors and told them their input was vital to our success and that I wanted this year to be their happiest. I asked if there was anything that we had missed so far. Kimiko calmly stated that she wanted to play the last game on our home field. (We had scheduled it at the city park with lights to help draw a larger crowd.) I told her it would be no problem to change the game so that they could finish their WIU career on the field where they had spent so much of their lives.

strengths and interests, these range from serving as the recruiting coordinator to being the pitching coach, junior varsity team coach, and strength and conditioning coach, to name a few. The rest of the coaching responsibilities are shared. I want and need their input and make it clear when they are hired that we are a team within a team. I let them know that we will work together for the best of the team, each of us focusing on our strengths, and that I am interested in what they think and how they feel the program is going. Finally, after the season is over, I ask the assistants to fill out an evaluation of the program as well as to evaluate me. I have shared my office with my assistant for the last

10 years, and that lends itself to a comfortable exchange of ideas.

Early in the year, I meet with the assistant to discuss her role as a coach on the team. I ask her what she would like to learn and to accomplish and what areas she feels are her strong points. We then lay out each of the areas of the program and how the responsibilities will be divided and shared. Each month, we review how all jobs are coming along. These are very informal meetings, and the purpose is to give feedback to the assistant and to assess the status of the program. At this time, I will let the assistant know if she needs to communicate better, or if she should be more positive or more assertive. When evaluating my assistants, I go by my own personal observations.

There is so much to coaching that new assistants, as well as veterans, look forward to and need feedback. Most coaches probably do not tell their assistants nearly enough how important they are to the overall health of the team. It is important for leaders to show appreciation for the things that help the program flourish. A coach's job sometimes goes unappreciated, so it is up to you to make it known to your assistants that their efforts and ideas are an integral part of the success of the team.

EVALUATION DURING THE SEASON

I want to hear from our players because I believe they will give insight into what is and is not working in the program. This feedback comes about not only through their words, but also through their actions. Are they conditioned well enough? Did we overtrain? Are they excited about the team? I ask all the players from time to time if they like certain things we are doing or if they have any suggestions. Our coaches meet with our captains once each week (for a breakfast or a lunch) to share ideas and to let them hear me ask the question, "How is your team and how are your teammates doing?" I believe that healthy teams talk and everyone loses or wins together. I want the players to realize this and to bring their concerns to the coaches or the captains so that we can all work out problems and find solutions.

It Has to Be a Give-and-Take

When coaching athletes, you give a lot. You give your time, thoughts, ideas, experiences, conversations, counseling skills—essentially you give your all. When the athletes respond by only taking, you run dry. It is important that they give back and know that they should and are welcome to give back. My assistant coach and I were in our weekly lunch with our captains, and we were trying to talk to them about how we like to hear "thank you" and "good job" as much as they do. To make this point, my assistant looked at one of the captains and said, "There is someone on the team who brings something new to practice every day. She always says 'Hello' and gives all she has that day. Who do you think it is?" Both captains shook their heads and named different teammates. My assistant went on a bit and then said, "She is sitting with you now," and nodded her head in my direction. Both the captains claimed it was a trick question as they looked down. My assistant spoke clearly and replied, "My point is that Coach is on the team also, and gives every day. Just like you didn't think of her when I asked the question, her contributions are often overlooked." The captains shook their heads in agreement and smiled as if a light had gone on. I thanked my assistant for the nice words. Coaching is fun and a great job to have. It becomes satisfying when you see that you make a difference or when an athlete stops for a moment to thank you for something you have done for her. The athletes need to know that they are in a relationship that involves give-and-take. It is your job as a coach to make them aware of this relationship.

I believe the best way to evaluate is to write down or log what your strengths and weaknesses are *during* the season, not just after it. I make it a habit to carry note cards to every practice and game. On these cards, I write down things that stand out, whether it is a good play or a mental error. I review the card with the players after the practice or game, and then I incorporate drills into practice to help us strengthen what we are weak at. When this is

done, I drop the card into a file to be reviewed at the end of the season. The information gives me great feedback on what we struggled with and what our stronger areas were. The cards help me remember and feel more confident that I am not overlooking anything, plus they serve as a journal and are easy to keep.

POSTSEASON EVALUATION

Just as we do a postseason evaluation of our players, we also evaluate ourselves as coaches and the overall health of the program. Successful coaching is an ongoing process of looking for areas that need strengthening, and acknowledging the things that have gone well. I try to study the successful programs and coaches in the country and to follow some of their examples. Whenever a top 10 coach is speaking at a clinic or at a coaches' convention, I try to attend.

The postseason evaluation involves taking an honest look at my staff, my team, our opponents, and myself. If I feel I need to replace staff members because of failure to meet my team's goals and objectives, then it must be done. Evaluation is sometimes painful, and the decisions you make for the program's best interests may be even more painful, but if you expect to succeed, change may be in order.

At the end of the season, I hand out program evaluation forms to my players for them to complete (see figure 17.1). After all forms are collected, I (and sometimes my assistants) meet with each player individually to acknowledge the athlete's strengths and weaknesses and to assess her future with the team. I will let each player know the role I see her playing the next season, along with the amount of her scholarship. I go over her single-season highlights and her career accomplishments. Finally, I present a plan of action for her to follow throughout the summer.

As coaches, we give our players the power to recognize their own strengths. This is a sense of empowerment that we are put in a position to use. And through that comes control over our players' ideas, efforts, dreams, and

Figure 17.1 Program Evaluation Form

Confidential—do not include your name.
Please be honest and constructive as you complete this evaluation. Your input into our program is vital for the future. On the scales below, 1 is the lowest rating and 5 is the highest.

1. I learned effective softball strategies and skills:

   1   2   3   4   5

2. My individual performance of softball skills and strategies improved:

   1   2   3   4   5

3. I enjoyed playing softball this season:

   1   2   3   4   5

4. The coaching staff helped me develop as a player:

   1   2   3   4   5

5. The coaching staff helped me develop as a person:

   1   2   3   4   5

6. Players were treated fairly on the team:

   1   2   3   4   5

7. Players on the team respected team rules:

   1   2   3   4   5

8. Practices were well organized, challenging, and fun:

   1   2   3   4   5

9. The role I played in games was the best for the program:

   1   2   3   4   5

10. I feel more positive about the program now than I did at the beginning of the season:

   1   2   3   4   5

Your choice for the Most Valuable Player _____

Your choice for the Most Improved Player _____

Player you respect the most on the team _____

Player you respect the least on the team _____

Did the team live up to your expectations? Why or why not? _____

_____

Was training beneficial? Why or why not? _____

_____

(continued)

Figure 17.1 *(continued)*

What would you change (if anything) regarding any aspect of the program?

_____

_____

What do we need to do in order to win the conference championship next spring?

_____

_____

What can the coaching staff do to make the softball program better than it was this past season?

_____

_____

What is the best thing about being a softball player?

_____

_____

What is the worst thing about being a softball player?

_____

_____

What changes would *you* make to eliminate the worst things about the program?

_____

_____

performances. We nourish them to be self-actualizing. We empower them and protect them. We hold keys—pride, loyalty, discipline, heart, mind, and confidence—and with these keys we unlock the door to opportunity and possibility.

I want you to use this book to help your student-athletes grow on the field and off. Use this as a guide to develop your own philosophy, not only within the science of coaching, but the art of coaching as well. Play ball!

I chose my career because I loved sport—the sheer joy and exhilaration and the knowledge that a sport experience can be truly empowering.

INDEX

PLEASE NOTE: The italicized *f* following a page number represents a figure on the page indicated.

ABOUT THE AUTHORS

Kathy Veroni

Roanna Brazier

Kathy Veroni is one of the most successful coaches in NCAA softball history, with more than 875 wins to her credit at Western Illinois University. Including her time as head coach of a women's premier fastpitch team, she won more than 1,250 games in her fastpitch coaching career. In 34 seasons at WIU, Veroni built a balanced program that enjoyed academic and athletic success while providing players with an excellent experience as collegiate athletes. She served as president of the National Fastpitch Coaches Association (NFCA) and has been inducted into the NFCA Hall of Fame, the Illinois State University Athletic Hall of Fame, and the Illinois Amateur Softball Association Hall of Fame. Veroni has been a speaker at coaching clinics throughout the Midwest and runs numerous camps and clinics for coaches and youth in western Illinois.

Roanna Brazier was head coach at Ohio University for nine years and an assistant for three years before signing on as a pitching instructor at Club K, a softball training facility in Nashville, Tennessee. During her tenure at Ohio, Brazier's players earned all-conference and all-region honors. She also served as head coach of a USA all-star team in the summer of 2003. From 1987 to 1990, Brazier was an All-Big Eight Conference performer at the University of Kansas. While pitching and playing first base, Brazier, a three-time all-conference selection, set six Jayhawk season and career records, including innings pitched and victories. In 1990, she earned All-Midwest Region accolades after posting a 28-7 record with a 0.93 ERA.